TOXIC TORTS
IN A NUTSHELL

FOURTH EDITION

By

JEAN MACCHIAROLI EGGEN
Professor of Law
Widener University School of Law

A Thomson Reuters business

Mat #40954314

Nutshell Series, In a Nutshell and the Nutshell Logo are
trademarks registered in the U.S. Patent and Trademark Office.

COPYRIGHT © 1995 WEST PUBLISHING CO.
© West, a Thomson business 2000, 2005
© 2010 Thomson Reuters
    610 Opperman Drive
    St. Paul, MN 55123
    1–800–313–9378
Printed in the United States of America

ISBN: 978–0–314–92282–3

For Jeff and Don

III

PREFACE TO FOURTH EDITION

Toxic torts now command a prominent position in the American civil justice system. As the fourth edition of this Nutshell goes to press, actions have been filed related to matters as diverse as environmental and economic harm from the oil spill in the Gulf of Mexico, personal injuries claimed by U.S. military service personnel in Iraq and Afghanistan from exposure to burn pits operated by contractors, and patients' exposure to radiation from medical CT scanners. The first decisions addressing the relationship between greenhouse gas emissions and climate change are working their way through the courts. And we are on the cusp of a proliferation of toxic tort actions related to new technologies, such as nanotechnology, and new substances, as evidenced by the recently certified Chinese drywall class action. This dynamic growth of toxic torts is not likely to abate.

In the month of June alone, the Gulf oil spill has spawned an unprecedented amount of legal action on all fronts. The commercial fishing industry has brought lawsuits for economic injuries to its livelihood. Environmental groups have brought citizens suits under the federal environmental laws to halt damage to the coastal environment. Governmental entities have attempted regulation, sought legislation, and entered the litigation arena. Spill cleanup workers have complained of illness associated with exposure to the oil spill, and landowners are suffering damage to their private property. The massive scope of the oil spill's impact has meant that many of the actions are class actions. Already there has been promise of a $20 billion fund to reimburse injured parties. But no one knows the scope of those who will be injured, or the ultimate cost of the harm. The Gulf oil spill is only the latest example of a mass toxic tort that will occupy lawmakers and litigants well into mid-century. Broad-spectrum incidents, such as the Gulf oil spill, are the very definition of a toxic tort.

In the five years since the publication of the third edition of this Nutshell, the number and complexity of the issues in toxic tort litigation have grown. Moreover, the amount of judicial innovation in this area of the law—both sui generis and in applying existing doctrines to new situations—is impressive. But the task ahead of the legal profession continues to be daunting. And, as the Gulf oil spill demonstrates, relentless. This Nutshell examines the ongoing judicial efforts to develop a workable jurisprudence of toxic injury and identifies and assesses the most prominent innovations. Toxic tort law is truly one of the most dynamic and challenging areas of the law. I hope this Nutshell captures both its breathtaking scope and its analytical depth.

I would like to extend my gratitude and appreciation to my research assistant, Eric Laury, who has assisted tirelessly and intelligently in updating the material in this Nutshell, while also co-blogging with me on nanotechnology and the law. I would also like to acknowledge my late colleague, Robert Justin Lipkin, who taught me the true meaning of the scholarly enterprise.

JEAN MACCHIAROLI EGGEN

Wilmington, Delaware
June 2010

OUTLINE

___

OUTLINE

OUTLINE

Page

OUTLINE

TABLE OF CASES

References are to Pages

A

TABLE OF CASES

B

TABLE OF CASES

C

D

E

F

G

H

I

J

K

L

M

N

O

P

R

S

T

U

V

W

Y

Z

TABLE OF STATUTES

UNITED STATES

UNITED STATES CONSTITUTION

UNITED STATES CODE ANNOTATED

7 U.S.C.A.—Agriculture

11 U.S.C.A.—Bankruptcy

15 U.S.C.A.—Commerce and Trade

TABLE OF STATUTES

POPULAR NAME ACTS

CIVIL RIGHTS ACT OF 1964

COMPREHENSIVE ENVIRONMENTAL RESPONSE, COMPENSATION AND LIABILITY ACT

TABLE OF STATUTES

**COMPREHENSIVE ENVIRONMENTAL RESPONSE,
COMPENSATION AND LIABILITY ACT**

TABLE OF STATUTES

TABLE OF STATUTES

TABLE OF STATUTES

OFFICIAL CODE OF GEORGIA ANNOTATED

HAWAII REVISED STATUTES

ILLINOIS SMITH–HURD ANNOTATED

WEST'S ANNOTATED INDIANA CODE

IOWA CODE ANNOTATED

KANSAS STATUTES ANNOTATED

LI

TABLE OF STATUTES

TABLE OF STATUTES

SOUTH CAROLINA CODE

TENNESSEE CODE ANNOTATED

V.T.C.A., CIVIL PRACTICE AND REMEDIES CODE

UTAH CODE ANNOTATED

VIRGINIA CODE

FEDERAL RULES OF CIVIL PROCEDURE

TABLE OF STATUTES

FEDERAL RULES OF CIVIL PROCEDURE

TABLE OF STATUTES

FEDERAL RULES OF CIVIL PROCEDURE

FEDERAL RULES OF EVIDENCE

CODE OF FEDERAL REGULATIONS

TABLE OF STATUTES

CODE OF FEDERAL REGULATIONS

TOXIC TORTS
IN A NUTSHELL

FOURTH EDITION

CHAPTER ONE

INTRODUCTION TO THE STUDY OF TOXIC TORTS

A. WHAT IS A TOXIC TORT?

The term "toxic torts" encompasses a wide variety of claims, both private and public. To some extent, characterizing this law as "torts" is a misnomer. A toxic tort action may be a civil lawsuit, an administrative action for clean-up of hazardous waste, a workers' compensation claim, or any other of a multitude of actions. What do these actions have in common? What themes tie them together? And why should these particular kinds of actions— tort or otherwise—be treated as a separate category in the law? It is important initially to understand the answers to these questions and to comprehend the various contexts in which a toxic tort may arise. This chapter explores the characteristics of a toxic tort to provide the basis for a more detailed understanding of the kinds of claims and defenses that this book will discuss.

1. Exposure to a Toxic Substance

Toxic tort actions involve substances as diverse as asbestos, silicone gel breast implants, prescription drugs, chemical compounds, radiation, and hazardous waste. The harm claimed is equally diverse. Claimants may seek compensation for personal injuries or property damage. But claimants may also seek to recover for discrimination in the workplace or for the costs of cleaning up a contaminated site. In general, however, the claims involve the release of and exposure to—or threatened release of and exposure to—one or more substances alleged to be "toxic." The definition of what is "toxic" may vary, depending upon the context in which it appears. Generally, the use of the term in legal circles is looser than its use in medical or scientific circles. A broad, workable definition is given in the Toxic Substances Control Act (TSCA), 15 U.S.C.A. § 2606(f) (West 2010), where, in the context of the manufacture of chemical substances and mixtures, imminent hazard is described as involving "the manufacture, processing, distribution in commerce, use, or disposal of [a substance that] is likely to result in . . . injury to health or the environment." Similarly, in the Hazard Communication Standard promulgated by the Occupational Safety and Health Administration (OSHA), a "health hazard" is defined as "a chemical for which there is statistically significant evidence based on at least one study conducted in accordance with established scientific principles that acute or chronic health effects may occur in exposed employees." 29 C.F.R. § 1910.1200(c) (2010).

Human or property exposure may occur in a wide variety of ways. The New York statute of limitations that governs actions relating to toxic exposures enumerates the methods of exposure as follows: "absorption, contact, ingestion, inhalation, implantation or injection." N.Y. Civ. Prac. L. & R. 214–c (McKinney 2010). Exposure may be knowing, as with a prescription drug, or unknowing, as with a contaminated drinking water supply.

The substances that give rise to toxic tort actions have certain characteristics that distinguish them from the instrumentalities that give rise to traditional tort actions, such as motor vehicle accidents. These also tend to be many of the same substances selected by the federal Government for regulation, either generically or specifically, in programs administered by a variety of agencies, such as the Environmental Protection Agency, the Food and Drug Administration, and OSHA. For example, in the Hazard Communication Standard, OSHA has required certain actions to be taken with regard to chemicals that may be classified as "carcinogens, toxic or highly toxic agents, reproductive toxins, irritants, corrosives, sensitizers, hepatotoxins [(toxic to liver)], nephrotoxins [(toxic to kidneys)], agents which act on the hematopoietic [(blood)] system, and agents which damage the lungs, skin, eyes, or mucous membranes." 29 C.F.R. § 1910.1200(c) (2010). Substances and processes of concern under TSCA include those causing such effects as "carcinogenesis, mutagenesis, teratogenesis, behavioral disorders, [and] cumulative or synergistic effects." TSCA, 15 U.S.C.A. § 2603(b)(2)(A) (West 2010). Carcinogenesis relates to the capability of the substance to cause cancer. Teratogenesis refers to a birth defect caused by maternal exposure during fetal development that may cause the fetus to be malformed. Mutagenesis is somewhat different. It refers to the inducement of genetic mutations caused by changes in DNA. Genetic mutations may express themselves at various times and in various ways. The injurious effects can appear directly in the person exposed to a particular substance. Or, the gene may be inherited, and the harmful expression of the gene may manifest itself in a subsequent generation. For example, a plaintiff might allege that her cancer was caused by her grandmother's ingestion of a prescription drug while the grandmother was pregnant with the plaintiff's father, who has remained healthy. The plaintiff might allege that the in utero exposure caused a genetic mutation in the father that was passed on to the plaintiff, causing her to develop cancer.

Often the substances involved in toxic tort actions are new compounds, and sometimes they can be obscure. In addition, the complaint in a toxic tort action may set forth circumstances in which several or many substances were commingled in some fashion. Thus, it may be necessary to examine the synergistic effects associated with the combination of substances alleged. Two or more separate substances may combine and interact in a way that becomes harmful only upon interaction or in a way that enhances the harmful effects of the substances. Further, some substances may cause deleterious effects only upon prolonged or cumulative exposure. The subtleties of the scientific issues involving the toxicity of substances indicate the need for attorneys practicing in this area of the law to have a basic understanding of scientific or engineering principles as well as to keep current on scientific knowledge relevant to their cases.

2. Latency Period

In general, in a toxic tort action, the full effects of exposure are not immediately apparent. This is either because the injury does not manifest itself immediately or because the harm goes undiscovered for a period of time. Injuries such as cancer, birth defects, and genetic mutations necessarily require a latency period for their development. Asbestos exposure presents a classic example of a long latency period between exposure and the onset of symptoms. Asbestos workers rarely exhibited any evidence of serious asbestos-related disease at the time of initial exposure or shortly thereafter. It was not uncommon for workers to develop asbestosis, a chronic and degenerative lung condition, or malignant mesothelioma, a form of lung cancer associated with asbestos exposure, many years after initial exposure and often many years after exposure had ceased. Latency periods of ten to thirty years appear frequently in the cases. *See* Borel v. Fibreboard Paper Prods. Corp., 493 F.2d 1076 (5th Cir.1973). Latency periods may not stop at several decades. The example given earlier of genetic harm demonstrates the possibility that injuries could manifest themselves generations after the initial exposure.

The long latency periods associated with toxic tort claims generate many problems that are unusual in the standard tort action. For example, statutes of limitations and rules of accrual have needed to be modified to encompass toxic tort actions, in which the time of the defendant's action and the discovery of the injury are separated by expanses of time. Furthermore, the collection of evidence and even the identification of tortfeasors become more difficult with the passage of time due to missing or imperfect records and lapsed memories. Virtually every aspect of tort law has been challenged by the novel claims and scientific issues that are presented in a toxic tort action.

Latent illness need not require decades or years to develop. The law has recognized that even very short latency periods, such as a few weeks, will trigger many of the same the problems as illnesses developing over longer periods of time. Thus, the Second Circuit Court of Appeals held in Bano v. Union Carbide Corp., 361 F.3d 696 (2d Cir.2004), that a latent injury manifesting a few weeks after initial exposure should be treated the same as injuries with longer latency periods for purposes of the special New York discovery statute of limitations.

3. Scientific Uncertainty and Causation Problems

Due to the latency period between exposure to the substance and the onset of symptoms, it is often difficult for a plaintiff to establish the necessary causal link between the substance and the injury.

The likelihood of multiple intervening causes is greater with the passage of time. Further causal complications arise from the fact that many of the diseases alleged by toxic tort plaintiffs occur in background levels in the general population, and not just among those persons who have been exposed to the substance in question. For example, persons who were exposed to radiation during the United States Government's atomic testing program in the 1940s and 1950s have claimed that they developed leukemia and other cancers as a result of their exposures. The same illnesses occur in the general population as a result of numerous other causes, such as heredity, exposure to other environmental substances, or exposure to radiation in other contexts; sometimes, they occur inexplicably and, apparently, spontaneously. *See* Allen v. United States, 588 F.Supp. 247 (D. Utah 1984). As a result, in many instances it is virtually impossible to determine with any measure of certainty whether a plaintiff's illness arose from the defendant's product or conduct, or whether that plaintiff still would have developed the illness in the absence of the alleged exposure.

A related complicating factor in toxic tort litigation is the inability of science to connect many illnesses to their precise causes. The etiology of many illnesses, such as many cancers, autoimmune diseases, and neurological damage, is not completely understood in the medical community. At the least, scientific knowledge is constantly evolving. Often, determination of levels of exposure that could cause injury, and the kinds of injury produced by certain exposures, are open to reasonable debate in the scientific literature and among scientific researchers generally. Accordingly, clinical evidence of the plaintiff's physical condition or of the progression of the disease may not provide the solid evidence of causation that is useful in other kinds of tort claims.

Consequently, it is not unusual for a plaintiff in a toxic tort action to bring a claim for which evidence of the cause-in-fact is lacking. Courts are now faced with the issue of whether or to what extent to allow such claims. The strongest evidence of causation in a toxic tort action is probabilistic evidence. Such evidence by its very nature can only demonstrate whether the particular substance to which the plaintiff was exposed was *capable* of producing the injury alleged. Probabilistic evidence cannot establish that exposure to the substance was the actual cause of the particular plaintiff's injury. It merely deals in probabilities, never in certainty.

Even where plaintiffs have been allowed to maintain actions without traditional cause-in-fact evidence, the end result has not necessarily been favorable to plaintiffs. For example, in numerous cases in which plaintiffs have alleged birth defects as a result of in utero exposure to the prescription drug Bendectin, the actions have been dismissed either because the plaintiff's primary probabilistic evidence was deemed inadmissible under the applicable evidentiary standard or because the court deemed the probabilistic evidence to be insufficient to raise a triable question of fact. *See, e.g.*, DeLuca v. Merrell Dow Pharmaceuticals, Inc., 791 F.Supp. 1042 (D.N.J.1992) (summary judgment dismissing the action for insufficient expert evidence).

4. Reliance on Expert Scientific Testimony

The problems of causation outlined above, and discussed in greater depth in Chapter Eight, render it necessary for the parties to a toxic tort action to focus closely on establishing or refuting a legally cognizable connection between the exposure alleged and the injury suffered by the plaintiff. In a conventional tort action, causal connections could be established to the jury by circumstantial evidence on matters often within the jury's knowledge and experience. The scientific and medical nature of toxic torts, however, requires the presentation of evidence about which few persons have the requisite level of knowledge or experience.

In a conventional personal injury action, the testimony of a treating physician often is sufficient to establish the relationship between the defendant's product or conduct and the plaintiff's injuries. In toxic tort actions, the testimony of a treating physician on causation is often successfully challenged when unaccompanied by scientific studies. Thus, in the traditional motor vehicle accident, a plaintiff suffering from traumatic head injury typically will rely upon the treating physicians to describe the condition and to offer opinions from their professional knowledge and experience on the existence of brain damage and the degree of recovery expected.

In contrast, in a toxic tort action, the treating physicians may know relatively little about the causation of the illness and, in some cases, may not even know of the exposure. Their task of treating the illness in some instances will be the same regardless of whether it was caused by exposure to a toxic substance or arose otherwise. Even where treating physicians offer causation opinions based upon their clinical experience and medical knowledge, those opinions may face tough challenges in the courts. Thus, to prove causation, toxic tort plaintiffs often must rely upon statistical information and reports of laboratory studies.

In determining the role that scientific evidence will play in the resolution of a toxic tort claim, courts are called upon to consider the relationship between medical or scientific causation and legal causation. The level of certainty required to establish a causal relationship in scientific matters is upwards of ninety-five percent certainty. In contrast, the preponderance-of-the-evidence standard applied in most civil actions in the United States is a mere fifty-one percent. Courts have been reluctant to recognize legal causation in the absence of scientific concurrence, however. Consequently, parties and their attorneys must focus their attention on the reliability and quality of the expert testimony that supports their respective positions.

In addition, toxic tort claims have involved an unprecedented variety and number of experts. For example, a claim for personal injuries arising out of seepage of hazardous chemicals into the groundwater system beneath a disposal site and, ultimately, into the plaintiffs' drinking water supply could involve all of the following experts: chemist, industrial toxicologist, chemical engineer, environmental engineer, hydrogeologist, epidemiologist, and a wide variety of medical subspecialists, depending upon the injuries alleged. Considering that both plaintiffs and defendants will need experts to support their positions, the expert component of the litigation could become very time consuming and costly, and those factors could dictate the course of the litigation.

5.   The Role of Risk

The causation problem is one example of the role that risk plays in toxic tort litigation. Probabilistic evidence is based upon risk; that is, it provides the court or jury with evidence of the risk of developing a certain illness as a result of exposure to a particular substance. Statisticians skilled in the area of epidemiology have created models that estimate the level of risk of illness from exposure to a substance. This is one form of risk analysis and is frequently used by both plaintiffs and defendants in toxic tort litigation. *See generally* David E. Lilienfeld, Paul D. Stolley, & Abraham M. Lilienfeld, Foundations of Epidemiology 226–28 (3d ed. 1994). Translating statistical risk into legally cognizable standards has been problematic, however, and resistance to employing concepts of risk to form the basis of legal claims is pervasive.

Contemporary life carries with it certain risks that citizens perceive to be dangerous. Whether those fears are reasonable or not, aggrieved persons have sought relief both in the courts and through governmental regulation for adverse effects arising from those risks, and courts have increasingly been willing to recognize risk as a basis for claims. Claims by toxic tort plaintiffs for emotional distress absent signs of physical injury, for increased risk of disease, and for medical surveillance without a current medical condition all rely to some degree on risk as their foundation. In these types of claims, the plaintiff is seeking some form of relief purely on the basis of the risk of contracting some disease in the future.

Risk also forms the basis for environmental regulation. Regulatory officials consider the health and environmental effects of substances when determining whether to develop standards for or limitations on the manufacture, use, and disposal of those substances. Regulatory response to risk is often substance-specific and relatively narrow in focus. For example, OSHA standards exist for only a small percentage of the many substances that could be regulated in the occupational setting. This has led some to be critical of the current approach to use of risk in the regulatory process. *See* Hon. Stephen Breyer, Breaking the Vicious Circle 10–51 (1993) (arguing that Congressional and regulatory responses to risk tend to reflect public perceptions rather than risk analysts' priorities).

The disciplines of risk assessment and risk management have blossomed in recent decades and have become important tools for the management and reduction of toxic and environmental risks, both by means of regulation and through the judicial system. In general, risk assessment involves the identification of potentially hazardous substances and a determination of the effects on humans of certain levels of exposure to the substances. Through the use of interdisciplinary methodologies and statistical extrapolation, the analysts attempt to predict the effect on populations of exposure to the identified substances. They also seek to characterize the substances with regard to the hazards they pose, such as whether a particular substance is carcinogenic.

Risk management, on the other hand, is a broader process and, in many ways, is more subjective than risk assessment. The risk manager's task is to determine the optimum means for addressing the risks identified by the risk assessment process. Ideally, the risk manager would be aware of the limitations of the data used. The risk management process is conducted in light of society's goals and policies, including the manner in which the risk information will be used by the legal system. *See generally* Carnegie Comm'n on Science, Technology and Government, Risk and the Environment: Improving Regulatory Decision Making (1993) (discussing and evaluating the roles of risk assessment and risk management in the environmental regulatory process). For example, determining where to dispose of hazardous waste involves the weighing of conflicting policies, such as fairness considerations in using a site that may be located in a lower-economic neighborhood compared to the availability and low cost of the same site.

The appropriate use of the risk assessment methodologies and proper interpretation of the data collected through the process are matters that continue to be open to dispute. Public perceptions, policy goals, and partisan political affiliations all play a role in the assessment and management of risk, whether through the regulatory process or in the court system.

6. Massive Scope

The exposures that form the basis of toxic tort lawsuits often affect many people. On occasion, the numbers have reached into the thousands or tens of thousands. Some exposures occur at approximately the same time and under the same circumstances, as with the attacks of September 11, 2001 and their aftermath, when numerous persons were exposed to a toxic air mix of chemicals, asbestos, and other substances. *See generally* Jean Macchiaroli Eggen, *Toxic Torts at Ground Zero*, 39 Ariz. St. L.J. 383 (2007). In contrast, some mass exposures have occurred to many people over a long period of time, up to several decades, and under a variety of circumstances. The use of asbestos insulation products in construction is an extreme example, but drug product liability cases present a similar pattern.

A special problem in many mass toxic tort actions involves the extent to which future claimants— those who have been exposed, but who have not manifested any symptoms of disease at the time of the litigation—should be or can be included in a settlement or judgment. The inclusion of future claimants in current litigation stretches the scope of the litigation indefinitely, and it would be a rare case indeed where the number of ultimate claimants could be predicted with accuracy.

The sheer magnitude of much toxic tort litigation has created significant judicial management problems. Judges may be faced with questions involving the use of the class action device or other aggregative procedures to manage the litigation more efficiently. Pretrial practice, including discovery, necessarily takes on a heightened role in mass toxic tort litigation. Moreover, the wealth of scientific evidence that the parties seek to introduce calls for special expertise and specialized judicial management. All these factors combine to make the road to resolution a protracted and challenging process.

B. CONVERGENCE OF PUBLIC LAW AND PRIVATE LAW

The developing law of toxic torts exhibits a blend of principles arising from the common law and standards and approaches rooted in the regulatory aspects of public law. In 1980, when the Comprehensive Environmental Response Compensation and Liability Act (CERCLA), 42 U.S.C.A. §§ 9601–

9675 (West 2010) (also known as the "Superfund" statute), was enacted, Congress declined the opportunity to include remedies for personal injuries within the statute. Instead, the statute offered a remedial scheme allowing administrative and judicial actions by the Government—and, in some limited circumstances, by private parties—for matters relating to the clean-up of hazardous substances released into the environment. With a great deal of overlap, the law of toxic torts has evolved in the gap between traditional tort doctrine and public law. The result has had a synergistic effect, spinning off new legal territory that requires a jurisprudence of its own. Courts are gradually working their way toward that new jurisprudence.

Attorneys whose practices encompass toxic torts may also be spending significant amounts of time involved in OSHA matters, handling state workers' compensation claims before an administrative law judge, or defending citizens suits for administrative penalties authorized under the federal environmental laws. The methodologies and standards employed in the public sector with respect to toxic substances often differ from the standards that have evolved under the common law. A case filed by flight attendants for injuries alleged to have been suffered as a result of their exposures to environmental tobacco smoke while working allows reflection on some of these issues. As workers, the claimants would have workers' compensation claims against their employers. They would also have product liability claims against the cigarette manufacturers. Public law issues emerge as well, with the Government regulating smoking on airplanes, and OSHA and EPA contemplating whether to regulate environmental tobacco smoke in the workplace.

What does a company's compliance with regulatory standards mean for plaintiffs seeking redress for injuries associated with the regulated activity or product? This question is complex, but it is central to many toxic tort cases. While the answer is equally complex, a basic understanding of the interaction between private law and public law is crucial for attorneys practicing in this area.

CHAPTER TWO

THEORIES OF LIABILITY: PRODUCTS

The law of toxic torts has several provenances. One major source has been the relatively new law of product liability. Another major source has been the more traditional law of torts related to the land, such as nuisance and trespass. A third source has been the regulatory arena of environmental and occupational regulation. Chapters 2, 3, and 4 look at these topics. This Chapter will focus primarily on claims against sellers of products. Where appropriate, the discussion will take note of the areas in which interaction between tort law and public law is inevitable.

A. PRODUCT LIABILITY LAW AND TOXIC TORTS

1. The Emergence of the Law of Toxic Product Liability

Product liability law developed from the need in modern society to provide consumers with a means of recovery for injuries that occurred from defective products. Product liability law focuses on the condition of the product and, at least theoretically, far less on the conduct of the product seller. Older law either required a contract between the injured person and the product seller or focused exclusively on the conduct of the seller. To understand the need for a law of product liability for injuries from toxic products, it is useful to examine two cases in the context of asbestos personal injury litigation, one applying the older law and then a major case applying product liability law.

Asbestos is a highly fire-resistant naturally occurring mineral that has been incorporated into insulation products. These insulation products had a vast array of uses, a small sampling of which are roofing, building shingles, flooring, ceiling tiles, boilers in ships and buildings, and brakes in motor vehicles. Asbestos is a fiber, and the fibers were bonded into the insulation materials. The danger existed that the fibers would escape into the air when workers were cutting or otherwise working with the insulation materials, and also when the products deteriorated over time or were otherwise disturbed in situ. The fibers were small enough to be inhaled, where they lodged in the lung tissue and could begin a disease process. The so-called "signature diseases" of asbestos exposure in the workers were asbestosis and mesothelioma. Asbestosis is a progressive fibrosis of the lung tissue caused by fibers lodged in the lung, which, although not malignant, may be fatal. Mesothelioma is a form of lung cancer that affects the pleural lining, the sac around the lungs. Many workers have claimed other illnesses, particularly other kinds of cancer, and some of these other illnesses have been shown to have a likely causal relation to asbestos exposure. The illnesses often had a long latency period, and it was not uncommon for a diagnosis of asbestos-related disease to come many years after exposure to asbestos had ceased. An excellent discussion of the characteristics of asbestos and the nature of asbestos-related illness, as well as a detailed survey of the earliest asbestos actions, may be found in Chapter 1 of Paul Brodeur, Outrageous Misconduct (1985).

Most of the asbestos personal injury litigation has arisen from the exposure of workers who used asbestos insulation products in the course of their employment. Unable to bring actions against their employers because of the operation of the workers' compensation laws, they brought suit against the manufacturers of the products they handled.

Early toxic tort actions evinced a reluctance on the part of courts to apply the emerging law of product liability to claims of injury from exposure to toxic substances. A typical example was Bassham v. Owens–Corning Fiber Glass Corporation, 327 F.Supp. 1007 (D.N.M.1971). The *Bassham* court refused to treat a claim by an asbestos worker under the law of product liability, holding that occupational disease claims were not injuries of the sort contemplated by the law of product liability. The long latency period between exposure to the asbestos and manifestation of the disease was a major factor in distinguishing the claim from the standard product liability claim in which an immediate injury occurs as a result of contact with a defective product. As the court stated, "[t]here was nothing sudden or rapid that happened," making it difficult to determine when an injury occurred. The judicial attitude in *Bassham* was fairly common until the mid–1970s.

Borel v. Fibreboard Paper Prods. Corp., 493 F.2d 1076 (5th Cir.1973) was the seminal case that applied the law of strict product liability to workplace-related asbestos injury. The plaintiff, an industrial insulation worker, brought an action against several manufacturers of asbestos-containing insulation materials for failure to warn of the hazards associated with handling asbestos. The plaintiff alleged that he had developed both asbestosis and mesothelioma from his exposure to asbestos in the workplace over a thirty-three year period.

Applying Texas law, the court held the manufacturers liable under a product liability theory for failure to adequately warn the plaintiff of the hazards of the asbestos-containing products with which he worked. In so doing, the court examined the medical literature regarding the effects of asbestos on workers and concluded that evidence of causation existed. The *Borel* court's decision to hold the manufacturers strictly liable was significant as the leading departure from the line of cases from which *Bassham* was derived. It was also noteworthy because the jury, which had found the defendants negligent on Borel's separate negligence claim, had assigned some measure of fault to Borel himself. Under the applicable law of contributory negligence, the plaintiff was unable to recover anything on the negligence claim because he bore some of the responsibility for his injuries. But under the law of strict product liability, in which contributory negligence was not a defense, the plaintiff's fault was no impediment to recovery.

Once the *Borel* court presented its well-reasoned opinion in applying strict product liability to asbestos-related occupational disease, a flood of asbestos litigation entered the court systems. That flood has never abated. Furthermore, strict product liability law was applied to a variety of other products alleged to cause latent illness in plaintiffs.

2.   The Restatements of Torts

The concept of strict product liability developed long before the Restatement (Second) of Torts codified the doctrine in 1965. Justice Traynor's famous concurrence in Escola v. Coca Cola Bottling Co., 150 P.2d 436 (Cal.1944) articulated a doctrine of product liability that moved beyond negligence to absolute liability for marketing a defective product that caused injury to humans. Justice Traynor minimized reliance upon concepts of contract law—such as privity and warranties—in favor of creation of an independent tort remedy. He stated that "public policy demands that responsibility be fixed wherever it will most effectively reduce the hazards to life and health inherent in defective products that reach the market." The sellers of products, whether the manufacturers, distributors, or retailers, are the persons in that position. The justification for the new doctrine was the changing relationship between product manufacturers and consumers. Not only are modern consumers more alienated from the manufacturing processes than were their counterparts in the Nineteenth Century, but modern products are considerably more technologically or chemically complex.

Strict product liability law embodies the policy position that the costs of injuries can best be borne by the manufacturers and sellers of the products because they are in the best position to spread the costs of accidents associated with those products across society in the price of the product and through insurance. As a matter of equity, product liability law reflects public expectations that sellers stand behind the products that they develop or sell.

In 1965, the Restatement (Second) of Torts appeared in final form, containing a remarkable new section recognizing the strict liability of product sellers. For more than thirty years, this document was the subject of both glorification and scorn. The states adopted the *Second Restatement*, in whole or in part, reinterpreted it, and developed their own doctrines where the *Restatement* was lacking. The case law of strict product liability that controls in most jurisdictions today is a creature of the *Second Restatement*. In 1998, however, the American Law Institute produced a new Restatement (Third) of Torts: Products Liability, which attempted to address and resolve the key issues raised by the earlier *Restatement* and by state courts throughout the country. The *Third Restatement* evidences the increasing importance of product liability litigation in the landscape of tort law and takes a strong position on some major issues that have appeared in the litigation.

a. *Restatement (Second) of Torts § 402A*

Section 402A of the *Second Restatement* provides as follows:

(1) One who sells any product in a defective condition unreasonably dangerous to the user or consumer or to his property is subject to liability for physical harm thereby caused to the ultimate user or consumer, or to his property, if

(a) the seller is engaged in the business of selling such a product, and

(b) it is expected to and does reach the user or consumer without substantial change in the condition in which it is sold.

(2) The rule stated in Subsection (1) applies although

(a) the seller has exercised all possible care in the preparation and sale of his product, and

(b) the user or consumer has not bought the product from or entered into any contractual relation with the seller.

Thus, no privity between the injured party and the manufacturer or other seller is required for liability to attach. Moreover, no attention to the seller's fault is necessary, at least theoretically. *See generally* Greenman v. Yuba Power Products, Inc., 377 P.2d 897 (Cal.1963).

The only requirements of Section 402A are that the defendant be "in the business of selling" the product, that the product be "in a defective condition unreasonably dangerous," and that the plaintiff be an "ultimate user or consumer." Implicit in Section 402A is the additional requirement that the plaintiff prove that the product caused the injuries alleged. Section 402A strict liability claims based upon asbestos, cigarettes, prescription drugs, and medical devices have proliferated since the 1970s, but the lawsuits are by no means limited to these products. A product may be defective in several different ways, and it is not uncommon to find more than one type of defect alleged in a plaintiff's complaint.

b.   *Restatement (Third) of Torts: Products Liability*

The multitude of judicial decisions in the area of product liability law in the three decades after the 1965 publication of Section 402A necessitated another, closer look at how product liability law had evolved. After several years of controversial drafts, the ALI's Restatement (Third) of Torts: Products Liability emerged in final form in 1998. While the document was an effort to restate the law of product liability in this country as it has evolved since the *Second Restatement*, courts continue to struggle with the underlying premises and practical applications of product liability doctrine. The vast majority of existing product liability case law from recent years is an outgrowth of the *Second Restatement*; however, courts have begun to cite and discuss the

Third Restatement explicitly. In some respects, the *Third Restatement* was nothing new, as it reflected the current state approaches. But in other respects, its take on certain rules was very controversial.

B. THEORIES OF LIABILITY FOR DEFECTIVE PRODUCTS

Unlike its predecessor, the *Third Restatement* goes into great detail about the different categories of product defects. *See* Restatement (Third) of Torts: Products Liability § 2. Furthermore, in contrast to the *Second Restatement*, the *Third Restatement* articulates the separate tests for each type of product defect. These tests generally accurately reflect the trends in the states. The *Third Restatement* also explicitly addresses certain troublesome issues with which the courts have dealt, but which were not addressed in the *Second Restatement*. The different approaches of Section 402A and the *Third Restatement* will be integrated into the discussions of the product liability theories below.

1. Design Defect

Claims for defective design allege that all units in a product line present an unacceptable hazard to the ultimate user or consumer. The defect is designed into the product. In toxic tort cases, claims for defective design appear across many different kinds of products, including prescription drugs, cigarettes, chemical compounds, and a range of consumer products from drain cleaners to plastic baby bottles.

Much of the controversy generated by Section 402A was directed at the interpretation of the meaning of "defective condition" for the purpose of imposing strict liability. With respect to design defects, two distinct approaches have emerged for defining the concept. The first is commonly known as the consumer expectation test. This test derives from comment i of 402A, which defines "unreasonably dangerous" as "dangerous to an extent beyond that which would be contemplated by the ordinary consumer who purchases it, with the ordinary knowledge common to the community as to its characteristics." Although this test sounds relatively easy to apply, it is often difficult to apply in cases involving alleged toxic products, where the reasonable consumer's expectations may be unclear. Moreover, anomalous results could be achieved in situations in which the danger was known or obvious (no liability), even though the product was extremely hazardous and could easily have been designed to be safer.

Over time, courts addressing design defect claims have favored a risk-utility, or risk-benefit, balancing test, according to which the product will be deemed defective where the product's danger outweighs its utility. This test usually incorporates an examination of whether alternative designs were available that would have eliminated the risks of the product. It also necessarily includes consideration of the costs of developing a safer product. Courts are in disagreement as to the relative weight to be given to these various factors when applying a risk-utility analysis. In addition, consumer groups have complained that the risk-utility test allows manufacturers to be immunized from liability for design defects for very hazardous products simply because of the products' high degree of utility.

There is no getting around the fact that the risk-utility test for product defects is very similar to the risk-utility test used in negligence to determine whether the defendant breached a duty to the plaintiff. In the well-known case of United States v. Carroll Towing Co., 159 F.2d 169 (2d Cir. 1947), Judge Hand set out the risk-utility analysis as a formula, B<PL, according to which negligence would exist where the burdens (costs) of making the activity safer were on balance less than the probability that harm would occur multiplied by the magnitude of the harm that could result. This is not unlike the risk-utility test used in product design defect cases, and many have questioned whether design defect claims are merely subject to a negligence analysis. *See, e.g.*, Martin A. Kotler, Products Liability and Basic Tort Law 159–60, 183–84 (2005). In jurisdictions adopting the risk-utility test, product designs are judged by a discrete test that contains many factors. Those factors have been assembled into a test in the *Third Restatement*.

The Restatement (Third) of Torts: Products Liability abandons the consumer expectation test in favor of the risk-utility test. Referring to this test in language common to the doctrine of negligence, the *Third Restatement* calls it a "reasonableness test." Stated more specifically, the test for a design defect is "whether a reasonable alternative design would, at reasonable cost, have reduced the foreseeable risks of harm posed by the product and, if so, whether the omission of the alternative design by the seller or a predecessor in the distributive chain rendered the product not reasonably safe." Restatement (Third) of Torts: Products Liability, cmt. d to § 2.

Wright v. Brooke Group Ltd., 652 N.W.2d 159 (Iowa 2002), which adopted the *Third Restatement*'s test, may indicate the direction that many state courts will take. The Iowa Supreme Court, on certified questions of law from the Northern District of Iowa, first traced the history of product liability law in the state. After adopting Section 402A, the Iowa Supreme Court had moved toward a dual test, incorporating both risk-utility analysis and consumer expectations. In the 1990s, the court eliminated strict liability in failure-to-warn cases, and in *Wright*, the court adopted the test in Section 2 of the *Third Restatement* for design defect claims. The court favored the *Third Restatement* test because "[t]he rules are stated functionally rather than in terms of traditional doctrinal categories," such as negligence or strict liability.

Numerous factors enter into the determination of a design defect in the *Third Restatement*'s test. Courts are often asked to evaluate the role of industry custom and practice in design defect claims. As a general rule, industry practice is relevant to the determination of product defect, but is not necessarily dispositive. Conformity with industry practice does not automatically mean that the product seller will not be liable. The existence of an open and obvious danger is also relevant, but in contrast to the consumer expectation test, does not of itself preclude a finding of product defect. Comment f proposes numerous factors that may be considered in determining whether a design defect exists, but notes that a plaintiff need not present evidence on all factors. These factors include matters related to the product claimed to be defective—such as the foreseeability of the harm and whether the product contained appropriate instructions or warnings—as well as the effect that any proposed alternative design would have on production costs, product longevity, and the like. The impact of a proposed alternative design on corporate earnings would not be an appropriate consideration in determining design defect, however.

The *Third Restatement* clearly states that in making his or her prima facie case, a plaintiff claiming a design defect "must prove the availability of a technologically feasible and practical alternative design that would have reduced or prevented the plaintiff's harm." Cmt. f. Earlier drafts of this section drew criticism from the plaintiff bar because of the high costs of expert testimony to determine the alternative design and prove this element of the case. In response, the final version of the section states that "the plaintiff is not required to establish with particularity the costs and benefits associated with adoption of the suggested alternative design" and that expert testimony on this issue would not be required in every case. Moreover, the Restatement emphasizes that this requirement "should not be construed to create artificial and unreasonable barriers to recovery." Cmt. f.

The states tend to use either a version of the risk-utility test or a version of the consumer expectation test. In Fabiano v. Philip Morris Inc., 847 N.Y.S.2d 901 (N.Y. Sup. Ct. 2007), a trial court applied the New York version of the risk-utility test in a case brought by a smoker alleging, among other claims, that the cigarettes he smoked were defectively designed. The New York test had been set forth in Voss v. Black & Decker Mfg. Co., 450 N.E.2d 204 (N.Y. 1993) and included the following factors:

(1) the product's utility to the public as a whole, (2) its utility to the individual user, (3) the likelihood that the product will cause injury, (4) the availability of a safer design, (5) the possibility of designing and manufacturing the product so that it is safer but remains functional and reasonably priced, (6) the degree of awareness of the product's potential danger that can reasonably be attributed to the injured user, and (7) the manufacturer's ability to spread the cost of any safety-related design changes.

The *Fabiano* court applied this test and concluded that the plaintiff's design defect claims withstood summary judgment.

Some states have stayed with the consumer expectation test of the *Second Restatement*. In another smoker case, a Florida court rejected the risk-utility analysis and applied Florida's "ordinary consumer expectations" test to a design defect claim. In Liggett Group, Inc. v. Davis, 973 So.2d 467 (Fla. App. Ct. 2007), the court held that proof of a safer alternative design was not required and that the jury could reasonably have found that a design defect existed solely on the basis of the consumer expectation test.

In Godoy v. E.I. du Pont de Nemours & Co., 768 N.W.2d 674 (Wis. 2009), the Wisconsin Supreme Court stood firm on the use of the *Second Restatement*'s consumer expectation test for design defects. The case involved injuries from exposure to lead paint, specifically white lead carbonate pigment. The court held that even though the danger of the paint was not readily apparent to the consumer, a "claim for defective design cannot be maintained where the presence of lead is the alleged defect in design, and its very presence is a characteristic of the product itself. Without lead, there can be no white lead carbonate pigment." Whether the seller failed to properly warn of the hazards inherent in the product was a separate issue, the court said.

2. Failure to Warn

Failure to warn of the hazards of an allegedly toxic product is generally treated as a separate liability theory. It also constitutes a product defect. The leading failure-to-warn case in the area of toxic torts is Borel v. Fibreboard Paper Products Corp., 493 F.2d 1076 (5th Cir.1973), previously discussed. A major difficulty in applying the developing law of warning defects to toxic torts is the unknowability of hazards at the time of the manufacture and sale of the product. Thus, an issue has arisen as to whether the seller may defend against the action on the ground that it did not know, nor could it have known, the consequences of the product's use at the time of the plaintiff's exposure. The general rule in almost all jurisdictions is that defendant product sellers may defend on this ground. This "state-of-the-art" defense is discussed in more detail under product defenses, *infra*. In light of this knowability requirement, the analysis of failure to warn in the product defect context is virtually identical to negligence.

In general, the seller of the product is under a duty to disclose only foreseeable risks associated with the product. In *Borel*, for example, the court examined closely the development of scientific knowledge regarding the hazards of working with asbestos insulation products before concluding that the risks were foreseeable as early as the 1930s. Even very small foreseeable risks may trigger liability. In Davis v. Wyeth Laboratories, Inc., 399 F.2d 121 (9th Cir.1968), the court held that a manufacturer of polio vaccine had a duty to warn consumers of the risk that one person in one million would contract polio through taking the vaccine. The court stated:

> There will, of course, be cases where the personal risk, although existent and known, is so trifling in comparison with the advantage to be gained as to be de minimis. Appellee so character-

izes this case. It would approach the problem from a purely statistical point of view: less than one out of a million is just not unreasonable. This approach we reject. When, in a particular case, the risk qualitatively (e.g., of death or major disability) as well as quantitatively, on balance with the end sought to be achieved, is such as to call for a true choice judgment, medical or personal, the warning must be given.

Furthermore, the manufacturer will be held to the "knowledge and skill of an expert," another negligence concept. Thus, the manufacturer has an affirmative obligation to keep aware of current scientific developments related to its products, as well as to conduct its own reasonable inquiry into the effectiveness and safety of the products. The *Borel* court stated:

> The manufacturer's status as an expert means that at a minimum he must keep abreast of scientific knowledge, discoveries, and advances and is presumed to know what is imparted thereby. But even more importantly, a manufacturer has a duty to test and inspect his product. The extent of research and experiment must be commensurate with the dangers involved.

Even where a risk-utility analysis leads to the conclusion that the utility of the product outweighs its risks—thereby resulting in the conclusion that the product is not defectively designed—inadequate warnings will not be excused. The court in *Borel* emphasized the importance of adequate warnings.

The court stated: "The utility of an insulation product containing asbestos may outweigh the known or foreseeable risk to the insulation workers and thus justify its marketing. The product could still be unreasonably dangerous, however, if unaccompanied by adequate warnings."

The *Borel* court followed Section 402A. In the *Third Restatement*, the test is whether "the foreseeable risks of harm posed by the product could have been reduced or avoided by the provision of reasonable instructions or warnings by the seller ... and the omission of the instructions or warnings renders the product not reasonably safe." § 2(c). Although the language seems to address defendants, the warning requirements in the *Third Restatement* focus on whether the existing warnings, or lack thereof, made the *product* not reasonably safe to the plaintiff and what level of warning could convey the necessary information. *See generally* cmt. i to § 2.

3. Manufacturing Defect

A manufacturing, or production, defect relates to a product that was produced out of conformity with the product line's design and the manufacturer's intent. The classic example of a manufacturing defect is one of the cases in which a decomposed mouse was found in a bottle of soda. *See, e.g.,* Shoshone Coca–Cola Bottling Co. v. Dolinski, 420 P.2d 855 (Nev.1966). Although toxic tort actions may certainly arise from manufacturing defects, such claims are less frequent in the toxic tort context than are design defects or failure to warn. Nevertheless, a manufacturing defect claim may arise where, for example, a foreign chemical contaminates a batch of a particular product.

In Weber v. Fidelity & Casualty Ins. Co., 250 So.2d 754 (La.1971), the plaintiff brought an action against the manufacturer of a cattle dip and its insurer for damages associated with the application of the dip. The plaintiff alleged that several of the cattle to which the dip had been applied had died shortly after the application and that his two minor sons had become ill from mixing the dip. The plaintiff claimed that excessive amounts of arsenic must have been present in the dip to cause the ill effects. The product, although designed to contain arsenic, had not been designed to contain an amount that could cause the harm alleged. The court held that the plaintiff had made out a prima facie case for a manufacturing defect.

The rule for manufacturing defects tends to be more straightforward than the rules applicable to design defects or failure to warn. Indeed, the *Third Restatement* states the rule as one of absolute liability. Thus, it allows liability "when the product departs from its intended design even though all possible care was exercised in the preparation and marketing of the product." Restatement (Third) of Torts: Products Liability § 2(a). The rule of absolute liability is justified by the policy goal of encouraging manufacturers to invest in product safety measures and to raise the level of quality control during the production process. The rule also discourages manufacturers from allowing certain numbers of flawed products to enter the market as a cost-conserving measure. The reasoning for applying absolute liability to distributors and retailers, in addition to product manufacturers, is not only that sellers are in a better position than consumers to spread the loss, but that the threat of liability will encourage them to deal with responsible manufacturers.

4.   Prescription Drugs Under the Third Restatement

Section 6 of the Restatement (Third) of Torts: Products Liability proposes a rule for application of product liability to sellers of prescription drugs and medical devices that differs somewhat from Section 2's rule for other products. Section 6 provides a more specific test for liability related to prescription drugs and separates manufacturer liability from distributor/retailer liability.

For prescription drug manufacturers, the *Third Restatement* retains the three categories of liability, but with some modifications. The theory of manufacturing defect is unchanged. With regard to defective design, however, the risk-utility test embodied in Section 6 is intended to be more rigorous than its counterpart in Section 2(b). Section 6(c) states:

A prescription drug or medical device is not reasonably safe due to defective design if the foreseeable risks of harm posed by the drug or medical device are sufficiently great in relation to its foreseeable therapeutic benefits that reasonable

health-care providers, knowing of such foreseeable risks and therapeutic benefits, would not
prescribe the drug or medical device for any class
of patients.

Comment b makes clear that a design defect could
not be found if a reasonable health care provider
would prescribe the drug to anyone at all under any
circumstance. Thus, if the drug has any utility to
any class of patients, no design defect would exist,
notwithstanding the existence of high risks and
harmful effects to other patients.

It is unclear whether Section 6(c) will gain widespread acceptance among the states, though courts
generally favor some measure of immunity for prescription drug manufacturers. In Gebhardt v. Men-
tor Corp., 191 F.R.D. 180 (D.Ariz.1999), the court
applied Section 6(c), but held that the plaintiff did
not establish that physicians would not prescribe
the device for any class of patients. But in Mele v.
Howmedica, Inc., 808 N.E.2d 1026 (Ill.Ct.App.2004),
the court rejected any version of Section 6(c) because it could not be reconciled with state product
law under Section 402A in general and the consumer expectation test in particular.

Section 6(d) specifies that liability for inadequate
instructions or warnings may arise from failure to
properly warn or instruct prescribing health care
providers or the patient. Liability for failure to
warn the patient, however, will arise only if "the
manufacturer knows or has reason to know that
health-care providers will not be in a position to

reduce the risks of harm in accordance with the warnings or instructions." Comment e explains that this type of situation would usually arise only in a clinic environment where individual evaluation by a physician has not occurred, such as a mass vaccine inoculation program. Thus, Section 6(d)(1) retains the "learned intermediary" rule, which imposes on the health care provider the primary responsibility to instruct or warn of a drug's or medical device's risks in most circumstances. The learned intermediary doctrine is discussed in more detail *infra*.

Liability of a retail seller or other distributor of a prescription drug or medical device is limited under the *Third Restatement*. Such sellers would be absolutely liable for a manufacturing defect, as defined in Section 2(a). Beyond that, a retail seller or other distributor would be liable only for its own negligence. *See* § 6(e).

C. OTHER THEORIES OF LIABILITY

1. Negligence

The *Borel* case demonstrated the perils of relying upon a negligence theory in a latent disease case in the era when contributory negligence barred recovery by plaintiffs in most jurisdictions. Without question, most toxic product plaintiffs would prefer to rely upon strict liability theories than upon negligence. But whether negligence is asserted as a fallback position or as the only available claim under the circumstances of the case or in the applicable jurisdiction, plaintiffs will need to prove the standard negligence prima facie case. This traditionally requires the plaintiff to prove the elements of duty, breach of duty, cause-in-fact, proximate causation, and actual damages. The standard of care defining the duty, and the existence of a breach of the duty, may be difficult to prove where a latency period exists between the time of the exposure and the manifestation of illness. It requires the plaintiff to demonstrate both the defendant's knowledge of the hazards at the time of exposure and the foreseeability of harm to the plaintiff.

Actions based upon HIV-contaminated blood products present examples of the problems of latent-illness negligence claims. While the supplying of blood and other body parts is generally considered a service, rather than a product, negligence claims against the suppliers of blood products are quite similar to negligence claims involving other products. The blood-product negligence claims have tended to focus upon the time at which the blood suppliers became aware of the bloodborne nature of AIDS and the availability of steps to screen donated blood for HIV. With respect to the applicable standard of care, courts differ as to whether the supplier can rely upon industry practices at the time of collection to establish its duty.

In general, a blood supplier is held to a professional standard for a skilled provider of the same services. In Doe v. American Red Cross Blood Services, 377 S.E.2d 323 (S.C.1989), the court interpreted this to mean that the blood supplier must "conform to the generally recognized and accepted practices in his profession" at the relevant time. But other courts have held that mere compliance with industry practices cannot by itself establish the defendant's compliance with due care. In United Blood Services v. Quintana, 827 P.2d 509 (Colo. 1992), the court stated:

> In a professional negligence case ... a plaintiff should be permitted to present expert opinion testimony that the standard of care adopted by the school of practice to which the defendant adheres is unreasonably deficient by not incorporating readily available practices and procedures substantially more protective against the harm caused to the plaintiff than the standard of care adopted by the defendant's school of practice....

> In the instant case, [the blood supplier's] compliance with the Food and Drug Administration's recommendations and with the guidelines developed by the national blood banking community was some evidence of due care, but was not conclusive proof that additional precautions were not required.

In *Quintana*, the jury, on remand, found the defendant negligent notwithstanding its compliance with the industry standards. Not all cases have reached the same result, however. *See, e.g.*, Doe v. Miles Laboratories, Inc., 927 F.2d 187 (4th Cir.1991) (holding that the defendant blood clotting factor manufacturer had not breached the applicable standard of care after examining industry custom, governmental regulations, and medical profession standards at the relevant times); *see also* McKee v. Miles Laboratories, Inc., 675 F.Supp. 1060 (E.D.Ky. 1987) (dismissing negligence claims for failure to show violation of the standard of care).

The HIV cases have tended to focus on the timing of the defendant's conduct as well as the reasonableness of the conduct. In Kozup v. Georgetown University, 663 F.Supp. 1048 (D.D.C.1987), the court apparently held that blood suppliers that complied with industry standards prior to 1985—when the ELISA test for screening blood for the presence of HIV antibodies was developed and implemented in the blood industry—could not as a matter of law be negligent for failure to test blood, notwithstanding the existence of another, less reliable, testing procedure. In contrast, the New Jersey Supreme Court held that a blood bank association was negligent for failure to recommend that its member blood banks implement surrogate testing to reduce the risk of HIV-contaminated blood. In Snyder v. American Association of Blood Banks, 676 A.2d 1036 (N.J.1996), the court held that the association owed a duty of care to the plaintiff, who had contracted HIV from a transfusion in 1984, prior to the availability of the ELISA test. The court stated that the association should have recommended to its members that they use a form of testing that sought to identify persons at risk of carrying HIV by identifying common characteristics in a majority of persons who developed AIDS. In this instance, testing for antibodies to hepatitis B would have eliminated from the blood supply a substantial amount of HIV-contaminated blood. The court was not swayed by the defendants' arguments that use of the surrogate test would have been costly and would have caused the blood banks to reject too much blood. Similarly, whether a defendant breached its duty by failing to screen out high risk blood donors has depended upon the date of the exposure in relation to the knowledge of the defendant regarding the risk of HIV transmission in human blood. *See, e.g.*, Hoemke v. New York Blood Center, 912 F.2d 550 (2d Cir.1990) (no negligence for a transfusion occurring in 1981).

The issue of timing is not unique to the HIV cases. The latency period that is characteristic of toxic torts creates the timing problem. Courts and juries that have the benefit of hindsight when examining the conduct of defendants must make determinations of what was objectively known or subjectively knowable at the time of the defendant's actions. While this is not exactly new, longer latency periods confuse and complicate these determinations.

2. Implied Warranties

Warranty claims are a creature of the law of contracts, and in particular the law of sales. Before plaintiffs were allowed to sue in tort for defective products, warranty claims were the most important type of claim for injuries from products. Warranty claims continue to be asserted in many toxic tort actions, typically along with negligence and strict product liability claims. Perhaps because warranty claims derive from the law of contracts, these claims tend to be given less emphasis than other claims in judicial decisions in the area of toxic torts. Nevertheless, they continue to be recognized as prominent among the claims in the toxic product plaintiff's arsenal. *See, e.g.*, Cipollone v. Liggett Group, Inc., 505 U.S. 504 (1992) (asserting warranty claims along with strict product liability claims, negligence, and fraud). Some courts, however, merge claims for implied warranties and strict liability on the theory that they are mirror images of one another, the former in contract and the latter in tort. *See* Freeman v. Hoffman–La Roche, Inc., 618 N.W.2d 827 (Neb.2000).

Article Two of the Uniform Commercial Code (U.C.C.), adopted in virtually every state, supplies the basic rules governing claims for breach of implied warranties. The U.C.C. does not require that the person making the warranty claim be in privity of contract with the seller of the product. The extent to which persons related or unrelated to the buyer may rely upon the implied warranties will depend upon which alternative set forth in U.C.C. § 2–318 the state has enacted. These alternatives range from the more restrictive (family members, household members, and guests of the buyer) to the quite liberal (persons who could bring product liability actions in tort).

a. *Implied Warranty of Merchantability*

Uniform Commercial Code § 2–314 establishes an implied warranty of merchantability in a contract of sale in which the seller is "a merchant with respect to goods of that kind." U.C.C. § 2–314(1) (2008). To be merchantable, the product must, at a minimum, be "fit for the ordinary purposes for which such goods are used" (§ 2–314(2)(c)), be "adequately contained, packaged, and labeled as the agreement [of sale] may require" (§ 2–314(2)(e)), and "conform to the promises or affirmations of fact made on the container or label if any" (§ 2–314(2)(f)).

A valid claim for breach of the implied warranty of merchantability will not exist if the use of the product was not its ordinary use. For example, in Rynders v. E.I. du Pont de Nemours & Co., 21 F.3d 835 (8th Cir.1994), the court addressed claims for personal injuries by persons who had received implants designed to correct temporomandibular joint (TMJ) disorders. The implants were manufactured by a non-party medical supplier using Teflon, an industrial material manufactured by the defendant. The court held that the plaintiffs had not stated claims for breach of the implied warranty of merchantability because there was sufficient evidence demonstrating that the defendant du Pont had developed Teflon for industrial purposes and not for medical use. Thus, the use of the product was not its ordinary purpose and could not give rise to a claim under that warranty theory.

b. *Implied Warranty of Fitness for a Particular Purpose*

A warranty of fitness for a particular purpose is also implied in the sale of a product, where appropriate. U.C.C. § 2–315 provides that

[w]here the seller at the time of contracting has reason to know any particular purpose for which the goods are required and that the buyer is relying on the seller's skill or judgment to select or furnish suitable goods, there is . . . an implied warranty that the goods shall be fit for such purpose.

As distinguished from an implied warranty of merchantability, this section does not require the seller of the product to be a "merchant" of the type of goods sold. Furthermore, the section provides that the seller must know that the buyer will be relying on the seller's skill or judgment.

The "particular purpose" must be different from the ordinary purpose for which the product is used. The seller's knowledge that the consumer intends to use the product for a certain purpose would not trigger this warranty if that purpose falls within the ordinary range of uses for that product. Thus, in Unified School District v. U.S. Gypsum Co., 788 F.Supp. 1173 (D.Kan.1992), where the plaintiff sought damages for the removal of asbestos-containing materials from its schools, the court was correct in dismissing the claim for breach of implied warranty for a particular purpose because the asbestos-containing materials had been used for their intended purpose.

3. Misrepresentation Claims

a. Express Warranty

In addition to implied warranties, product sellers may make express warranties to consumers. The rule of express warranties also derives from the Uniform Commercial Code. U.C.C. § 2–313 provides that a seller makes an express warranty by "affirmation of fact or promise made" (§ 2–313(1)(a)), by "description of the goods" (§ 2–313(1)(b)), or by a "sample or model" (§ 2–313(1)(c)), any of which must have been made a part of the basis of the bargain between the seller and the buyer. Breach of an express warranty essentially creates a strict liability, as the product need not be shown to be defective for the breach of warranty claim to lie. Nor need the plaintiff demonstrate reliance on the warranty, unless the seller affirmatively proves lack of reliance. U.C.C. § 2–313 (2008), comments. *See* Unified School District v. U.S. Gypsum Co., 788 F.Supp 1173 (D.Kan.1992) (applying Kansas law). A certain amount of exaggeration, or "puffing," is tolerated before the seller's representations will be considered an express warranty.

Recent amendments to Section 2–313 could potentially convert the section into three, depending on how much of the amendments a state chooses to adopt. Amended Section 2–313 restricts the warranty to the "immediate buyer," but retains the requirement that the representation be a basis of the bargain. The other amendments apply to a "remote purchaser"—someone who "buys or leases goods from an immediate buyer or other person in the normal chain of distribution," § 2–313A(b)—and apply different requirements to each, depending on whether the warranty was made in the packaging,

§ 2–313A, or in advertisements to the public, § 2–313B.

b. Misrepresentation

Misrepresentation claims may be based on strict liability, negligence, or intentional or fraudulent conduct. A strict tort liability claim for misrepresentation is set forth in the Restatement (Second) of Torts and is recognized in many jurisdictions. Section 402B of the *Second Restatement* provides:

> One engaged in the business of selling chattels who, by advertising, labels, or otherwise, makes to the public a misrepresentation of a material fact concerning the character or quality of a chattel sold by him is subject to liability for physical harm to a consumer of the chattel caused by justifiable reliance upon the misrepresentation, even though
>
>> (a) it is not made fraudulently or negligently, and
>>
>> (b) the consumer has not bought the chattel from or entered into any contractual relation with the seller.

Here, as with Section 402A, the seller must be "in the business of selling chattels." The section also focuses on the public nature of the misrepresentation, such as—but not limited to—advertisements and other forms of sales promotions.

Moreover, in contrast to express warranty theories under the U.C.C., Section 402B expressly requires "justifiable reliance" by the consumer on the representations made by the seller. What constitutes justifiable reliance? In Gunsalus v. Celotex Corp., 674 F.Supp. 1149 (E.D.Pa.1987), the court dismissed the plaintiff's misrepresentation claims arising out of cigarette advertisements that the plaintiff alleged misrepresented the health and safety aspects of smoking. The plaintiff alleged reliance on certain advertisements in which the manufacturer made representations that the specific brand of cigarettes was soothing to the throat. The court held that the ads were "not the kind of representations upon which reasonable people would rely; they suggest only that a smoker might enjoy Pall Mall cigarettes more than other brands." The court further noted that once the plaintiff had tried the particular cigarette brand, his decision to continue smoking that brand was based upon his own taste choices and/or his alleged addiction, not upon the seller's representations.

Section 9 of the Restatement (Third) of Torts: Products Liability touches upon misrepresentation claims involving the marketing of a product. Essentially, Section 9 succinctly restates the prevailing principles that a product seller may be held liable for material misrepresentations that are fraudulent, negligent, or innocent. Comment b incorporates section 402B from the *Second Restatement*. Comment d emphasizes that a plaintiff alleging a claim of misrepresentation regarding a product need not prove that the product was defective at the time of the sale to have a viable misrepresentation claim.

D. REGULATORY DUTY TO DISCLOSE

Product manufacturers have certain regulatory duties under the Occupational Safety and Health Act (OSHAct), the primary statute governing health issues in the workplace, that may create liabilities beyond the direct liability to an injured user or consumer. One such liability is imposed by the Hazard Communication Standard, 29 C.F.R. § 1910.1200 (2010). The Hazard Communication Standard requires chemical manufacturers and importers to evaluate, by considering the available scientific information, the chemicals produced or imported by them to determine the hazards associated with the chemicals. Further, the manufacturers and importers must create a material safety data sheet (MSDS) for each hazardous chemical, which shall travel with the chemical when it leaves the hands of the manufacturer or importer and is transferred to a distributor or employer. The manufacturer or importer is also required to label the chemicals with "appropriate hazard warnings," which should include a description of the target organ effects of exposure to the chemicals. Martin v. American Cyanamid Co., 5 F.3d 140 (6th Cir.1993). In other words, "eye irritant" would be insufficient, but "may cause blindness" would give the necessary target organ effect. Upon receiving the MSDS and the labeled chemicals, the employers then are obligated to pass the information on to their employees who come into contact with the chemical, pursuant to certain defined regulatory procedures. *See generally infra* Chapter 5, Sec. C.4. As with all matters related to the OSHAct, any liability incurred for violations would be owed to the Government through fines or penalties. The OSHAct does not create a private cause of action for persons who claim injury from violations of the Act and its regulations.

E. PRODUCT LIABILITY DEFENSES

Toxic tort claims stretch the law of product liability beyond its originally intended limits. Accordingly, it is within the context of toxic tort actions that courts have been asked to apply certain product defenses in new ways. This has been particularly notable with respect to the unknowable character of many hazards at the time the product was sold. While this information is always relevant to negligence claims, and is usually relevant in product liability claims, dissenting arguments raise important policy questions about the role of strict liability in the legal system.

1. State-of-the-Art Defense

The state-of-the-art defense has been asserted in product liability claims where the defendant alleges that it did not know, and could not reasonably have known, of the hazards of the product at the time the product was placed on the market. The defense has been widely recognized in failure-to-warn cases. *See, e.g.*, Anderson v. Owens–Corning Fiberglas Corp., 810 P.2d 549 (Cal.1991). Courts generally agree that "[s]tate of the art includes all of the available knowledge on a subject at a given time, and this includes scientific, medical, engineering, and any other knowledge that may be available." Lohrmann v. Pittsburgh Corning Corp., 782 F.2d 1156 (4th Cir.1986). This includes reasonable testing and the information that reasonable testing should have produced. Most courts accept the fact that by allowing the state-of-the-art defense in failure-to-warn claims under Section 402A and comment j, "negligence concepts to some extent have been grafted onto strict liability . . . and liability is no longer entirely 'strict.'" Owens–Illinois, Inc. v. Zenobia, 601 A.2d 633 (Md.1992).

Almost all courts allow the state-of-the-art defense in failure-to-warn cases. See, e.g., Anderson v. Owens–Corning Fiberglas Corp., 810 P.2d 549 (Cal. 1991). Courts following Section 402A have typically read comment j on warnings to allow the defense. In the Third Restatement, the state-of-the-art defense is expressly and categorically endorsed. Comment m to § 2 of the Third Restatement specifically references toxic chemicals, prescription drugs, and medical devices, stating: "[P]laintiff should bear the burden of establishing that the risk in question was known or should have been known to the relevant manufacturing community. The harms that result from unforeseeable risks . . . are not a basis for liability."

A vocal—and controversial—minority view has been expressed by the New Jersey Supreme Court in an early failure-to-warn case involving asbestos workers. In Beshada v. Johns–Manville Prods. Corp., 447 A.2d 539 (N.J.1982), the court refused to allow the state-of-the-art defense, even though the extent and timing of the defendants' knowledge of the hazards associated with their asbestos-containing products were in dispute. The court examined the policies underlying the law of product liability— most particularly, risk spreading and deterrence— and concluded that undiluted strict liability best served the goals of the tort system. Moreover, the court expressed concern that undertaking the task of determining what was scientifically knowable at a particular point in time would consume judicial resources and ultimately lead to jury confusion.

The *Beshada* court's opinion points out both sides of the policy argument regarding allowance of the state-of-the-art defense:

> One of the most important arguments generally advanced for imposing strict liability is that the manufacturers and distributors of defective products can best allocate the costs of the injuries resulting from those products. The premise is that the price of a product should reflect all of its costs, including the cost of injuries caused by the product. This can best be accomplished by imposing liability on the manufacturer and distributors. Those persons can insure against liability and incorporate the cost of the insurance in the price of the product . . . .

With respect to deterrence, the court noted that the level of the state of the art at a particular moment in time is affected by the level of research and development conducted by the industry at that time. The court stated: "By imposing on manufacturers the costs of failure to discover hazards, we create an incentive for them to invest more actively in safety research."

In 1984, shortly after the *Beshada* case, the New Jersey Supreme Court allowed the state-of-the-art defense in a product liability action against drug manufacturers. Feldman v. Lederle Laboratories, 479 A.2d 374 (N.J.1984). The court in *Feldman* expressly limited *Beshada* to its facts, presumably the unique circumstances of asbestos litigation. Some courts might disagree as to the propriety of the distinction made by the New Jersey Supreme Court in these cases. When asbestos manufacturers raised the question of the constitutionality of this distinction between asbestos cases and other types of cases, they were rebuffed. *See* In re Asbestos Litig., 829 F.2d 1233 (3d Cir.1987) (holding that the classifications were not unconstitutional).

Similarly, the Montana Supreme Court, on a certified question from a federal district court, has emphatically stated that Montana does not recognize the state-of-the-art defense in strict product liability actions generally. Rather, in Sternhagen v. Dow Co., 935 P.2d 1139 (Mont.1997), a case involving exposure to an agricultural chemical, the Montana Supreme Court held that knowledge of the hazards of the product should be imputed to the manufacturer for the same public policy reasons expressed in *Beshada*.

2. Unavoidably Unsafe Products

Some products may be incapable of being made completely safe for the use for which they were intended, but their usefulness may outweigh the risk of harm. The unavoidably unsafe product is the subject of comment k of Section 402A of the second Restatement, which states that "[s]uch a product, properly prepared, and accompanied by proper directions and warning, is not defective, nor is it unreasonably dangerous." The policy behind this defense is to encourage the development of useful and highly necessary products by allowing the seller to avoid liability associated with the inherent and unavoidable risks of those products. As comment k states, however, the seller remains under an obligation to provide an appropriate warning to the consumer regarding the risks associated with the product. Thus, comment k applies directly to design defects, but not to manufacturing defects or failure to warn claims.

The classic example of an unavoidably unsafe product is an experimental drug that could be quite beneficial for its therapeutic purpose, but that may carry with it significant risks. The battle on the application of comment k has been waged primarily in the arena of prescription drugs. Some courts have held that comment k is properly applied on a case-by-case basis. *See* Savina v. Sterling Drug, Inc., 795 P.2d 915 (Kan.1990); *see also* Hill v. Searle Laboratories, 884 F.2d 1064 (8th Cir.1989) (holding that only products "with exceptional social need" fall within comment k protection). The case-by-case analysis would seem to be consistent with the language of comment k itself, which provides various examples of the kinds of prescription drugs that would appropriately fall within the comment's protection, but which does not suggest that all prescription drugs—or all of any class of product—should be deemed unavoidably unsafe as a matter of law. *See* Hill v. Wyeth, Inc., 2007 WL 674251 (E.D. Mo. 2007) (holding that the determination of whether a prescription drug was unavoidably unsafe was for the jury); Ruiz–Guzman v. Amvac Chemical Corp., 7 P.3d 795 (Wash.2000) (holding that under right circumstances a pesticide could be considered unavoidably unsafe under case-by-case approach to comment k).

Other courts, in contrast, have read comment k as applicable to certain broad classes of claims. In particular, in Brown v. Superior Court, 751 P.2d 470 (Cal.1988), a DES drug case, the California Supreme Court held that all prescription drugs are deemed unavoidably unsafe. *Accord, e.g.*, Hahn v. Richter, 673 A.2d 888 (Pa. 1996). The court's concerns were that liability for prescription drug defects could drive manufacturers from the market, that liability could lead to protracted delays in new drugs reaching the market, and that manufacturers' insurance rates would soar. In Grundberg v. Upjohn Company, 813 P.2d 89 (Utah 1991), the Utah Supreme Court agreed, emphasizing the social benefit of prescription drugs. The *Grundberg* court noted that the Food and Drug Administration (FDA) often grants approval to market new drugs that contain known risks on the basis of their beneficial qualities. The court found that the regulatory process for licensing new drugs and providing post-market surveillance adequately balanced the drugs' risks with their benefits and was the proper forum for that analysis.

The *Second Restatement* had used the risk-utility test primarily in the context of unavoidably unsafe products, preferring the consumer expectation test for determining the existence of a product defect. The Restatement (Third) of Torts: Products Liability adopts the risk-utility test to determine design defects. Thus, it is not surprising that the *Third Restatement* jettisons the unavoidably unsafe defense as a distinct defense. The basic concept of the defense is inherent in the risk-utility test, however, and clearly the seller of a product with high utility that carries with it some risks, which could not have been made safer at the time, and that is accompanied by appropriate warnings, would escape liability.

The *Third Restatement*'s separate section on the liability of sellers of prescription drugs and medical devices does provide special protection from design defect claims. Section 6 of the *Third Restatement* adopts a rule that allows a prescription drug manufacturer to avoid liability for defective design claims if its product has any utility for any class of patients, regardless of the risks, provided that the drug is accompanied by appropriate instructions and warnings. This section suggests that the prescription drug manufacturer need not show a high utility for the drug—just any utility at all—to avoid liability. Comment b to Section 6 cites the FDA's regulatory system as the primary source of standards for drug design and as a major reason for granting deference to drugs that have undergone FDA approval. Nevertheless, the *Third Restatement* stops short of advocating an absolute immunity for prescription drug and medical device manufacturers along the lines of *Grundberg*, and these issues will continue to be worked out in the courts.

3. Sophisticated User Defense

In some commercial situations, the party to whom the product is delivered is in a position equal or superior to the seller to know the hazards of the product, particularly in the context of its industrial use. Courts have allowed a "sophisticated user" defense for suppliers where they have provided adequate warning of the hazards of the product to the purchaser. This defense is often employed in the context of bulk suppliers of chemicals to knowledgeable industrial intermediaries. Thus, in Adams v. Union Carbide Corp., 737 F.2d 1453 (6th Cir.1984), the court affirmed the trial court's grant of summary judgment in favor of Union Carbide, the manufacturer/supplier of the chemical toluene diisocyanate (TDI), which Union Carbide had sold to the plaintiff's employer, General Motors. The plaintiff alleged that Union Carbide should have directly warned the employees of General Motors. The court relied on Restatement (Second) of Torts § 388, comment n, finding that Union Carbide's safety manual, the MSDS (the information sheet on the hazards of the product provided by the supplier), and safety discussion sessions with General Motors officials satisfied Union Carbide's obligation to provide adequate warnings. The court held that Union Carbide reasonably relied upon General Motors to communicate the safety information to its employees.

In Oman v. Johns–Manville Corp., 764 F.2d 224 (4th Cir.1985), the court applied a balancing test to determine whether the manufacturer of asbestos-containing products had a duty to warn the employees of the purchaser of its products. The factors set forth in this test were:

> (1) the dangerous condition of the product; (2) the purpose for which the product is used; (3) the form of any warnings given; (4) the reliability of the third party as a conduit of necessary information about the product; (5) the magnitude of the risk involved; and (6) the burdens imposed upon the supplier by requiring that he directly warn all users.

In *Oman*, the court did not allow the sophisticated user defense because the product was extremely dangerous and little burden would be placed upon the manufacturer to provide the warning. Further, the record showed that the employer was unaware of the dangers until 1964, and, upon becoming aware, failed to communicate the dangers to its employees. Reaching a similar result, the court in Willis v. Raymark Industries, Inc., 905 F.2d 793 (4th Cir.1990) stated that "[t]he fact that an employer possesses knowledge of a product's dangers does not extinguish the manufacturer's liability unless the manufacturer can also show that it had reason to believe that the employer was or would be acting to protect the employees."

What, then, constitutes a sufficiently "sophisticated" user to trigger the defense? In Hoffman v. Houghton Chemical Corp., 751 N.E.2d 848 (Mass. 2001), the Massachusetts Supreme Judicial Court observed that it is often too difficult for suppliers of bulk products to warn the users of their products. The court noted that the purchasing company is typically in a different industry from the supplier, and the specific uses of the product by the purchaser's employees may be too remote for the supplier to foresee. Some intermediaries are truly "sophisticated." In Baker v. Monsanto Co., 962 F.Supp. 1143 (S.D.Ind.1997), the court ruled that the plaintiff's employer, Westinghouse Electric, fell clearly within the category of a sophisticated user. The plaintiff claimed personal injuries resulting from exposure to PCBs in dielectric fluids inside electrical equipment he repaired in the course of his employment. Westinghouse had established the specifications for the dielectric fluids that Monsanto manufactured for Westinghouse. Indeed, Westinghouse had specified both the chemical and physical properties of the fluids for the product, which was developed by Westinghouse after seventeen years of conducting its own research. Given that Monsanto had sent written warnings to Westinghouse regarding the hazards of some of its products, the court held that

Westinghouse was in a superior position to assess the hazards and establish safety measures for its own employees. Accordingly, Monsanto was not liable for failure to warn.

Where the employer can be shown to be in a position to adequately warn its employees, the inadequacy of the warnings from the supplier to the purchaser becomes irrelevant. Newson v. Monsanto Co., 869 F.Supp. 1255 (E.D.Mich.1994) involved the sale of polyvinyl butyryl (PVB) to Ford Motor Company for use in manufacturing shatterproof windshields. When workers brought suit against the supplier for respiratory injuries that they claimed were related to exposure to heated PVB, the court allowed the supplier to avoid liability on the basis that Ford was a sophisticated user of PVB. The court so held notwithstanding the fact that the supplier had not provided an adequate warning regarding the hazards of heated PVB. The court determined that Ford, which had several departments engaged in scientific research, could have learned of the hazards of heated PVB by conducting its own research and through its own past experience.

What should the result be when the employee who uses the product has superior knowledge of its hazards? Johnson v. American Standard, Inc., 179 P.3d 905 (Cal. 2008), involved an HVAC technician who claimed that chemical suppliers and equipment manufacturers should have warned him that his work would expose him to a dangerous gas. He also claimed that he was unaware of the hazard. The court said that if the plaintiff, a highly trained and skilled worker, knew or should have known of the specific danger, then the suppliers should be shielded from liability without the need to show that they had warned. This approach, the court acknowledged, was essentially a version of the rule of no liability for obvious dangers.

OSHA regulations may play a role in determining the knowledge of the industrial product user of the hazards of the substance in question. Thus, in Martin v. S.C. Johnson & Sons, Inc., 1996 WL 165039 (D.V.I.1996), the court held that the chemical manufacturer was reasonable in relying on the industrial user of the chemical to comply with the OSHA Hazard Communication Standard and pass on the manufacturer's warnings (contained in labels and material safety data sheets (MSDSs)) to its employees. A chemical manufacturer's duties pursuant to the Hazard Communication Standard are discussed in Section D, *supra*.

4. Learned Intermediary Doctrine

In contrast to the sophisticated user defense, which is typically raised in the context of an industrial setting in which the plaintiff is an employee of the party determined to be the "sophisticated user," the learned intermediary doctrine is sometimes raised when the product seller claims that other kinds of professional parties with superior knowledge had the responsibility to directly warn the product user of its hazards. The defense frequently arises in cases against manufacturers of prescription drugs. A majority of jurisdictions espouses the doctrine, which is based on the concept that the "purchaser's doctor is a learned intermediary between the purchaser and the manufacturer. If the doctor is properly warned of the possibility of a side effect in some patients, and is advised of the symptoms normally accompanying the side effect, there is an excellent chance that injury to the patient can be avoided." Sterling Drug, Inc. v. Cornish, 370 F.2d 82 (8th Cir.1966).

The *Third Restatement* incorporates the common-law learned intermediary doctrine into the section on liability of manufacturers of prescription drugs or medical devices for failure to warn. Section 6(d)(1) provides that the manufacturer is shielded from liability for failing to warn the ultimate consumer where it has given reasonable warnings of foreseeable harm to "prescribing and other health-care providers who are in a position to reduce the risks of harm in accordance with the instructions or warnings." Where the manufacturer knows that the physician or other health-care provider has a limited decision making role vis-à-vis the therapeutic relationship with patients, then the manufacturer will be required to directly warn the patients. Restatement (Third) of Torts: Products Liability, § 6(d)(2) & cmt. b. In turn, some states have adopted Section 6 of the *Third Restatement. See, e.g.,* Larkin v. Pfizer, Inc., 153 S.W.3d 758 (Ky. 2004); Freeman v. Hoffman–La Roche, Inc., 618 N.W.2d 827 (Neb.2000).

When asserted in a toxic tort action, the learned intermediary doctrine is analogous to the sophisticated user defense, relying upon the same underlying principles. In Swicegood v. Pliva, Inc., 2010 WL 1138455 (N.D. Ga. 2010) (slip op.), for example, the court held that the defendant product manufacturer could not rely on the physician intermediary to adequately warn the patient because there was sufficient evidence for a jury to conclude that the physician did not know the extent of the risk posed by the drug. The plaintiff in that case sued the manufacturer of a drug prescribed for short-term treatment of gastroesophageal reflux disease, claiming that the drug caused her to develop a movement disorder. The court refused to allow the learned intermediary defense.

Courts sometimes arrive at different results on similar facts, however. In Harrison v. American Home Products, Inc., 165 F.3d 374 (5th Cir.1999), the court held that the manufacturer of Norplant contraceptive had not been obligated to warn consumers directly about the product's risks because physicians played a significant role in prescribing the product and educating patients about its benefits and risks. In contrast, in Perez v. Wyeth Labs. Inc., 734 A.2d 1245 (N.J.1999), the New Jersey Supreme Court held that the manufacturer's mass advertisements of Norplant to the public opened the company to failure-to-warn claims by patients.

One recognized exception to the learned intermediary doctrine is in the context of mass immunization programs. For example, Davis v. Wyeth Labs.,

Inc., 399 F.2d 121 (9th Cir.1968) recognized an exception for mass polio immunizations at a clinic in which no real opportunity for physician consultation was available. Similarly, Allison v. Merck & Co., 878 P.2d 948 (Nev.1994) involved a vaccine program in which the manufacturer contracted with CDC to provide product information to patients. The court held that the manufacturer may not delegate its duty to warn and may be liable for failure to adequately warn the recipients of the vaccine. A second exception recognized by some courts involves oral contraceptives. The principle is similar to mass immunizations. Dispensing oral contraceptives frequently involves less physician input than other prescription drugs. *See* MacDonald v. Ortho Pharmaceutical Corp., 475 N.E.2d 65 (Mass.1985). Finally, New Jersey has recognized an exception for direct-to-consumer advertising of prescription drugs. *See* Perez v. Wyeth Labs. Inc., 734 A.2d 1245 (N.J.1999).

Some jurisdictions have rejected the learned intermediary defense. In State v. Karl, 647 S.E.2d 899 (W. Va. 2007), the Supreme Court of Appeals of West Virginia found the "justifications for the learned intermediary doctrine to be largely outdated and unpersuasive." The court pointed to the changes in prescription drug marketing and sales, which include much direct-to-consumer advertising and internet sales. The court also noted that the physician-patient relationship has undergone a dramatic change, particularly as a result of managed care, which has reduced the amount of time a physician spends with a patient. In commenting on the *Third Restatement*'s provisions, the court read Section 6(d)(2) as a strong qualification of the learned intermediary defense, because so many situations exist in which the physician is not in a position to adequately warn patients. Finally, as a matter of public policy, the court said that because prescription drug manufacturers receive substantial economic benefit from the sale of their products, they should bear a reciprocal duty to make certain that adequate warnings reach consumers.

5. Plaintiff's Culpable Conduct

The *Second Restatement*, drafted in the era when any contributory negligence on the part of the plaintiff generally barred the plaintiff's negligence claim, declared that contributory negligence should not be considered a defense to a strict liability claim. Restatement (Second) of Torts § 402A, cmt. n (1965). Assumption of the risk was available as a defense to a strict liability claim, however, provided that the plaintiff voluntarily and unreasonably encountered a known danger. This bifurcation of what is now commonly known as the culpable conduct defense no longer made sense following the adoption by most states of the doctrine of comparative negligence. This shift in the states is reflected in the *Third Restatement*, which adopts the use of apportionment of fault in strict liability actions.

The *Third Restatement* provides: "A plaintiff's recovery of damages for harm caused by a product defect may be reduced if the conduct of the plaintiff combines with the product defect to cause the harm and the plaintiff's conduct fails to conform to generally applicable rules establishing appropriate standards of care." Restatement (Third) of Torts: Products Liability § 17(a). This rule is broad enough to encompass conduct that would have been characterized previously as contributory negligence and at least some types of assumption of risk. In addition, the *Third Restatement* incorporates product misuse, alteration, and/or modification into the apportionment doctrine, stating that such conduct is relevant to a determination of comparative responsibility. *See* cmt. c. Comment b notes that the "generally applicable rules establishing appropriate standards of care" invoked in Section 17 vary from state to state.

6. Blood Shield Statutes

Virtually every state has enacted legislation shielding suppliers of blood, blood products, and other bodily fluids or tissues from defective product claims. In Royer v. Miles Laboratory, Inc., 811 P.2d 644 (Or.Ct.App.1991), the court interpreted the Oregon blood shield statute in a case brought by a hemophiliac who contracted hepatitis and HIV from a blood clotting product. The appellate court affirmed the trial court's dismissal of the strict liability claims on the basis of the statutory language, which provided:

The procuring, processing, furnishing, distributing, administering or using of any part of a human body for the purpose of injecting, transfusing or transplanting that part into a human body is not a sales transaction covered by an implied warranty under the Uniform Commercial Code or otherwise.

Or. Rev. Stat. § 97.300 (currently codified at Or. Rev. Stat. § 97.985 (2009)). Because the concept of strict liability in tort was essentially an offshoot of breach of warranty under the U.C.C., the court construed the statute to bar strict product liability claims against the manufacturer of the clotting product.

The policies underlying the blood shield statutes are several. First, the state legislatures feared that allowing strict liability against providers of blood and blood products would cause providers to leave the market. Second, the costs of liability, coupled with a diminished market, would raise the cost of blood products to a prohibitive level. Third, the blood industry had charitable beginnings, and the notion of treating its providers in a fashion similar to profit-making product manufacturers was distasteful. Consequently, providing blood and blood products has been traditionally viewed as a service, rather than as the sale of a product.

Most state blood shield statutes were developed in the pre-AIDS era, and at a time when the selling of blood and blood products was not considered big business. In many respects, these products are now sold in the same fashion as other products, with non-profit blood suppliers realizing profits from the sale and resale of blood. Blood products are distributed into the stream of commerce with markups in price at every stage leading to their ultimate destination. These factors raise the issue of whether blood shield statutes may be inappropriate for the claims and injuries of the new millennium. Nevertheless, courts continue to uphold the validity of the blood shield statutes. *See, e.g.*, Weishorn v. Miles–Cutter, 721 A.2d 811 (Pa.Super.1998).

A further reason for the legislative restrictions on the use of strict product liability claims is the difficulty in viewing contaminated blood and other human body parts as products in the traditional sense. This has been problematic both in a moral sense and as a matter of legal doctrine. Thus, contaminated blood is not seen as the kind of defect that Section 402A was intended to reach. Resembling a manufacturing defect more closely than a design defect, contaminated blood defies strict categorization into any of these theories. The fact that strict product liability is not available for claims arising from the sale of blood and blood products does not preclude claims based upon negligence, however. *See generally* Section C.1, *supra*.

F. LOOKING TO THE FUTURE: NANOTECHNOLOGY

Nanotechnology has been around for a while, but it is becoming more pervasive as new products and applications appear. What is nanotechnology? The National Nanotechnology Initiative (NNI) provides the following definition:

Nanotechnology is the understanding and control of matter at dimensions between approximately 1 and 100 nanometers, where unique phenomena enable novel applications. Encompassing nanoscale science, engineering, and technology, nanotechnology involves imaging, measuring, modeling, and manipulating matter at this length scale.

A nanometer is one-billionth of a meter. A sheet of paper is about 100,000 nanometers thick; a single gold atom is about a third of a nanometer in diameter. Dimensions between approximately 1 and 100 nanometers are known as the nanoscale. Unusual physical, chemical, and biological properties can emerge in materials at the nanoscale. These properties may differ in important ways from the properties of bulk materials and single atoms or molecules.

http://www.nano.gov/html/facts/whatIsNano.html. NNI lists developing uses as diverse as cancer treatments, nerve regeneration, efficient solar energy, and both industrial and consumer product enhancement. Thus, nanoparticles are frequently part of product design to give the product characteristics that are more useful and convenient. Notwithstanding this burst of technological ingenuity, the impact of nanotechnology on human health and the environment has been only sparsely studied, and nanotechnology is virtually unregulated in the United States. As an emerging technology with unknown risks, nanotechnology is likely to follow the path of other toxic torts in the areas of both private law and public law.

The FDA, the likely federal agency to regulate nanotechnology in pharmaceuticals and food products, currently takes a hands-off approach to food additives that contain engineered nanoparticles. The FDA does not require a food manufacturer to report additives that are deemed generally regarded as safe (GRAS) in the opinion of the manufacturer without FDA input. U.S. Government Accountability Office (GAO), Food Safety: FDA Should Strengthen Its Oversight of Food Ingredients Determined to Be Generally Recognized as Safe (GRAS) 26–27 (2010).

Some studies have shown the potential for health risks associated with useful nanoparticles in products. For example, researchers from UCLA conducted a laboratory study on mice to test the effects of the titanium dioxide nanoparticles regularly used in many consumer products, including cosmetics (especially sunblocks), food coloring, toothpaste, and paint. The researchers have heralded their study as the first animal study to demonstrate a connection between the particular substance and genetic harm. Trouiller et al., *Titanium Dioxide Nanoparticles Induce DNA Damage and Genetic Instability In vivo in Mice*, 69 Cancer Res. 8784 (2009). As the number and frequency of these kinds of studies increase, a better picture of the hazards of nanotechnology will emerge. It is likely that the earliest tort litigation will be based upon product liability claims and the other product-related claims set forth in this Chapter. For an overview of nanotechnology risk and thoughts on the litigation that is certain to come, see Ronald C. Wernette, *The Dawn of the Age of Nanotorts*, 24 Toxics L. Rptr. (BNA) 73 (Jan. 15, 2009).

So little is known about the health impacts of nanotechnology that there is no information about when and how humans are exposed to nanoparticles in ways that could be harmful. Thus, looking at nanotechnology through the prism of toxic torts, everything from exposure to injury to scientific proof remains uncertain, and all issues are on the table. For an ongoing discussion of the legal issues related to nanotechnology, see this author's blog at http://blogs.law.widener.edu/nanolaw/.

G. TORT REFORM MEASURES

No discussion of toxic tort causes of action would be complete without some mention of the reform movement. Tort reform has taken different shapes and has moved on several fronts, most notably various legislative initiatives both at the state and federal levels. It has generally taken the form of efforts to limit litigation, especially medical malpractice lawsuits and product liability litigation. Because of the heavy emphasis on product liability in the tort reform movement, this discussion of reform measures is included here in the chapter on toxic product liability. But tort reformers have also directed their efforts at tort litigation generally, and much of the discussion here applies to torts beyond product liability actions.

1. Federal Tort Reform Efforts

Efforts at federal product liability legislative reform have been considered for a number of years. These proposals would preempt the operation of state tort law in the areas covered by the legislation. Some federal measures have proposed broad reforms, whereas others have focused on specific kinds of suits (asbestos, medical malpractice, fast food). The issue of federal product liability law has been divisive, however, with representatives of industry and proponents of consumer protection facing off on a number of issues. Moreover, Congressional sentiments regarding tort reform have vacillated according to the political winds. Observers of Congress undoubtedly will continue to debate the benefits and disadvantages of such provisions for some time to come.

During the 1990s, various bills aimed at broad reform of product liability law were seriously considered in Congress. The bills tended to include many of the same provisions from year to year. Driven by industry and foes of strict product liability, but opposed by consumer groups and the plaintiffs' bar, debate on the proposed reforms has been vigorous. Often, the language in the bills was inflammatory, tending to stifle reasoned discussion. For example, in the proposed "Product Liability Reform Act of 1997" (S 648) offered in the 105th Congress, among the "Findings" that formed the basis of the bill was language characterizing the tort system as one of "excessive, unpredictable, and often arbitrary damage awards and unfair allocation of liability" (Tit. III, Sec. 2(a)(4)–(5)). The positions of these groups have become even more entrenched. Thus, it is not surprising that a satisfactory compromise measure has not yet been achieved. Moreover, with Congressional attention given over to the economic recession, the focus has been off of tort reform. As a perennial topic of debate, however, it is never off the table.

In general, the federal bills have attempted to abrogate the doctrine of strict product liability and establish negligence and warranty law as the only legal bases for the liability of a product seller. Punitive damages also have been a major focus of the reform efforts. Some measures have included caps on punitive damages and/or required proof of punitive damages claims by "clear and convincing" evidence. The bills often seek to abrogate the doctrine of joint and several liability. Other provisions have appeared, such as a requirement for a notice of claim in product liability actions, special statutes of limitations and statutes of repose, and special sanctions for frivolous actions or conduct that harasses the other party or causes undue delay in the litigation. Furthermore, some efforts have been made to include a provision for attorney fees to be paid to the prevailing party.

The various measures that continue to be introduced in Congress have galvanized both their proponents and their opponents. While it is possible that Congress will eventually pass some broad product liability reform, the exact parameters of such legislation are difficult to predict.

2. State Tort Reform

States continue to give attention to reforming tort law legislatively. One example is the Ohio tort reform package, passed in late 2004. The chief provision of the Ohio legislation is a cap of $500,000 on non-economic damages in non-catastrophic injury cases. The legislation also limits punitive damages to twice the amount of pain and suffering, plus special damages, with a separate provision designed to protect small businesses. It contains a ten-year statute of repose, as well as specific provisions prohibiting fast food lawsuits and claims against certain asbestos successor corporations. Ohio Rev. Code Ann. § 2315.18 (West 2010). An earlier Ohio tort reform package containing a similar cap on non-economic damages was ruled unconstitutional in 1999. But this time, the Ohio Supreme Court upheld the constitutionality of the reform measures. Arbino v. Johnson & Johnson, 880 N.E.2d 420 (Ohio 2007).

3. Joint and Several Liability Reform

Since the 1980s, state legislatures have embarked upon a mission to dramatically alter the operation of the doctrine of joint and several liability. Typically, the states have undertaken to abrogate, or to modify, joint and several liability in favor of several-only liability. There is a wide variation among these statutes, but the states are in general agreement that joint and several liability no longer serves the system effectively in all kinds of cases. Most states that have addressed the issue have abrogated joint and several liability and mandated several-only liability, but have imposed varying numbers of exceptions that would permit joint and several liability in some cases. Several of the exceptions are noteworthy because of their bearing on toxic tort litigation.

A common exception to several-only liability is hazardous waste litigation. *See, e.g.*, N.Y. Civ. Prac. L. & R. 1602(9) (McKinney 2010) (actions arising from releases into the environment of hazardous substances or hazardous wastes). Another exception is certain kinds of product liability actions. *See, e.g.*, N.J. Stat. Ann. § 2A:15–5.3(d) & (f) (West 2010) (negligent manufacture or use of hazardous or toxic substances except where fault can be apportioned). Some states have devised schemes based upon the defendant's percentage share of fault as determined by the jury at trial. When the defendant's liability exceeds a certain threshold percentage, joint and several liability applies. *See, e.g.*, Haw. Rev. Stat. § 663–10.9(3) (West 2010) (twenty-five percent or greater); Iowa Code Ann. § 668.4 (West 2010) (fifty percent or more).

The joint and several liability reforms are a logical outgrowth of the comparative negligence movement that overtook the state legislatures a decade earlier. The significant number of exceptions, however, indicates that total abrogation of joint and several liability may be inappropriate and unworkable in certain categories of cases, many of which affect toxic tort claimants.

CHAPTER THREE

THEORIES OF LIABILITY: LAND–BASED CLAIMS

When a toxic tort action arises from the defendant's activities on land, and/or affects the plaintiff's interest in property, the relationship between private law and public law becomes clearest. The activities out of which such claims may arise can be quite diverse, from the disposal of hazardous waste to ordinary industrial activity. While the law of torts provides remedies for such injuries, the law has been asked to stretch traditional causes of action to fit the toxic tort context. In addition, federal and state laws regulate many activities on the land, and defendant companies may be subject to additional regulatory liabilities beyond the strict operation of tort law. Most notably, private toxic tort actions may be associated with clean-up liabilities pursuant to the federal Comprehensive Environmental Response, Compensation, and Liability Act (CERCLA), also known as the Superfund law. The private state-law actions are set forth in this Chapter, whereas a more detailed discussion of CERCLA is presented in Chapter Four.

A. STRICT LIABILITY

The concept of land-related strict liability derives from the often-studied English case of Rylands v. Fletcher, 3 H.C. 774, 159 Eng.Rep. 737 (1865), which provided for absolute liability of owners or occupiers of land on which non-natural and hazardous activities were undertaken. Under this rule, the plaintiff need not show lack of due care on the part of the landowner defendant. Whereas *Rylands* was limited to situations in which the owner or occupier brings onto the land a thing that is "likely to do mischief if it escapes," modern American courts have expanded this doctrine to include any ultrahazardous activity, including the storage of hazardous chemicals on the property. *See* Cities Service Co. v. State, 312 So.2d 799 (Fla.Dist.Ct.App.1975) (holding that phosphate waste stored on property that contaminated an adjacent drinking water supply constituted a non-natural use of land and invoked the doctrine of strict liability).

A modern version of *Rylands* appeared in the Restatement (Second) of Torts §§ 519–520, which replaced the "ultrahazardous" language contained in the first Restatement with the concept of "abnormally dangerous activity" and a multi-factored test. Section 519 provides:

(1) One who carries on an abnormally dangerous activity is subject to liability for harm to the person, land or chattels of another resulting from the activity, although he has exercised the utmost care to prevent the harm.

(2) This strict liability is limited to the kind of harm, the possibility of which makes the activity abnormally dangerous.

Thus, reasonable care on the part of the landowner will not prevent liability if the activity is abnormally dangerous and the harm is associated with those dangerous qualities. The reasoning underlying strict liability for such activities is to require "[t]he defendant's enterprise ... to pay its way by compensating for the harm it causes." Restatement (Second) of Torts § 519, cmt. d (1965).

The principles set forth in the *Second Restatement* are in use in most states, in part because an accompanying section lists factors to help in identifying an abnormally dangerous activity. Section 520 sets forth these factors:

(a) existence of a high degree of risk of some harm to the person, land or chattels of others;

(b) likelihood that the harm that results from it will be great;

(c) inability to eliminate the risk by the exercise of reasonable care;

(d) extent to which the activity is not a matter of common usage;

(e) inappropriateness of the activity to the place where it is carried on; and

(f) extent to which its value to the community is outweighed by its dangerous attributes.

The factors incorporate a risk-utility analysis in that the value of the activity to the community

enters into the calculus and is to be balanced
against the degree of harm. Comment f to Section
520 makes clear, however, that all listed factors are
to be considered, but that no single factor will be
dispositive, and not all of them need be applicable
for a finding of abnormal danger.

In Sterling v. Velsicol Chemical Corp., 647
F.Supp. 303 (W.D.Tenn.1986), the district court
examined the activities of the defendant in maintaining a chemical waste burial site that allegedly
contaminated neighboring water wells. The court
determined that the defendant's activities satisfied
both the *Rylands* test and the *Second Restatement*
test for strict liability. The court applied the Section 520 factors and held that increased risk of
disease and diminished quality of life as a result of
exposure to the chemicals constituted a great risk
of harm. According to the court, the risk of harm
ultimately outweighed any value that the defendant's enterprise had to the community. As in
Sterling, a number of courts that have considered
the issue have held that the disposal or storage of
hazardous substances constitutes an abnormally
dangerous activity under the *Second Restatement*
test. *See, e.g.*, State Dep't of Envt'l Protection v.
Ventron Corp., 468 A.2d 150 (N.J.1983) (concluding that mercury and other toxic wastes are abnormally dangerous substances and that their disposal
is an abnormally dangerous activity).

In Abbatiello v. Monsanto Co., 522 F.Supp.2d 524
(S.D.N.Y. 2007), the plaintiffs used the theory in an
action against suppliers of polychlorinated biphe-

nyls (PCBs), who sold the PCBs to a General Electric Company facility manufacturing various electrical products. General Electric was also named as a defendant. The plaintiffs claimed that the PCBs were then released into the environment, causing the alleged harm. The court applied the *Second Restatement* rule and found that the magnitude of the potential harm from the releases was great and that the activity was not a matter of common usage. In particular, the court found pertinent the allegation that the defendant chemical companies were the sole manufacturers and suppliers of PCBs in the United States. On this basis, the court denied the motion to dismiss, finding sufficient fact questions as to whether this activity was abnormally dangerous.

In contrast, however, some courts have held that the handling of hazardous substances does not necessarily constitute an abnormally dangerous activity. *See* Avemco Insurance Co. v. Rooto Corp., 967 F.2d 1105 (6th Cir.1992); Arawana Mills Co. v. United Technologies Corp., 795 F.Supp. 1238 (D.Conn.1992); Richmond, Fredericksburg & Potomac Railroad Co. v. Davis Industries, Inc., 787 F.Supp. 572 (E.D.Va.1992). These cases tend to focus on the ability of the landowner to eliminate the hazards associated with the substances that they handled or stored.

Although most jurisdictions continue to rely on the *Second Restatement*, the Restatement (Third) of Torts: Liability for Physical and Emotional Harm § 20 (2005) contains a compressed rule, with fewer factors. The provision has the effect of elevating the importance of looking at whether the activity is one that is not of common usage. The section provides:

(a) An actor who carries on an abnormally dangerous activity is subject to strict liability for physical harm resulting from the activity.

(b) An activity is abnormally dangerous if:

(1) the activity creates a foreseeable and highly significant risk of physical harm even when reasonable care is exercised by all actors; and

(2) the activity is not one of common usage.

Comment a states: "Strict liability does not signify absolute liability. Even in cases covered by this Section, various limitations on liability apply and various defenses are available. . . ." One such defense is the plaintiff's culpable conduct. § 25.

B. TRESPASS

Historically, the tort of trespass applies to invasive actions that interfere with a person's possessory interest in property. In this sense, it is distinguishable from nuisance, which provides a broader claim for interferences with property, as discussed in the next section. Although the defendant need not have actually entered onto the plaintiff's property, the defendant must have caused the entry of a tangible substance onto the property. *See generally* Dan B. Dobbs, The Law of Torts § 50, at 95 (2000). Toxic torts have pushed the technical definition of such an invasion because toxic torts can involve microscopic substances in the air, water, or soil that invade the property of the plaintiff. Notwithstanding this new category of invasive substances, the case law indicates that the tort of trespass accommodates the evolution into toxic torts.

The Restatement (Second) of Torts § 158 sets forth the basic provisions of liability for trespass:

One is subject to liability to another for trespass, irrespective of whether he thereby causes harm to any legally protected interest of the other, if he intentionally

(a) enters land in the possession of the other, or causes a thing or a third person to do so, or

(b) remains on the land, or

(c) fails to remove from the land a thing which he is under a duty to remove.

The *Second Restatement* thus makes clear that liability for trespass exists for both direct and indirect invasions of property. Further, the invasion may be on the surface of the land, beneath the land, or in the air above the land. *See* § 158, cmt. i & § 159. With respect to the requirement of intent in the case of more indirect invasions, comment i explains: "[I]t is not necessary that the foreign matter should be thrown directly and immediately upon the other's land. It is enough that an act is done with knowledge that it will to a substantial certainty result in the entry of the foreign matter." *See generally* Dan B. Dobbs, The Law of Torts § 51, at 98–100 (2000).

Traditionally, a trespass action is maintainable even without a showing of harm, resembling a strict liability standard. Thus, nominal damages could be recovered by virtue of the invasion of the property alone. Toxic tort cases have called upon courts to interpret this principle in a different context from that in which the tort of trespass initially arose, as many such cases involve airborne particulates or invisible particles. In some instances, courts may be reluctant to allow traditional trespass claims under those circumstances.

In Brockman v. Barton Brands, Ltd., 2009 WL 4252914 (W.D. Ky. 2009) (slip op.), the court allowed a trespass claim involving emissions from a coal-fired liquor distillery. Although the court held that the odors of which the plaintiffs complained were insufficient to constitute trespass because they were not a physical invasion, the black particulates were a "visible and tangible presence on the property" of the plaintiffs. The court said that a physical interference with a plaintiff's possessory right to property will suffice as a basis for damages that go beyond mere nominal damages. In denying the motion to reconsider, the court restated that the black particles and black mold alleged demonstrate "actual physical invasion" of their property, and said that the plaintiffs' sampling evidence sufficed to support the physical invasion, even though only one sample had come from the property of a plaintiff. Brockman v. Barton Brands, Ltd., 2010 WL 231738 (W.D. Ky 2010) (slip op.) (denying motion to reconsider).

Some courts have recognized that a trespass may occur even where the invasion is by invisible substances. In Martin v. Reynolds Metals Co., 342 P.2d 790 (Or.1959), gases and particulate matter composed of fluoride compounds from an aluminum smelting operation that had drifted onto the land of the plaintiff were held to constitute a trespass. The court stated that it "prefer[red] to emphasize the object's energy or force rather than its size." The *Martin* court stated, however, that not all invasions are, as a matter of law, actionable in trespass: "[A] possessor's interest is not invaded by an intrusion which is so trifling that it cannot be recognized by the law.... [T]here is a point where the entry is so lacking in substance that the law will refuse to recognize it, applying the maxim de minimis non curat lex." This case indicates that despite the rigid historical pedigree of the law of trespass, courts may impose their own thresholds in certain categories of cases.

In Bradley v. American Smelting and Refining Co., 709 P.2d 782 (Wash.1985), the court went further and imposed a requirement of actual damage in another case involving invisible particulate matter. Acknowledging that "our concept of 'things' must be reframed" in light of modern usages of the land, the court agreed that invisible particles, at least in some circumstances, could constitute a trespassory invasion. Adopting a test announced in Borland v. Sanders Lead Co., 369 So.2d 523 (Ala. 1979), the *Bradley* court required a showing by the plaintiff of "substantial damages to the res."

The *Martin/Borland/Bradley* line of cases continues to have vitality in more recent toxic tort actions. The application of the principles of trespass vary from state to state, however. In Mercer v. Rockwell Int'l Corp., 24 F.Supp.2d 735 (W.D.Ky. 1998), the federal district court applied Kentucky law to a trespass claim involving the drainage of PCB-contaminated water onto the plaintiffs' land. The court stated that "[w]hen the 'thing' that has entered plaintiff's property is imperceptible to ordinary human senses, it does not so obviously infringe upon a landowner's right to exclusive possession." In these circumstances, violation of the right of exclusive possession exists "only when the substance actually damages the property." Citing *Bradley* with approval, the court held that to determine "actual harm," the plaintiffs would need to show that the amount of PCBs on their property presented an actual health hazard. Public perception that the property is unsafe provides no basis for a trespass claim absent actual damage. In *Mercer*, the plaintiffs failed to establish the actual harm required.

The technical requirements of the tort of trespass may make that theory less attractive to plaintiffs who seek remedies for interference with their rights and interests in their property. These requirements also include numerous privileges that may be asserted as defenses to a trespass claim. *See* Restatement (Second) of Torts §§ 191–211 (1965). The much greater flexibility of the law of nuisance makes nuisance claims a preferable course of litigation for many plaintiffs.

C. NUISANCE

Nuisance offers a broader theory than trespass for interferences with property. A nuisance may be the result of intentional or negligent conduct, or it may be associated with the performance of an abnormally dangerous activity. Not only does nuisance not require the physical invasion of the property that the law of trespass requires, but also the nature of the interests protected by the law of nuisance is broader than the possessory interest protected by the law of trespass. Two distinct doctrines of nuisance have evolved, private nuisance and public nuisance. The fundamental distinction between these two doctrines is founded in the nature of the interest that is protected.

1. Private Nuisance

A claim in private nuisance arises from the tortfeasor's unreasonable nontrespassory interference with a private individual's use and enjoyment of the individual's property. Restatement (Second) of Torts § 821D–F (1979). Although the harm suffered generally must be significant, the precise parameters of the right have always been vague, and toxic tort actions have offered courts the opportunity to apply private nuisance in a variety of circumstances. As a result, no unitary, precise definition of private nuisance has emerged. Some examples within the toxic tort context give a sense of the rights encompassed, and excluded, by this tort.

In Ayers v. Township of Jackson, 525 A.2d 287 (N.J.1987), the New Jersey Supreme Court allowed a private nuisance claim for diminution in quality of life arising from the contamination of the plaintiffs' drinking water supply, which caused inconvenience and discomfort for some time after its discovery. Following Restatement (Second) of Torts § 929, the court stated that plaintiffs could recover nuisance damages for inconvenience, discomfort, and annoyance in addition to damages for injury to their persons and proprietary interests.

In Abbatiello v. Monsanto Co., 522 F.Supp.2d 524 (S.D.N.Y. 2007), the court allowed a private nuisance claim to proceed against suppliers of PCBs and the manufacturer to whom the PCBs were sold, based upon releases of the substance into the environment from the manufacturer's facility. Under applicable New York law, the court said, every party that participates in the creation of the nuisance may be held liable on a private nuisance claim. In this case, the plaintiffs alleged that the suppliers knew of the hazards of PCBs and made a deliberate decision to conceal the dangers. The court found this sufficient to withstand a motion to dismiss.

In Adkins v. Thomas Solvent Co., 487 N.W.2d 715 (Mich.1992), the plaintiffs brought an action in nuisance to recover damages for depreciation in the value of their property as a result of groundwater contamination allegedly caused by the defendant company. The record showed, however, that the plaintiffs' property had not actually been contaminated and, further, that no such contamination was likely to occur in the future. The court refused to allow a nuisance claim under these circumstances, stating that "[c]ompensation for a decline in property value caused by unfounded perception of underground contamination is inextricably entwined with complex policy questions regarding environmental protection that are more suitably resolved through the legislative process." Even though the court acknowledged that in a proper nuisance case depreciation in the value of property could constitute an element of damages, it found this plaintiff's claim to be a " 'loss without an injury, in the legal sense.' "

One issue that is especially relevant in toxic tort litigation is whether a nuisance claim may be maintained solely for fear of future injury. In Koll–Irvine Center v. County of Orange, 29 Cal.Rptr.2d 664 (Cal. Ct.App.1994), the court rejected a private nuisance claim brought by commercial property owners in the vicinity of jet fuel storage tanks at an airport. The plaintiffs alleged that they feared the construction of the tanks in a location close to a commercial center created a danger of an explosion that interfered with their use of their property. The court held that the plaintiffs' private nuisance claim could not be based upon mere fear of future injury. In contrast, in two consolidated actions applying New Jersey law, which in turn relied on the *Second Restatement*, the court concluded that fear of future harm was sufficient to satisfy the requirement that the private nuisance resulted in "significant harm." Rowe v. E.I. du Pont de Nemours & Co., 262 F.R.D. 451 (D.N.J. 2009). The court relied on comment f to Section 821F of the *Second Restatement*, which states: "In determining whether the harm would be suffered by a normal member of the community, fears and other mental reactions common to the community are to be taken into account, even though they may be without scientific foundation or other support in fact." Thus, the court concluded, fear of future harm could constitute a substantial interference with a person's use and enjoyment of their property.

2. Public Nuisance

In Rowe v. E.I. du Pont de Nemours & Co., 262 F.R.D. 451 (D.N.J. 2009), the court distinguished between the plaintiffs who could maintain private nuisance claims and those who could not. In that groundwater contamination action, the court certified a small class of persons with private wells close to the release who had claims for private nuisance. The plaintiffs using the municipal water supply, on the other hand, could not rely on private nuisance, but they could rely on a theory of public nuisance. This distinction is an instructive starting point for a discussion of public nuisance.

Second Restatement § 821B characterizes public nuisance as an "unreasonable interference with a right common to the general public." The precise definition of public nuisance, however, is as elusive as that of private nuisance. *See generally* Dan B. Dobbs, The Law of Torts § 467, at 1334–38 (2000). Public nuisance claims may be established by statute with respect to certain enumerated activities. *See, e.g.*, Ariz. Rev. Stat. Ann. § 36–601(A) (West 2010) (listing certain conditions declared nuisances dangerous to the public health). Whether or not a statute exists, judicial determination has usually been necessary to define unreasonableness and determine who may bring a public nuisance action.

The *Second Restatement* defines "unreasonableness" as follows:

(a) Whether the conduct involves a significant interference with the public health, the public safety, the public peace, the public comfort or the public convenience, or

(b) whether the conduct is proscribed by a statute, ordinance or administrative regulation, or

(c) whether the conduct is of a continuing nature or has produced a permanent or long-lasting effect, and, as the actor knows or has reason to know, has a significant effect upon the public right.

Thus, it would not be necessary, except in actions falling within subsection (c), for the plaintiff to prove culpable conduct on the part of the actor. Typically, the public right is sought to be protected by a public entity. *See, e.g.*, State of New York v. Schenectady Chemicals, Inc., 459 N.Y.S.2d 971 (N.Y.1983) (state brought a public nuisance claim for clean-up expenses incurred with respect to a dump site at which the defendant company disposed of waste).

North Carolina v. Tennessee Valley Authority, 593 F.Supp.2d 812 (D.N.C. 2009), was a public nuisance action brought by the state on behalf of its citizens for air pollution from the TVA's coal-fired power plants in other states, claiming that it was a health risk to the citizens of North Carolina. After unsuccessfully attempting to obtain relief through the administrative structure of the federal Clean Air Act, the state brought suit. The court made findings of fact that the components of the pollution alleged were associated with premature mortality, including infant mortality, as well as chronic conditions such as asthma and bronchitis. There was also a body of scientific evidence indicating negative effects on the environment. The court acknowledged that "public nuisance principles ... are less well-adapted than administrative relief to the task of implementing the sweeping reforms that North Carolina desires," which included the use of costly pollution controls. Nevertheless, the court held that the emissions from one of the defendant's power plants in Tennessee constituted a public nuisance to the people of North Carolina. The court issued an injunction to abate the nuisance.

In Rhode Island v. Lead Industries Assn., Inc., 951 A.2d 428 (R.I. 2008), the state had less success with its public nuisance claim seeking cleanup of properties contaminated with lead paint. The Supreme Court of Rhode Island held that the hazards of the lead paint were not common to the general public, but only affected certain individuals in their homes. The court also held that the former lead paint manufacturers lacked control over the paint at the time of the alleged injuries. *See also* City of Saint Louis v. Benjamin Moore & Co., 226 S.W.3d 110 (Mo. 2007); In re Lead Paint Litig., 924 A.2d 484 (N.J. 2007).

While public nuisance claims are usually brought by a public entity, private individuals in toxic tort actions have sometimes brought claims for public nuisance. These plaintiffs essentially are acting as private attorneys general, seeking to vindicate public harms and to be compensated for their own damages. Questions arise as to the circumstances under which private citizens should be allowed to prosecute a public nuisance action. Restatement (Second) of Torts § 821C (1979) provides that a private citizen seeking to maintain a public nuisance action for damages "must have suffered harm of a kind different from that suffered by other members of the public exercising the right common to the general public that was the subject of interference." This has come to be referred to as the "special injury rule." With respect to actions seeking to enjoin or abate a public nuisance, the rule is broader, however. The plaintiff must satisfy the special injury rule, or be an appropriate public official, or have standing to either commence a citizens suit (pursuant to the federal environmental laws) or be a class member in a class action.

What constitutes a "special injury?" The courts emphasize that the harm alleged must be different in *kind*, not just in degree, to that suffered by members of the public. In Birke v. Oakwood Worldwide, 87 Cal.Rptr.3d 602 (Cal. App. Ct. 2009), the court considered a public nuisance action brought by a minor, through her father as guardian, relating to environmental tobacco smoke in the outdoor common areas of the apartment complex where she lived. The plaintiff claimed that allowing smoking in those areas interfered with the rights of a substantial number of persons to be free from health hazards (increased risk of lung cancer and heart disease) and alleged that she suffered a special injury because the smoke aggravated her pre-existing asthma. The court concluded that the plaintiff had pleaded a special injury.

The *Birke* court cited Restatement § 821C, comment d, which provides that physical harm "is normally different in kind from that suffered by other members of the public and [a public nuisance] action may be maintained." In Anderson v. W.R. Grace & Co., 628 F.Supp. 1219 (D.Mass.1986), the plaintiffs complained that the defendants had contaminated the groundwater that fed into their drinking water supply, thereby causing a variety of illnesses in the community. The court allowed the public nuisance claim because "[t]he right to be free of contamination to the municipal water supply is clearly a 'right common to the general public.'" The individual health problems of which the residents complained constituted the requisite special injury. *See also* Wood v. Picillo, 443 A.2d 1244 (R.I.1982) (allowing public and private nuisance claims for physical harm to persons residing near a chemical depository).

Anderson also addressed the elements of damages, which the court stated included compensation for diminution in property value, physical injuries, and emotional distress related to the physical injuries. While allowable recovery is broad, recovery on the basis of economic loss alone, without physical injury, may not be allowed, although the rules vary from state to state. *See* State of Louisiana ex rel. Guste v. M/V Testbank, 752 F.2d 1019 (5th Cir. 1985) (recovery for economic loss alone not allowed). *But see* In re Nautilus Motor Tanker Co., 900 F.Supp. 697 (D.N.J.1995) (recovery for economic loss allowed under New Jersey common law).

Absent individual harm, however, a private person will not be allowed to bring a public nuisance action even if the circumstances show an interference with a right common to the public. In Venuto v. Owens–Corning Fiberglas Corp., 99 Cal.Rptr. 350 (Cal.Ct.App.1971), the court held that individuals who complained of emissions from a plant that were polluting the air and causing health complaints among neighboring residents could not maintain an action for public nuisance because the same injuries were suffered by all residents. Likewise, in Brown v. Petrolane, Inc., 162 Cal.Rptr. 551 (Cal.Ct.App. 1980), the court refused to allow a public nuisance action brought by private citizens on the basis of fear of the proximity of explosive substances handled by the defendant. The court stated that the plaintiffs' fear did not constitute special injury because it was common to their entire community, even though differing in degree.

Public nuisance continues to play an important role in toxic tort litigation. It is a viable claim for public entities and also for private individuals who meet the special injury requirement. Public nuisance merges features of public law with features of private litigation; as such, it exemplifies the characteristic convergence of public and private law in the law of toxic torts.

D. CLAIMS AGAINST REAL ESTATE BROKERS

Some purchasers of residential property have claimed harm as a result of purchasing property that, unbeknownst to the purchaser, was contaminated with hazardous substances or was in proximity to a hazardous condition. Often in such instances, the responsible party may be indeterminable, insolvent, or no longer existent. Some plaintiffs have sought a remedy against the real estate broker who may or may not have known of the existence of the hazard.

Traditionally, the real estate broker was deemed to be the agent of the seller. Traditional rules governing the transfer of property emphasized the doctrine of caveat emptor, under which a purchaser of property had little or no recourse against the seller or the broker for claims arising out of defects on the property. Only where the broker engaged in some affirmative misrepresentation to the purchaser that constituted fraud—either passive or active—did the purchaser have a cause of action against the broker. This rule proved workable when the kind of defect contemplated was, for example, termite infestation, but became more difficult to justify in other contexts.

Thus, during the 1970s, courts began to erode the traditional rule and to imply a fiduciary relationship between the broker and the purchaser. Courts began to hold brokers liable for making representations without determining the actual condition of the property if the buyer inquired about the specific condition. Moreover, if the broker had information or a suspicion that should have prompted the broker to investigate the condition of the property, the broker could be liable for not doing so. *See* First Church of the Open Bible v. Cline J. Dunton Realty, Inc., 574 P.2d 1211 (Wash.Ct.App.1978). This shift in the law was grounded in the superior position of the broker to know or obtain information about the property. *See* Berryman v. Riegert, 175 N.W.2d 438 (Minn.1970).

Some courts have taken the fiduciary relationship a step further. In Bevins v. Ballard, 655 P.2d 757 (Alaska 1982), the seller had represented to the broker that the water well on the property was adequate, and the broker transmitted the information to the purchaser. Because under state law the seller would have been liable to the purchaser directly for misrepresentations, however innocent, the court imposed a similar liability on the broker for innocently transmitting the seller's misrepresentation. Due to the superior position of the broker, the court recognized an obligation on the part of the broker to investigate before passing along the seller's representations.

A few state courts have imposed on the broker a full duty to investigate. In these states, even where the broker has made no representations to the seller and is unaware of any latent defects, the broker may be liable for failing to investigate. *See* Easton v. Strassburger, 199 Cal.Rptr. 383 (Cal.Ct. App.1984) (holding that the real estate broker had an affirmative duty to conduct "a reasonably competent and diligent inspection" of the property and disclose all material facts to prospective purchasers); Robison v. Campbell, 683 P.2d 510 (N.M.Ct. App.1984) (noting that failure to investigate the property was considered by the trial court in determining that the broker had misrepresented the property's condition). Concepts of comparative negligence could mitigate this liability, however, where the purchaser inspected the property and could have learned of the defect.

Such cases raise significant questions regarding the extent of the broker's duty in the era of toxic torts. Must the broker go beyond the listed property and investigate neighboring property to determine the existence of hazardous substances? In Strawn v. Canuso, 657 A.2d 420 (N.J.1995), the New Jersey Supreme Court held that developers and selling brokers of new homes have an affirmative obligation to disclose to prospective purchasers the existence of off-site hazards that materially affect the value of the property. In *Strawn,* the plaintiffs were purchasers of new homes that were in the vicinity of a closed landfill that had been under investigation by the State because of the hazardous substances contained there.

Noting that the law has been slow to move away from the concept of caveat emptor, the court emphasized two policy issues that guided its decision— (1) the inequitable bargaining positions of the purchasers of residential property vis-á-vis the developers and their brokers and (2) the difference between the parties in relative access to information regarding the site. On this basis, the court limited its holding to professional sellers of real property, such as the developers and builders. Liability was thus extended to the brokers, agents, and salespersons representing the professional sellers in the transaction. The court stated:

> We hold that a builder-developer of residential real estate or a broker representing it is not only liable to a purchaser for affirmative and intentional misrepresentation, but is also liable for nondisclosure of off-site physical conditions known to it and unknown and not readily observable to the buyer if the existence of those conditions is of sufficient materiality to affect the habitability, use, or enjoyment of the property and, therefore, render the property substantially less desirable or valuable to the objectively reasonable buyer. Whether a matter not disclosed by such a builder or broker is of such materiality,

and unknown and unobservable to the buyer, will depend on the facts of each case.

Thus, the effect of the landfill on the value of the plaintiffs' property was a jury question to be determined at trial.

In circumstances less obvious than a closed landfill, would a broker necessarily possess the requisite expertise to make environmental judgments, and, if not, must an environmental engineer be called upon to conduct an investigation? If so, who pays for it? In the wake of the *Strawn* case, the New Jersey legislature addressed these problems and formalized the disclosure rules by enacting the New Residential Real Estate Off–Site Conditions Disclosure Act, N.J. Stat. Ann. § 46:3C–2 et seq. (2010), which requires that owners of certain types of sites disclose their existence to the municipality to create a repository of relevant off-site conditions.

E. OTHER THEORIES

1. Battery

Battery may be an available claim in situations in which the conduct of the defendant has gone beyond negligence. A claim of battery was allowed in Werlein v. United States, 746 F.Supp. 887 (D.Minn. 1990), a complex case that arose from the discharge of toxic chemicals by tenants at an army ammunition plant and another site. The plaintiffs were nearby residents who claimed injury from the release of the chemicals into the environment. The court defined the standard as requiring the plaintiff to prove that the defendant disposed of the toxic substances intending to cause an offensive or harmful contact or with the knowledge that such contact was substantially certain to occur. The court held that the plaintiffs had stated a claim for battery under the latter standard by alleging that the defendant "disposed of highly toxic substances into sandy ground directly above a regional aquifer."

In contrast, in Bogner v. Airco Inc., 353 F.Supp.2d 977 (C.D.Ill.2005), the court dismissed a battery claim in a wrongful death action based upon exposure to vinyl chloride in the workplace. After holding that workers' compensation did not bar a claim for intentional conduct by the employer, the court held that the employer's knowledge of the hazards of vinyl chloride and its failure to pass along that information to the employees did not rise to the level of an intentional tort. Thus, courts are capable of interpreting the "intent" requirement quite differently, and a claim of battery may be difficult to sustain.

In 2009 and 2010, Iraq War veterans filed suits against Halliburton Co., KBR Inc., and other contractors hired for waste disposal services, alleging harm to soldiers in Iraq and Afghanistan from burning open-air waste pits. In re KBR Burn Pit Litig., 09–MD–02083–RWT (D. Md., filed Mar. 9, 2010) (plaintiffs' first consolidated MDL complaint). One cause of action alleged was battery. The alleged basis for the harmful contact was two-fold—(1) improper design, management, and operation of the burn pits, thereby contaminating the air and (2) failure to properly monitor and assure the safety of water supplies. The plaintiffs alleged that the defendants acted knowing that the plaintiffs would come into contact with the contaminated air and water.

The need to rely upon a claim of battery is diminished in toxic tort actions, where plaintiffs usually have available negligence claims and may also have available strict liability claims. The problems of demonstrating intent may be a deterrent to plaintiffs. Plaintiffs seeking punitive damages, however, may include such a claim to support the punitive damages claim, as punitive damages claims require proof of conduct that is more egregious than mere negligence. Punitive damages are discussed in detail in Chapter Nine, *infra*.

2. Negligence Per Se

Toxic tort claims, with some exceptions, typically are not created by statute, but rather arise under the common law. Nevertheless, obligations imposed by statute or regulation may be relevant to the duty of the defendant toward the plaintiff. A plaintiff may attempt to show that the defendant violated a standard of conduct established by a statute or regulation and that in so doing must be held to be negligent per se. *See generally* Martin v. Herzog, 126 N.E. 814 (N.Y.1920). Where negligence per se is recognized, the statute giving rise to the claim must have been enacted to protect the class of persons of which the plaintiff is a member against the kind of harm that the plaintiff has suffered. *See generally*

Dan B. Dobbs, The Law of Torts § 134, at 315 (2000).

Negligence per se claims have had only limited success in toxic tort litigation; but some plaintiffs have had some measure of success with the theory. In Bagley v. Controlled Environment Corp., 503 A.2d 823 (N.H.1986), the court allowed a negligence per se claim based upon a state statute requiring operators of hazardous waste facilities to obtain a permit. The statute also required the operator to comply with statutory standards, to abide by any rule promulgated by the relevant agency, and to meet the terms and conditions of its particular permit. The court stated that in addition to the explicit standards stated in the statute or regulations, the conditions imposed in the defendant's permit created substantive standards that could serve as the basis for a negligence per se claim. In Anderson v. Minnesota, 693 N.W.2d 181 (Minn. 2005), the Minnesota Supreme Court allowed the plaintiff beekeepers to pursue their negligence per se claim based upon the defendant's alleged violation of state pesticide regulations requiring application in conformity with the label.

Some of the difficulties with allowing a negligence per se claim in environmental or toxic torts have been noted in the literature. First, negligence per se is a creature of an earlier time when community standards were embodied in statutory and regulatory standards. In contrast, environmental and products standards tend to be based upon sophisticated scientific data of varying degrees of uncertainty.

Even what appears to be the most objective standard in a statute or regulation—for example, a numerical standard, such as typically is contained in a permit under the environmental laws—may in fact have been based on scant scientific evidence. Or, the scientific basis may have been open to several reasonable interpretations, only one of which is reflected in the statutory standard. Or, the scientific evidence may be more complete or different at the time the action is brought from the evidence that formed the basis of the standard. Similar difficulties may arise with respect to identifying the harms that the statute or regulation was meant to remedy in relation to the harm that the plaintiff alleges. *See* Sheila Bush, *Can You Get There From Here? Noncompliance with Environmental Regulation as Negligence Per Se in Tort Cases*, 25 Idaho L. Rev. 469 (1988–1989). These arguments make a persuasive case for not allowing negligence per se in toxic tort actions. They suggest that a more sensible rule may be to treat violation of a statutory standard as evidence of negligence, but not per se negligence, in many toxic tort cases.

Consistent with these concerns, courts have held that a violation of the Occupational Safety and Health Act (OSHAct) will not be the basis for a negligence per se claim. In Elliott v. S.D. Warren Co., 134 F.3d 1 (1st Cir.1998), the court held that the defendant's failure to maintain a safe workplace and to warn of a dangerous condition, while constituting a violation of the OSHAct, did not give rise to a negligence per se claim by the plaintiff. The court reasoned that because the OSHAct does not create a private right of action, a violation of an OSHA regulation will not constitute negligence per se. The court concluded that the violation is merely evidence of negligence.

In contrast, the position of the Restatement (Third) of Torts: Products Liability has moved closer to a negligence per se concept. Section 4(a) provides that in a design defect or failure to warn case, "a product's noncompliance with an applicable product safety statute or administrative regulation renders the product defective with respect to the risks sought to be reduced by the statute or regulation." Comment d states that this rule "does not apply when a regulation merely suggests, but does not require, a safety feature."

F. LOOKING TO THE FUTURE: CLIMATE CHANGE LITIGATION

In 2010, climate change law is happening on all fronts—domestic and international, political and economic, statutory, regulatory, and civil litigation. Only some of the litigation touches directly on toxic torts, but the first cases will have a dramatic impact on future litigation and have the potential to either open the doors to substantial future litigation or seriously limit litigation. In 2009, three significant cases relying on the law of nuisance have tested these waters.

Connecticut v. American Elec. Power Co., 582 F.3d 309 (2d Cir. 2009), was the first of this trio and demonstrates the characteristics of this climate change litigation based upon the common law. Eight states, the City of New York, and three land trusts brought separate public nuisance actions against six electric power companies that owned and operated coal-fired power plants in twenty states. The relief sought was the abatement of the defendants' ongoing contributions to global warming. The court held that the plaintiffs had standing to bring their claims and that the common law of nuisance had not been displaced by any statute or current efforts in the political arena to manage greenhouse gases. The court also held that the plaintiffs had stated claims under the federal common law of nuisance.

Citing the Restatement (Second) of Torts § 821B (1979), the court held that the states and city had sufficiently stated an unreasonable interference with public rights, which included "the right to public comfort and safety, the right to protection of vital natural resources and public property, and the right to use, enjoy, and preserve the aesthetic and ecological values of the natural world." The court further ruled that the private parties, i.e. the land trusts, could maintain their public nuisance actions because they met the "special injury" rule by pleading harm that is different in kind from that of the general public, by virtue of their "missions to preserve ecologically sensitive land areas" and their ownership of land that is threatened with harm from the defendants' activities that contributed to global warming.

On the immediate heels of the *American Electric* case, a California federal district court decided Native Village of Kivalina v. ExxonMobil Corp., 663 F.Supp.2d 863 (N.D. Cal. 2009). The Village is an Inupiat Eskimo village on the barrier island of Kivalina, located seventy miles north of the Arctic Circle. Kivalina is protected from coastal storms and waves by Arctic sea ice for three seasons of the year, but the plaintiffs claimed that global warming has contributed to coastal erosion that requires relocation of the Village. The plaintiffs brought claims against various oil companies, power companies, and utility providers based upon public nuisance and related causes of action. The court's foremost concern was whether the action presented a nonjusticiable political question. The main issues were (1) whether the case would involve judicial resolution of questions textually committed by the Constitution to a branch of the Government other than the judiciary; (2) whether there was "a lack of judicially discoverable and manageable standards for resolving it;" and (3) whether the court would have to make an initial policy decision outside its usual judicial mandate. Baker v. Carr, 369 U.S. 186 (1962).

Ultimately, the court held that the case presented a political question that was outside the scope of the judicial branch of the Government. The court stated that for the action to proceed, the court would be required to make two general policy decisions. First, in determining whether the plaintiffs stated a claim for public nuisance, the court would be required to render judgment on the level of greenhouse gases in the atmosphere that is considered acceptable, given the utility of the defendants' activities. Second, the court said it would be required to determine which entities should bear the costs of global warming. Resolution of each of these issues, the court said, is an inherently executive and/or legislative task.

The third significant case was Comer v. Murphy Oil USA, 585 F.3d 855 (5th Cir. 2009). The plaintiffs were residents and landowners on the Mississippi Gulf coast who alleged that the defendant oil companies, electrical companies, and utilities caused massive emissions of greenhouse gases that contributed to global warming, causing warmer surface and water temperatures and rising sea levels. These effects, the plaintiffs alleged, added to the power of Hurricane Katrina, causing damage to private and public property. The putative class action alleged claims of public and private nuisance, negligence, trespass, unjust enrichment, fraudulent misrepresentation, and civil conspiracy. The district court had dismissed the claims for lack of standing and because they presented nonjusticiable political questions. The Fifth Circuit reversed in part and held that the nuisance, negligence, and trespass claims could proceed and that they did not present nonjusticiable political questions. The court noted that common-law tort claims and claims for damages (in contrast to claims for injunctive relief) are more likely not to present political questions. The court also observed that the major federal environmental statutes contain saving clauses preserving state common-law remedies, and predicted that any future legislation on greenhouse gas emissions would do likewise. After granting a rehearing en banc, the Fifth Circuit, in an unusual twist, declined to proceed with the rehearing for lack of a quorum and reinstated the district court's dismissal. Comer v. Murphy Oil USA, 2010 WL 2136658 (5th Cir. 2010).

It is possible that a split among the federal courts may be developing on the political question issue. Even if some of these common-law claims go forward, it is important to note that the plaintiffs will have significant difficulties proving causation. They will be required to demonstrate that the specific harm alleged was caused by the activities of the defendants in their actions. This is a daunting task. Not only do the plaintiffs face difficulties connecting the individual defendants to the harm, but, if the connection is made, the courts must deal with the potential indivisibility of the harm among the defendants whose emissions combined in the atmosphere. Causation issues are the subject generally of Chapter Eight.

CHAPTER FOUR
CERCLA LIABILITY
A. INTRODUCTION

The Comprehensive Environmental Response, Compensation and Liability Act (CERCLA), 42 U.S.C.A. §§ 9601–9675 (West 2010), is part of a broad federal scheme of regulation of industry. The enforcement provisions of CERCLA point out that a toxic tort defendant may be faced with an assault of actions on several fronts. Common-law torts may be only a portion of the defendant's worries. Attorneys should be prepared to advise and defend their clients in all these areas involving public, as well as private, law.

The role of CERCLA is different from the other environmental statutes. CERCLA is primarily focused upon cleanup of hazardous substances that have been released into the environment and hazardous substance emergencies, whereas many other federal environmental statutes tend to focus upon the ongoing regulation of various enterprises and activities by means of permits as well as other requirements. When CERCLA was initially enacted in 1980, Congress debated but rejected the option of including a provision for a private right of action for personal injuries. Consequently, CERCLA contains no private right of action for damages for persons who claim to have been injured by the releases encompassed by the statute, although it does contain a savings clause that recognizes the rights of private individuals to pursue their tort claims under state law. CERCLA § 310(h). Instead, the CERCLA provisions focus primarily on the right of the Government to enforce the cleanup regulations against parties deemed to be statutorily responsible. As with the other major federal environmental statutes, CERCLA also contains a citizens suit provision that permits private individuals, under certain circumstances, to step into the shoes of the Government and enforce the statute against alleged violators. CERCLA was significantly revised by the Superfund Amendments and Reauthorization Act of 1986 (SARA), with many of the amendments reflecting case law prior to that date. Several other major amendments have been made in the years since SARA, including clarifications of the innocent landowner defense, provisions clarifying the potential liability of lenders, and regulatory provisions on the redevelopment of brownfields.

B. ENFORCEMENT SCHEME

The applicability of CERCLA is triggered by the release or threatened release of a hazardous substance into the environment from a facility. A "facility" is defined broadly as "any site or area where a hazardous substance has been deposited, stored, disposed of, or placed, or otherwise come to be located." CERCLA § 101(9). The process by which the Government identifies a site appropriate for response action and determines the proper action is the National Contingency Plan (NCP). CERCLA § 105. Appropriate sites are placed on the National Priorities List (NPL) based upon a ranking of hazards. A decision to remedy is based upon cost considerations as well as the nature and magnitude of the hazard. A large portion of CERCLA centers on factfinding: determining hazardous substances, identifying dangerous sites, and requiring the reporting of information regarding releases of hazardous substances into the environment.

CERCLA provides several mechanisms by which responsibility for the cleanup of hazardous substances in the environment can be imposed upon persons statutorily deemed responsible for the release or threatened release. These persons are called "potentially responsible parties" (PRPs). First, the President, through the Attorney General, may commence either an administrative or judicial action against any PRP for abatement of the condition or for other appropriate action. CERCLA § 106. The trigger for such an action is the occurrence of "an imminent and substantial endangerment to the public health or welfare or the environment because of the actual or threatened release of a hazardous substance." CERCLA § 106(a). Failure to comply with such an order could lead to civil penalties of $25,000 a day plus treble costs. Second, the Government may conduct the cleanup, through hiring contractors, funded from the Superfund—a fund created pursuant to CERCLA for this purpose—and subsequently seek reimbursement from a PRP. CERCLA §§ 104, 111. The Government may not make a claim against the Fund unless efforts to find the PRPs or require them to conduct the cleanup have been exhausted. If the Government conducts the cleanup, PRPs have no right to preenforcement judicial review of the chosen remedial action. CERCLA § 113(h); Lone Pine Steering Committee v. EPA, 777 F.2d 882 (3d Cir.1985). Third, CERCLA contains provisions for settlement between a PRP and the Government designed to induce a timely settlement and expedite cleanup. CERCLA § 122.

While CERCLA does not provide a private right of action for damages for personal injuries, it does allow a private cause of action for response costs, which has been the subject of much judicial attention recently. Section 107(a)(4)(B) makes clear that response costs incurred by "any other person" may be sought from a PRP, provided that the cleanup was "consistent with the National Contingency Plan." Furthermore, Section 113(f) provides for contribution claims against "any person who is liable or potentially liable" under CERCLA § 107.

C. LIABILITY

To make a prima facie case for cleanup costs, the following elements must be demonstrated:

(1) a release or threatened release

(2) into the environment

(3) from a facility

(4) of a hazardous substance

(5) in which response costs have been incurred.

The same liability standards apply to actions brought by the Government against PRPs to force cleanups, except that the Government is asking the PRP to bear the costs of the cleanup. "Response" costs include both "remedial" and "removal" action. "Remedial" action is action consistent with a permanent remedy at the site, CERCLA § 101(24), whereas "removal" refers to any immediate action taken to prevent, minimize, or mitigate damages to the public or the environment, CERCLA § 101(23).

For a party to become liable for cleanup costs, a "release" or threatened release must have occurred. CERCLA § 101(22) defines "release" as:

> any spilling, leaking, pumping, pouring, emitting, emptying, discharging, injecting, escaping, leaching, dumping, or disposing into the environment (including the abandonment or discarding of barrels, containers, and other closed receptacles containing any hazardous substance or pollutant or contaminant....

A release must be into the "environment." The term "environment" is broadly defined to include navigable waters, surface water, groundwater, drinking water supply, land surface and subsurface, and ambient air. CERCLA § 101(8). CERCLA does not cover releases within the workplace, from motor vehicle exhaust, or due to a nuclear incident, as those matters are regulated by other federal statutes. CERCLA applies to both active and inactive sites.

In addition, the release must be from a "facility." CERCLA § 101(9) gives "facility" a very broad definition, which includes:

(A) any building, structure, installation, equipment, pipe or pipeline (including any pipe into a sewer or publicly owned treatment works), well, pit, pond, lagoon, impoundment, ditch, landfill, storage container, motor vehicle, rolling stock, or aircraft, or (B) any site or area where a hazardous substance has been deposited, stored, disposed of, or placed, or otherwise come to be located....

A "facility" does not include a consumer product in consumer use, however.

When a release or threatened release has occurred, the cleanup becomes the responsibility of the PRPs enumerated in Section 107. Traditionally, liability under CERCLA has been deemed to be strict, and joint and several. The landmark 2009 United States Supreme Court decision in Burlington Northern & Santa Fe Railway Co. v. United States, 129 S.Ct. 1870 (2009), held that CERCLA did not mandate joint and several liability in every case, however, and that CERCLA liability would be subject to common-law standards. In so ruling, the Court approved the line of cases addressing this subject, which began with United States v. Chem–Dyne Corp., 572 F.Supp. 802 (S.D.Ohio 1983). The *Chem–Dyne* court stated: "If the harm is divisible and if there is a reasonable basis for apportionment of damages, each defendant is liable only for the portion of the harm he himself caused." Following *Chem–Dyne*, numerous courts observed the same guiding principles, but reached varying results on the facts of the individual cases. Thus, in United States v. Monsanto Co., 858 F.2d 160 (4th Cir. 1988), involving a site with the commingled waste of many generators, the court held that the defendants had not sufficiently established divisibility of harm. In *Burlington Northern*, the Court quoted the Restatement (Second) of Torts § 433A and stated: "[A]pportionment is proper when 'there is a reasonable basis for determining the contribution of each cause to a single harm.'" The Court then upheld the determination of the district court that the PRP in question was liable for only nine percent of the harm. The Court was quick to note that a PRP seeking to establish apportionment has the burden to prove that a "reasonable basis" for apportionment exists.

What is the overall impact of *Burlington Northern* on the subject of CERCLA joint and several liability? First, the Supreme Court has acknowledged that the lower-court cases declining to treat joint and several liability as mandatory under CERCLA are correct. Second, common-law standards, as set forth in the *Second Restatement*, provide the basis for CERCLA apportionment. Thus, "when two or more persons acting independently caus[e] a distinct or single harm for which there is a reasonable basis for division according to the contribution of each, each is subject to liability only for the portion of the total harm that he has himself caused." Restatement (Second) of Torts, §§ 433A, 881 (1976). In contrast, where the harm is indivisible, joint and several liability must be imposed. Third, the burden remains on the PRP to prove divisibility. Fourth, the Court held that the district court's determination of apportionment satisfied the "reasonable basis" standard, even though the district court had not used any causation or fault factors, but rather a calculation related to percentage of the land, percentage of time leasing the property, and proportion of the PRP's substances that contributed to the overall release. The Court emphasized that equity considerations must play no role in the apportionment analysis.

While *Burlington Northern* invites PRPs to attempt to show divisibility of damages so as to reduce their individual liabilities, it is not at all clear that a dramatic shift in results will occur. This point was made by the federal district court in United States v. Iron Mountain Mines Inc., 2010 WL 1854118 (E.D. Cal. 2010), which stated that *Burlington Northern* does not require apportionment in all cases and does not change the manner of determining apportioned shares. Because waste from different sources is often commingled at a site, apportionment remains difficult to demonstrate and will depend on the specific facts of each case. Still, *Burlington Northern* is sure to exert substantial influence on litigants, courts, and agency settlements for years to come.

A PRP is liable for both Government response costs and private response costs. To recover costs, governmental cleanup actions must not be "inconsistent" with the NCP, whereas private cleanups must be "consistent" with the NCP, a distinction made explicit in the statute. CERCLA § 107(a)(4)(A) & (B). In addition, a PRP may be liable for natural resource damages and for health assessments pursuant to the Agency for Toxic Substances and Disease Registry, an agency within the Public Health Service established by CERCLA.

D. POTENTIALLY RESPONSIBLE PARTIES

CERCLA § 107(a) sets forth the categories of entities that comprise "potentially responsible parties," or PRPs. The liability of PRPs is deemed to be strict liability, but some defenses are available.

1. Current Owners and Operators

This category includes current owners and operators of a vessel or facility. CERCLA § 107(a)(1). The statutory language refers to "any person owning or operating such facility" or "owning, operating, or chartering by demise, such vessel." No qualifications are placed upon this definition, and because of the strict liability nature of CERCLA, no showing need be made of the culpability of an owner or operator to hold that party liable. In State of New York v. Shore Realty Corp., 759 F.2d 1032 (2d Cir.1985), the owner of the site was held liable for costs even though it had not participated in the disposal of waste on the site and had not owned the property at the time of disposal. Moreover, the court also held the officer and stockholder of Shore Realty liable as an "operator" of the facility because he managed the corporation and was in charge of the facility under scrutiny.

As the *Shore Realty* case suggests, "owners" and "operators" are generally viewed separately, though a single entity could be both an owner and an operator. But for the entity to be a PRP, it need only satisfy the definition of either owner or operator. A common question that has arisen in this context under CERCLA is the extent to which a parent corporation may be held liable for cleanup costs incurred in response to actions of a subsidiary. In United States v. Bestfoods, 524 U.S. 51 (1998), the United States Supreme Court established a two-part test to answer this question. Under this test, a parent corporation may be liable directly or indirectly. Direct liability requires that the parent corporation "manage, direct, or conduct operations specifically related to pollution, that is, operations having to do with the leakage or disposal of hazardous waste, or decisions about compliance with environmental regulations." Mere management or "actual control" alone does not lead to direct CERCLA liability; rather, the test for direct liability requires management of the activities of a subsidiary that may give rise to CERCLA liability. *See* Datron, Inc. v. CRA Holdings, Inc., 42 F.Supp.2d 736 (W.D.Mich. 1999) (holding that the parent corporation was not directly liable even though its corporate policy required the subsidiary to comply with waste disposal laws, and the parent's general counsel was involved in responding to litigation related to the contamination). Dual officership or directorship of the parent and subsidiary corporations is not dispositive of liability, but a rebuttable presumption exists that management is acting in the subsidiary's best interests. Consolidated Edison Co. v. UGI Utilities, Inc., 310 F.Supp.2d 592 (S.D.N.Y.2004).

Courts applying the *Bestfoods* direct liability test have continued to demand a substantial level of management of the operations giving rise to the release. In Yankee Gas Services Co. v. UGI Utilities, Inc., 616 F.Supp.2d 228 (D. Conn. 2009), the court examined the activities of a parent utility company that owned another company operating nine manufactured gas plants in Connecticut. Although the court concluded that the company was "a vigilant parent that conducted detailed ... oversight of its subsidiaries in Connecticut," that oversight did not rise to the level of managing or conducting operations of the subsidiaries. Therefore, the parent was held not to be an "operator" of the facility within the meaning of CERCLA § 107(a)(1).

In the alternative, the *Bestfoods* Court stated that a parent corporation may be liable indirectly for cleanup costs incurred by its subsidiary. Under this theory, the Supreme Court stated, a parent corporation could incur liability for cleanup costs related to activities of its subsidiary if facts exist to pierce the corporate veil. The Court did not elaborate further on the indirect liability test.

In the years since CERCLA was enacted, conflict also arose over the extent to which a lender may be considered an "owner or operator" of a facility for the purpose of incurring liability for cleanup costs. This question is critical in the common situation in which a bank or other lender holds a security interest in the property, typically a mortgage. The definition of owner or operator in Section 101(20)(A) of CERCLA excludes lenders, but only if they have not "participated in the management" of the facility. A decade of debate and confusion ensued regarding the interpretation of the phrase "participated in management," with attempts by EPA, the federal courts, and Congress to clarify the precise meaning. The tortuous road of interpretation culminated in an amendment to CERCLA addressing this issue.

The 1996 Lender Liability Amendments to CERCLA contained some significant new provisions. The essence of these provisions has been to clarify that "participation in management" requires some actual participation in the management of or in the operational affairs of the facility. In this respect, lender liability is similar to the direct liability standard for parent corporations set forth in *Bestfoods*. Merely being in a position to influence or participate does not constitute "participation" within the meaning of the Lender Liability Amendments. CERCLA § 101(20)(F). Furthermore, Congress set forth two liability triggers, requiring that the lender either (1) exercise specific control over and take responsibility for the hazardous substance practices of the facility or (2) exercise more general control or responsibility over the management or operational affairs of the facility, such as the conduct of day-to-day decision making. Generally, a lender is allowed to foreclose on property and sell its collateral, provided that it takes steps to divest itself of the facility at an early date. The more post-foreclosure activity a lender is engaged in, the greater the risk that liability will attach. Furthermore, the amendments provide additional guidance to lenders by setting forth a list of activities that generally, without more, would not result in liability under the above test, such as merely holding a security interest or conducting an inspection of the facility. CERCLA § 101(2)(F)(iv)(I–IX).

2. Former Owners and Operators

At least some past owners and operators are considered PRPs under the statute. CERCLA § 107(a)(2) establishes the liability of

> any person who at the time of disposal of any hazardous substance owned or operated any facility at which such hazardous substances were disposed of. . . .

In contrast to current owners and operators, former owners and operators will be liable only if they owned or operated the facility at the time of disposal of any hazardous substance at the facility or if they knew of a release, but failed to disclose it to a purchaser.

In an effort to refine the liability rule for prior owners and operators, some courts have addressed the question whether a prior owner may be held liable for passive migration of hazardous substances on its site without its knowledge or culpability. The question is a tricky one because rejecting liability under those circumstances seems to fly in the face of CERCLA's strict liability standard. Nevertheless, some federal appellate courts have held that a prior owner is not liable for cleanup costs for passive migration. In United States v. CDMG Realty Co., 96 F.3d 706 (3d Cir.1996), the parties agreed that no waste had been dumped at the facility during the prior owner's tenure, but the current owner argued that "disposal" had occurred by reason of the passive spreading of contaminants. The court held that the prior owner was not liable for cleanup costs under CERCLA merely on the basis of passive migration of the contaminants. Similarly, the Second Circuit held, in ABB Industrial Systems, Inc. v. Prime Technology, Inc., 120 F.3d 351 (2d Cir.1997), that a prior owner was not liable merely for passive migration of contaminants where the prior owner "merely controlled a site on which hazardous chemicals have spread without that person's fault." Other courts have expressed an opposing view on this issue. *See, e.g.,* Stanley Works v. Snydergeneral Corp., 781 F.Supp. 659 (E.D.Cal.1990) (holding that ongoing migration of hazardous substances at a site constitutes disposal under CERCLA).

3. Arrangers for Disposal

Another category of PRP is set forth in CERCLA § 107(a)(3), which establishes liability for

> any person who by contract, agreement, or otherwise arranged for disposal or treatment, or arranged with a transporter for transport for disposal or treatment, of hazardous substances owned or possessed by such person, by any other party or entity, at any facility or incineration vessel owned or operated by another party or entity and containing such hazardous substances. . . .

Essentially, liability under this section is triggered by being an "arranger." Industrial generators of hazardous waste are the principal group of entities that fall within the scope of this subsection, although the section certainly is not limited to industrial generators, and the use of the language "arranged for disposal" makes clear that Congress intended this category to reach beyond generators. Thus, contracting and arranging for disposal seem to be the targeted elements for liability, and courts have interpreted this section broadly.

An example of an arranger that was not a generator occurred in Emergency Technical Services Corp. v. Morton International, 1993 WL 210531 (N.D.Ill. 1993). In that case, a consultant who actually arranged the disposal, including choosing the site, was held liable as an arranger under § 107(a)(3). *But see* Amcast Industrial Corp. v. Detrex, 2 F.3d 746 (7th Cir.1993) (no arranger liability for accidental spill by a common carrier where chemical manufacturer shipped products to customers using the carrier).

In Burlington Northern & Santa Fe Railway Co. v. United States, 129 S.Ct. 1870 (2009), the Supreme Court clarified the meaning of "arranged for disposal." *Burlington Northern* was an action against various parties involved in the storage and distribution of agricultural chemicals on a parcel of land owned by certain railroads. The company that operated the business at the time of disposal had become insolvent and ceased operations at an earlier date. These actions were against other entities alleged to be PRPs under CERCLA. One of the defendants was Shell Oil Company, which had sold a pesticide to the company operating the distribution business on the property. Shell objected to being categorized as an "arranger" for the purpose of CERCLA liability. The Court held that "under the plain language of the statute, an entity may qualify as an arranger under § 9607(a)(3) when it takes intentional steps to dispose of a hazardous substance." In contrast, the Court said, "[i]t is ... clear that an entity could not be held liable as an arranger merely for selling a new and useful product if the purchaser of that product later, and unbeknownst to the seller, disposed of the product in a way that led to contamination." Acknowledging that "the question whether § 9607(a)(3) liability attaches is fact intensive and case specific," the Court held that Shell did not have the requisite intent, even though it was aware that "minor, accidental spills" occurred during the distribution process. In addition, the Court noted that when Shell became aware that spills were occurring, it took steps to encourage that its product would be handled safely by the distributor.

What is meant by "intentional steps to dispose of a hazardous substance" beyond the situation of a party that merely sold "a new and useful product" that was improperly disposed of by the purchaser? There is no doubt that the *Burlington Northern* decision will reduce the number of parties categorized as "arrangers" under CERCLA and that, as a result, the decision indirectly questions whether strict liability applies to arrangers. Accordingly, it may impact cases similar to earlier cases in which strict liability was applied. In United States v. Aceto Agricultural Chemicals Corp., 872 F.2d 1373 (8th Cir.1989), where the generator had no knowledge that the particular site would be used for disposal, the court imposed arranger liability. In GenCorp, Inc. v. Olin Corp., 390 F.3d 433 (6th Cir.2004), the Sixth Circuit held that an arranger need not actively participate in disposal to be liable as an arranger under CERCLA. Mere constructive ownership or possession of the waste was sufficient. Some earlier cases held otherwise, however, ruling that for a party to "arrange for disposal," the party must have taken some affirmative steps to the party's own advantage. In Morton Int'l, Inc. v. A.E. Staley Manufacturing Co., 343 F.3d 669 (3d Cir.2003), the court held that the party must not just own or possess the hazardous waste, but must "demonstrate either control over the process that results in a release of hazardous waste or knowledge that such a release will occur during the process." Each of these cases involved different and sometimes intricate relationships between the alleged arranger and the party operating the business. The *Burlington Northern* arranger standard is certain to require intense scrutiny of the unique factual circumstances of each case.

For those entities falling within the "arranger" category, relief may be available if they are able to demonstrate that their waste did not actually contribute to the release or was a divisible portion of the harm. The other portion of the *Burlington Northern* decision, discussed more fully in Section 3.C above, allows for apportionment of liability. The burden is on the arranger to demonstrate a reasonable basis for apportionment. *See also* United States v. Alcan Aluminum Corp., 990 F.2d 711 (2d Cir. 1993) ("[C]ommingling is not synonymous with indivisible harm, and Alcan should have the opportunity to show that the harm caused . . . was capable of reasonable apportionment. It may present evidence relevant to establishing divisibility of harm, such as, proof disclosing the relative toxicity, migratory potential, degree of migration, and synergistic capacities of the hazardous substances at the site."); United States v. Alcan Aluminum Corp., 964 F.2d 252 (3d Cir.1992) ("If Alcan can establish . . . that the harm is capable of reasonable apportionment, then it should be held liable only for the response costs relating to that portion of harm to which it contributed."); In re Bell Petroleum Services, Inc., 3 F.3d 889 (5th Cir.1993) ("If the expert testimony and other evidence establishes a factual basis for making a reasonable estimate that will fairly apportion liability, joint and several liability should not be imposed in the absence of exceptional circumstances.").

4. Transporters

CERCLA § 107(a)(4) sets forth the liability of a transporter of hazardous substances by identifying as a PRP

> any person who accepts or accepted any hazardous substances for transport to disposal or treatment facilities, incineration vessels or sites selected by such person, from which there is a release, or a threatened release which causes the incurrence of response costs, of a hazardous substance.

In addition, CERCLA § 101(26) defines the terms "transport" or "transportation" as follows:

> the movement of a hazardous substance by any mode, including pipeline ..., and in the case of a hazardous substance which has been accepted for transportation by a common or contract carrier, the term[s] ... shall include any stoppage in transit which is temporary, incidental to the transportation movement, and at the ordinary operating convenience of a common or contract carrier, and any such stoppage shall be considered as a continuity of movement and not as the storage of a hazardous substance.

The terms of the statute indicate that the transporter will be liable only if it selected the site, and the majority of jurisdictions interpret the statute broadly. *See* United States v. South Carolina Recycling & Disposal, Inc., 653 F.Supp. 984 (D.S.C. 1984). It is irrelevant whether or not the transporter was a common carrier; if the transporter chose the site, liability will attach. United States v. Hardage, 750 F.Supp. 1444 (W.D.Okla.1990). The transporter may not avoid liability by arguing that the generator or some other PRP collaborated in choosing the waste site or that the transporter did not make the ultimate decision in choice of site. Tippins Inc. v. USX Corp., 37 F.3d 87 (3d Cir.1994) (noting, however, that the transporter must take some active role in site selection for liability to attach). But one court has held that if a flow control ordinance requires the transporter to use the particular site, the transporter may escape CERCLA liability. Miami County Incinerator Qualified Trust v. Acme Waste Management Co., 61 F.Supp.2d 724 (S.D.Ohio 1999).

E. DEFENSES

The statutory defenses to a CERCLA action for cleanup costs are located primarily in Section 107(b) of the Act. Boilerplate language precludes liability for releases caused solely by an act of God or an act of war, CERCLA §§ 107(b)(1)–(2), with the emphasis on the "solely" requirement. Section 107(b) also provides for a third-party defense under limited circumstances. In 1986, Congress enacted, as part of SARA, what has become known as the "innocent landowner defense," which appears in the definitional section of CERCLA, Section 101(35), rather than in Section 107. Other procedural and substantive defenses to cost recovery actions may exist, including the possible availability of equitable defenses. *See* William H. Rodgers, Jr., Environmental Law § 8.8, at 793–94 (2d ed. 1994) (discussing the division of authority on the availability of equitable defenses in CERCLA actions). Though not technically a defense, Section 107(*o*) sets forth an exemption for certain very narrowly defined "de micromis" parties. The exemption applies only to arrangers and transporters and sets forth a ceiling for the amount of waste and a deadline for disposal for a PRP to qualify for the exemption.

To understand the potential CERCLA liability of clients who may also be defending separate toxic tort actions, the third-party defense and the innocent landowner defense are the most important.

1. Third–Party Defense

A defense to CERCLA liability may be available to a PRP in situations in which the release of the hazardous substances was due solely to

> an act or omission of a third party other than an employee or agent of the defendant, or than one whose act or omission occurs in connection with a contractual relationship, existing directly or indirectly, with the defendant. . . .

CERCLA § 107(b)(3). Not only does "contractual relationship" apply to contracts for disposal, transportation, or other handling of the waste, but it also refers to real property transactions. *See* CERCLA § 101(35)(A) (defining "contractual relationship" to include real property transactions and setting forth an innocent landowner defense with regard to real property transactions under a limited set of circumstances). By its terms, therefore, the defense is not available to a broad spectrum of persons related to the defendant in a variety of contractual relationships. *See, e.g.,* Shapiro v. Alexanderson, 743 F.Supp. 268 (S.D.N.Y.1990) (no defense where PRP asserting it is the landowner and the third party is the operator of the landfill).

Section 107(b)(3) sets forth two additional requirements. Section 107(b)(3) states:

[T]he defendant [must establish] by a preponderance of the evidence that (a) he exercised due care with respect to the hazardous substance concerned, taking into consideration the characteristics of such hazardous substance, in light of all relevant facts and circumstances, and (b) he took precautions against foreseeable acts or omissions of any such third party and the consequences that could foreseeably result from such acts or omissions. . . .

The combination of requirements in CERCLA § 107(b)(3) makes the third-party defense very difficult to use in most cases, causing Professor Rodgers to refer to it as "nine parts loser." *See* William H.

Rodgers, Jr., Environmental Law § 8.8, at 797–98 (2d ed. 1994) (noting that courts may decide to restrict the defense to situations involving third-party "outsiders," commonly referred to as "midnight dumpers").

2. Innocent Landowner Defense

The innocent landowner defense, a creature of the 1986 SARA amendments, and amended again in 2002, is found in the exception to the definition of "contractual relationship" in CERCLA § 101(35)(A). After stating that "contractual relationship" includes real property transactions, the section proceeds to delineate a defense for circumstances in which

the real property on which the facility concerned is located was acquired by the defendant after the disposal or placement of the hazardous substance on, in, or at the facility, and one or more of the [following] circumstances ... is also established by the defendant by a preponderance of the evidence:

(i) At the time the defendant acquired the facility the defendant did not know and had no reason to know that any hazardous substance which is the subject of the release or threatened release was disposed of on, in, or at the facility.

The other stated circumstances apply to governmental entities and to persons acquiring the property by inheritance or bequest and are separate from the innocent landowner defense.

The property owner must have conducted "all appropriate inquiries" at the time it acquired the property to be able to rely upon the innocent landowner defense. In general, the landowner must demonstrate:

(1) that "appropriate inquiries" were conducted prior to the date on which the party acquired the property;

(2) that inquiries were made into "the previous ownership and uses of the facility in accordance with generally accepted good commercial and customary standards and practices"; and

(3) that the party "took reasonable steps" to stop continuing releases and avoid future releases, and to "prevent or limit" any harm caused by releases that had already occurred.

CERCLA § 101(35)(B)(i).

In the early years of CERCLA, courts construing the innocent landowner defense were on their own in deciding the extent of the inquiry that the defendant must have conducted at the time of acquiring the property. In United States v. Serafini, 706 F.Supp. 346 (M.D.Pa.1988), the court refused to hold as a matter of law that lack of an on-site visual inspection precluded the defendant from relying on the innocent landowner defense. This suggested that each defendant's inquiry should be examined on a case-by-case basis in light of the customs and circumstances presented. In United States v. Pacific Hide and Fur Depot, Inc., 716 F.Supp. 1341 (D.Idaho 1989), the court established a sliding scale for evaluating landowners' inquiries, requiring the most stringent review in commercial property transactions and the least stringent in cases of inheritance or bequest. But some courts have been quite strict in reviewing the defendants' inquiry about the condition of the site. *See, e.g.,* In re Hemingway Transport, Inc., 993 F.2d 915 (1st Cir. 1993).

The 2002 amendments to the innocent landowner defense provided more detailed standards for "all appropriate inquiries" and included provisions to transition landowners into the more precise standards. The amendments also firmly establish that stricter requirements apply to owners of commercial property than residential or other noncommercial property. On November 1, 2006, the EPA's final rule for conducting "all appropriate inquiries" became mandatory for property purchased after that date. *See* 40 C.F.R. § 312.20 et seq. (2010). This rule establishes more comprehensive requirements for the inquiry than previously applied.

Finally, if the party can establish the above requirements, the party must additionally demonstrate that it met the requirements in Section 107(b)(3)(a) and (b) by exercising due care with respect to the hazardous substance and taking precautions against the acts or omissions of third parties. Thus, the burden on the landowner is very high.

In addition, the 2002 CERCLA amendments added a "contiguous owner" defense that is analogous to the innocent landowner defense for owners of adjacent property. CERCLA § 107(q). The same general requirements apply, including the requirement of "all appropriate inquiries." As a separate matter, certain "bona fide prospective purchasers" may be able to limit their statutory liability even though they knew of contamination on the property at the time of purchase. Among other things, the property owner must cooperate with the Government on cleanup efforts. CERCLA § 107(r).

F. PRIVATE PARTY ACTIONS AND CONTRIBUTION CLAIMS

One of the most vigorously litigated issues under CERCLA in recent years has involved the mechanisms by which private parties may seek reimbursement for response costs they incurred, either by Government mandate or by voluntarily cleaning up a release. These questions involve examining two separate sections of CERCLA, § 113(f) and § 107(a).

When a PRP incurs response costs pursuant to an order by or agreement with the Government, that party may seek to recover some or all of the response costs from other PRPs. *See, e.g.*, Bedford Affiliates v. Sills, 156 F.3d 416 (2d Cir.1998); Centerior Service Company v. Acme Scrap Iron & Metal Corp., 153 F.3d 344 (6th Cir.1998); New Castle County v. Halliburton NUS Corp., 111 F.3d 1116 (3d Cir.1997); Pinal Creek Group v. Newmont Mining Corp., 118 F.3d 1298 (9th Cir.1997). Section 113(f)(1) provides in part:

Any person may seek contribution from any other person who is liable or potentially liable under section 9606 of this title or under section 9607(a) of this title.... In resolving contribution claims, the court may allocate response costs among liable parties using such equitable factors as the court determines are appropriate.

This equitable allocation standard is markedly different from the strict/joint and several liability standard employed to determine liability in the first instance under Section 107 of CERCLA.

Section 107(a) also addresses private party actions against PRPs for response costs the private party incurred. Although this section is somewhat confusing because it is a subsection of (a)(4) which defines transporter liability, it clearly was intended to apply more generally. Thus, after stating that a PRP is liable to the U.S. Government, a State, or an Indian tribe for response costs, the section proceeds to state that any PRP "shall be liable for ... (B) any other necessary costs of response incurred by any other person consistent with the national contingency plan."

The United States Supreme Court placed an important limitation on contribution claims in Cooper Industries, Inc. v. Aviall Services, Inc., 543 U.S. 157 (2004). The Court limited the availability of Section 113(f) contribution actions to PRPs who have been sued in a civil action under CERCLA § 106 or § 107(a), including settlements of those actions. The case left open a number of issues, but initially was followed strictly. For example, in Elementis Chemicals Inc. v. T H Agriculture & Nutrition, 373 F.Supp.2d 257 (S.D.N.Y.2005), the court held that a PRP that voluntarily cleaned up its own property was barred by *Cooper Industries* from bringing a contribution action against another PRP. The role of Section 107(a) in private party actions remained unclear.

In 2007, the Supreme Court addressed private party actions under Section 107 in United States v. Atlantic Research Corp., 551 U.S. 128 (2007). Answering the question on everyone's minds after *Cooper Industries*, the Court held that CERCLA § 107(a) does, in fact, provide a PRP with a cause of action to recover from other PRPs the response costs it voluntarily incurred. The Court noted that "the remedies available in §§ 107(a) and 113(f) complement each other by providing causes of action 'to persons in different procedural circumstances.'"

One distinction between liability under Section 107(a) and liability for contribution under Section 113(f) is that the former is based upon joint and several liability, whereas the latter is based upon equitable principles. Where joint and several liability is the standard, liability may be subject to apportionment under the rule of Burlington Northern & Santa Fe Railway Co. v. United States, 129 S.Ct. 1870 (2009), as discussed in Section 3.C *supra*.

In contribution actions under Section 113(f), courts have employed a broad variety of factors to equitably allocate response costs. For example, in

United States v. Davis, 31 F.Supp.2d 45 (D.R.I. 1998), the court stated that "the dominant factor in determining each party's equitable share of liability is the extent to which the response costs are attributable to waste for which that party is directly responsible." In Browning–Ferris Industries of Illinois Inc. v. Ter Maat, 13 F.Supp.2d 756 (N.D.Ill. 1998), the court stated that "the truest measure to assess equitably the liability in this case is to consider the conduct of the parties" and "liability should be based on a percentage of fault rather than a percentage of volume or a percentage based on a particular waste stream." These cases suggest the broad discretion granted to courts by the statutory language directing them to use "such equitable factors as the court determines are appropriate."

G. SETTLEMENT

CERCLA § 122 contains settlement provisions that are designed to encourage cost recovery by giving PRPs an incentive to come forward and take responsibility for the release or threatened release. The Government is authorized to give the PRP with which the agreement has been made a covenant not to sue with respect to future liability, but only after all remedial action has been completed. CERCLA § 122(f). An exception to the covenant not to sue exists for releases arising out of conditions unknown at the time of the agreement. CERCLA § 122(f)(6). To further induce settlement, and to protect a PRP who settles its present and future liabilities with respect to a site, Section 113(f) shields the settling PRP from liability for contribution to other PRPs while maintaining the settling PRP's right to seek contribution from others. CERCLA § 113(f)(2), (3)(B).

A settlement with fewer than all PRPs in no way discharges the remaining PRPs from their statutory liability, unless the settlement agreement so provides. The settlement "reduces the potential liability of the others by the amount of the settlement." CERCLA § 113(f)(2). Although this pro tanto setoff rule appears to allow the nonsettling PRPs to benefit from a high settlement by the settling PRP (a settlement in excess of the settling PRP's equitable share), the preservation of contribution claims for the settling PRP renders this advantage illusory. On the other hand, if the settling PRP settles low (below its equitable share), the nonsettling PRPs may be required to pay an amount in excess of their percentage shares with no recourse against the settling PRP. Presumably, this scheme would have the effect of inducing PRPs to settle with the Government.

A special settlement provision addresses PRPs who are considered "de minimis." Section 122(g) provides for an expedited settlement with PRPs whose portion of the response costs is deemed to be minimal, as determined by one of two tests. The first test requires the PRP's contribution to the site to be minimal in *both* amount and toxicity, in comparison to the other hazardous substances at the site. The second test applies only to PRPs who are owners of the real property on which the facility is located, and requires that the owner did not "conduct or permit" any hazardous waste activities at the site and did not contribute to the release or threat of release. Further, the owner must not have "purchased the real property with actual or constructive knowledge that the property was used for the generation, transportation, storage, treatment, or disposal of any hazardous substance." CERCLA § 122(g)(1). In addition, the de minimis settlement must represent a minor portion of the overall response costs associated with the release. As with standard settlements under CERCLA, de minimis settlements relieve the settling PRP from liability for contribution to other PRPs arising out of the release that is the subject of the settlement. *See* CERCLA § 122(g)(5); Dravo Corp. v. Zuber, 13 F.3d 1222 (8th Cir.1994).

In recent years, the length and complexity of settlement negotiations between the Government and PRPs have become protracted, thus defeating the goal of using settlements to provide a faster means of achieving cleanups than enforcement actions. In September 2009, however, EPA announced a new policy to move settlements to completion more quickly. The new policy would aggressively expedite negotiations on the specifics of the cleanup and authorize regional EPA offices to use unilateral administrative orders when settlement is not forthcoming.

H. SAVINGS CLAUSE

CERCLA contains a provision expressly saving a person's right to pursue tort claims under state law for matters related to any release of a hazardous substance into the environment. Section 310(h) provides:

> This chapter does not affect or otherwise impair the rights of any person under Federal, State, or common law. . . .

This section makes clear that CERCLA was not intended to preclude individuals' private rights of action for personal injuries and property damage. Thus, the remedial scheme in CERCLA operates separately from the tort remedies available under state law.

I. CITIZENS SUITS

CERCLA, following the precedent of other federal environmental statutes, contains a citizens suit provision that allows "any person" to bring an action directly against a "person . . . who is alleged to be in violation of any standard, regulation, condition, requirement, or order" pursuant to CERCLA. CERCLA § 310(a)(1). Alternatively, the action may be brought against a Government officer (including the EPA Administrator) for failure to perform any non-discretionary act or duty pursuant to the Act. CERCLA § 310(a)(2). The term "person" refers to a corporation or a governmental entity, as well as a natural person. Citizens are not entitled to private monetary damages under this provision. Rather, the remedies available are injunctive relief to enforce the standard or regulation and, with respect to a Section 310(a)(1) citizens suit, civil penalties.

The citizens suit provision permits persons to act as private attorneys general to remedy violations that have not otherwise been remedied under the other provisions of the Act. As such, in many ways it is the federal statutory complement to the public nuisance action. It is a dramatic illustration of the confluence of public and private remedies in the area of toxic torts. The citizens suit does not, however, authorize citizens to force a cleanup. Rather, it enables citizens to seek enforcement of a Government cleanup order. Additionally, CERCLA further restricts the ability of citizens to interfere with remedial action at a particular site. *See* CERCLA § 113(h)(4) (providing that a citizens suit "may not be brought with regard to a removal where a remedial action is to be undertaken at the site").

The statute sets forth certain threshold limitations on commencement of the action. First, notice of the alleged violation must be sent to the EPA, the state, and the alleged violator at least sixty days before the action is commenced. CERCLA § 310(d)(1). Second, a citizens suit may not be commenced if the Government "has commenced and is diligently prosecuting an action" under the Act. CERCLA § 310(d)(2). The purpose of this second limitation is to allow focus on agency enforcement without the distraction and potential conflict of the citizens suit.

Much of the case law interpreting the scope of citizens suits has developed within the context of other federal environmental statutes. Many similar issues arise with respect to CERCLA citizens suits. In Steel Company v. Citizens for a Better Environment, 523 U.S. 83 (1998), the Supreme Court held that for a plaintiff in a citizens suit to have standing to sue, the plaintiff must establish three elements: (1) injury-in-fact, (2) causation of the injury by the conduct of the defendant, and (3) the likelihood that the relief sought will redress the injury. *Steel Company* involved a citizens suit brought for past violations of the Emergency Planning and Community Right to Know Act (EPCRA), 42 U.S.C.A. § 11046(a)(1) (West 2010). The Court ruled that the injunctive relief sought could not redress the wholly past nature of the violations, even though the injunctive relief was fashioned to prevent future violations of EPCRA. The logical result of *Steel Company* is a requirement that plaintiffs in citizens suits must allege continuing violations of the relevant statute or order when seeking injunctive relief to assure future compliance. The Supreme Court had also addressed the meaning of ''in violation'' so as to trigger citizens suit liability under the Clean Water Act, 33 U.S.C.A. §§ 1251–1387 (West 2010). The Court has held that violations must be ongoing or recurring, and not isolated past incidents, for a citizens suit to be proper.

Gwaltney of Smithfield v. Chesapeake Bay Foundation, 484 U.S. 49 (1987). *See also* Coalition for Health Concern v. LWD, Inc., 60 F.3d 1188 (6th Cir. 1995) (holding that the CERCLA citizens suit provision requires allegation of "continuous or intermittent violations").

CHAPTER FIVE

LIABILITY OF EMPLOYERS

Issues of toxic exposures in the workplace present the paradigmatic public and private law model. The product liability theories discussed in Chapter Two may certainly arise within the context of the workplace. But, as this chapter will explore, product liability becomes an option for the injured worker outside of the employer-employee relationship. This chapter addresses liabilities that inhere directly in the employment relationship. Many of the rules that apply in the workplace are not rules that derive from the law of torts, however. The workplace is primarily a public law forum, and statutory regulation and administrative law tribunals play prominent roles in the investigation of the impact of hazardous substances and the resolution of claims related to toxic exposures.

A. WORKERS' COMPENSATION

1. Historical Perspective

Interest in occupational illness in America was piqued in the 1930s with the attention drawn to workplace victims of silicosis. A bias existed, however, against recognizing occupational disease as a legitimate injury meriting compensation. Early concerns for a flood of claims related to occupational disease that could create economic havoc in industry caused lawmakers to be reluctant to provide mechanisms of recovery for occupational disease victims. *See generally* Arthur Larson, *Occupational Diseases Under Workmen's Compensation Laws*, 9 U. Rich. L. Rev. 87 (1974); Richard Robblee, *The Dark Side of Workers' Compensation: Burdens and Benefits in Occupational Disease Coverage*, 2 Indus. Rel. L.J. 596 (1978).

The workers' compensation schemes that evolved during the early part of the Twentieth Century, and that were in place in virtually every state by about 1920, originally did not include a remedy for occupational disease. Workers' compensation arose as a result of an increase in workplace accidents directly tied into the industrial revolution. The quid pro quo arrangement of workers' compensation provided a no-fault remedial scheme for employees injured during the course of employment and protection for employers from liabilities to their employees outside of workers' compensation for employment related injuries. The system was designed to treat worker injuries as a cost of industry to be spread to consumers of the products manufactured. *See* 1 Arthur Larson, Larson's Workers' Compensation Law § 1.04(2) (2009). Eventually, occupational disease claims came to be treated within the workers' compensation system, but with an ambivalence that has yet to be fully resolved. While workers' compensation typically provides compensation for medical expenses and lost wages, as well as a relatively small statutory amount above that, it does not include recovery for pain and suffering.

Although workers' compensation usually bars a separate claim against the claimant's employer arising out of the same incident, tort actions against third parties, such as the manufacturers of equipment used in the production process, are allowed. The now common situation of injured asbestos insulation workers presents a perfect example. In such cases, the workers usually may not bring suit against their employers (e.g. contractors) due to the operation of the workers' compensation laws, but may bring tort actions against the third-party manufacturers of the asbestos containing products. *See, e.g.,* Borel v. Fibreboard Paper Prods. Corp., 493 F.2d 1076 (5th Cir.1973).

Because the workers' compensation system has tended to be less responsive to occupational disease claims than to accidental injuries, and because of the attraction of large jury verdict awards for tort claims, workers have attempted to find legal loopholes that would permit them to bring tort actions against their employers, even where their claims fit within the scope of workers' compensation. One must bear in mind, however, that the difficulty of proving the defendant's culpable conduct in a civil action makes workers' compensation an attractive primary remedy.

2. Occupational Disease Statutes

Because workers' compensation statutes require that the injury have occurred within the course of employment, occupational disease claims have been treated with skepticism due to the difficulty of assuring that an illness was work-related. Two particular problems arise within this context. First, occupational diseases often are identical to illnesses existing in the general population, and may not be unique to the claimant's occupation. Second, the long latency periods associated with the manifestation of many illnesses make it difficult to demonstrate that an illness was in fact work-related and was not the result of intervening causes.

This skepticism led to restrictive treatment of occupational disease in the workers' compensation laws of most states. Limitations on occupational disease claims abound. For example, some statutes allow occupational disease workers' compensation claims only when the worker had been exposed to the toxic substance in the workplace for a certain length of time. Or, statutes in some states require employment for a certain length of time before the claim will be covered by workers' compensation. *See, e.g.*, Cal. Lab. Code § 5500.5 (West 2009) (fours years of employment, but 2010 proposal would change to one year). Further, some states require that the illness must manifest itself within a designated period of time following the worker's last exposure to the alleged substance or the worker's last day of employment for the employer. *See, e.g.*, 820 Ill. Comp. Stat. 310./1(d) & (f) (2008) (within two years of last exposure); S.C. Code Ann. § 42–11–70 (2008) (within one year of last exposure). Limitations such as these obviously cannot provide equitable rules in all occupational illness situations, and the distinctions they embody often seem arbitrary.

In general, occupational disease statutes require that for an illness to be compensable, it must be associated with the worker's specific occupation and not be an "ordinary disease of life." *See, e.g.*, 820 Ill. Comp. Stat. 310./1(d) (2008); Md. Code Lab. & Empl. § 9–101(g) (2009) (as interpreted in case law). To ensure this, one type of occupational disease statute provides a list of diseases that are compensable. *See, e.g.*, Pa. Stat. Ann. tit. 77, § 1208 (West 2009). These scheduled illnesses typically are those that are considered "signature diseases" related to a specific exposure, such as asbestosis. A claim brought for a listed disease will be presumed to be sufficiently associated with the workplace in which the claimant was exposed to the offending substance to satisfy the work-relatedness requirement. Most statutes allow occupational disease claims where the illness is "peculiar to" the worker's occupation, either as a sole requirement or as a supplement to a schedule of diseases. *See, e.g.*, Mich. Comp. Laws Ann. § 418.401(2)(b) (West 2009). For diseases associated with exposure to toxic substances, determination of whether a claimant's illness falls within this definition may be problematic. This is particularly true where the disease alleged has a long latency period and/or appears in background levels in the general population. Diseases "common to the general population," to which the general public is exposed outside of the claimant's workplace, will not be compensable, even if the claimant can make a reasonably good showing that he or she developed the disease as a result of a workplace exposure. *See, e.g.,* Pa. Stat. Ann. tit. 77, § 1208 (West 2009). The line between covered illness and noncovered illness tends to be blurred, however.

An often overlooked limitation on occupational disease claims is that they must be suffered by *employees.* This may seem obvious, but especially in the area of reproductive and genetic injury, persons related to the worker, such as a spouse or children, may claim to have been injured as a result of the worker's employment exposure to toxic substances. For example, a child of a worker may suffer a birth defect that allegedly was caused by the worker's exposure to a substance in the course of his or her employment. These third parties will probably be limited to the tort law—which may or may not provide recovery for the kind of claim brought and which may be subject to more stringent causation requirements than the work-relatedness requirement of workers' compensation law—for a remedy. *See generally* Jean Macchiaroli Eggen, *Toxic Reproductive and Genetic Hazards in the Workplace: Challenging the Myths of the Tort and Workers' Compensation Systems,* 60 Fordham L. Rev. 843 (1992) (discussing the problems third-party family members face in proving a sufficient causal connection between toxic exposure and injury to recover under either tort or workers' compensation law). More importantly, these third parties will not be limited by the exclusivity of the workers' compensation system and will be free to fully raise their tort claims and seek the available tort remedies. *Cf* Snyder v. Michael's Stores, Inc., 945 P.2d 781 (Cal. 1997) (tort action against the employer of the mother of the plaintiff child exposed to toxic substances in utero was not barred by the exclusivity of California workers' compensation statute).

3. Exclusivity of Remedy

The concept of workers' compensation as an exclusive remedy bars workers from bringing tort actions against their employers for work-related illness. In return, the worker obtains expedited compensation without the need to show fault on the part of the employer. The worker also is not restricted by the traditional tort doctrines of contributory negligence, assumption of the risk, and the fellow servant rule. One of the seeming paradoxes of occupational disease claims, however, is that the worker need not actually recover under workers' compensation for a tort action to be barred. Consider the example presented by Cole v. Dow Chemical Co., 315 N.W.2d 565 (Mich.Ct.App.1982). In *Cole*, workers complained of sterility as a result of occupational exposure to the chemical DBCP. The claims were held to be covered under the Michigan occupational disease statute, but presented noncompensable injuries. Subsequently, the workers brought actions against their employer in state court. The court dismissed their actions because the injuries were alleged to arise from exposures in the workplace setting. The court considered it irrelevant that the workers' compensation tribunal had refused to compensate the workers. *Cf.* Akef v. BASF Corp., 702 A.2d 519 (N.J.Super.Ct.App.Div.1997) (holding that a worker rendered sterile by workplace exposure had suffered a "permanent partial total disability" that was compensable under the workers' compensation statute).

In contrast, however, where the occupational illness is deemed noncovered, the claimant should be allowed to commence a tort action against the employer. For example, in McCarthy v. Department of Social & Health Servs., 759 P.2d 351 (Wash.1988), the plaintiff had been denied workers' compensation benefits because her chronic lung condition, which she alleged arose from a severe reaction to environmental tobacco smoke in the workplace, was not a covered illness within the state occupational disease statute. The court allowed her civil suit against the employer to proceed on that basis.

The situation presented in the *Cole* case demonstrates the kinds of problems faced by many occupational disease claimants whose injuries are alleged to be related to exposures to toxic substances in the workplace. Because such claims confront numerous statutory hurdles and are often challenged vigorously by employers and insurance carriers, close questions can result in noncompensable injuries. Where, as in *Cole*, claimants have no direct recourse in the courts, legitimately injured workers could be left with no remedy. There is no question that such toxic claims present significant problems for the legal system. Determining precisely how to go about handling these claims to balance all the interests of the parties will continue to be a major challenge in both the public and private legal arenas.

Some issues have arisen regarding the appropriate standard for determining when a disease is work-related. The most reasonable standard, and one that a number of courts have adopted, is that the claimant show that the workplace exposure was a "substantial contributing factor" to the claimant's illness. Thus, in Manske v. Workforce Safety & Ins., 748 N.W.2d 394 (N.D. 2008), the North Dakota Supreme Court applied the "substantial contributing factor" test where the decedent worker, a smoker exposed to asbestos in the workplace, had died of lung cancer. The court held that although smoking may have been a cause of the disease, the focus of the inquiry should be on whether asbestos exposure was a substantial contributing cause. *Accord* Lindquist v. City of Jersey Fire Dept., 814 A.2d 1069 (N.J. 2003).

4. Exceptions to Exclusivity

Most states recognize at least some exceptions to exclusivity, which allow claimants to bring actions directly against their employers in addition to collecting workers' compensation benefits. These exceptions exist in addition to the right to bring an action against a third party, such as the manufacturer of equipment or substances used during the course of employment. These exceptions generally are construed quite narrowly, however. Exceptions may appear in the state workers' compensation statute or may arise through judicial interpretation.

a. *Intentional Misconduct of Employer*

One circumstance that will give rise to special treatment is where the employer acted with the knowledge that injury to the worker was substantially certain to occur. Some jurisdictions treat this situation within the workers' compensation statute, typically establishing an increased benefit for intentional misconduct. In many jurisdictions, however, the employee may bring an independent civil action against the employer for injuries arising from such conduct. "Substantial certainty" of injury is typically a requirement; gross negligence or recklessness usually will not qualify to meet this exception. *See generally* 6 Arthur Larson, Larson's Workers' Compensation Law §§ 103–104 (2009). With respect to toxic workplace exposures, the major question becomes whether workers may bring tort actions against their employers when the conduct of which they complain is knowledge of workplace hazards coupled with failure to warn workers or remove the hazards.

The more traditional approach is exemplified by Franklin v. Tedford, 18 So.3d 215 (Miss. 2009). Employees of a furniture manufacturer brought claims for battery against their employer, claiming that the employer had intentionally exposed them to high levels of neurotoxic glue fumes. The Mississippi Supreme Court reaffirmed the intentional tort exception to exclusivity, but also reaffirmed state law requiring that the plaintiff show "actual intent to injure the employee." The court ruled that fact questions existed in this case.

Not all jurisdictions interpret intentional conduct in such a traditional manner. In Zagorianos v. United Painting Co., 1996 WL 682183 (Ohio Ct.App. 1996), a sandblaster sued his employer for injuries incurred as a result of exposure to lead paint dust. The worker claimed that the employer had intentionally exposed the workers to the lead paint dust. The court held that deliberate behavior by the employer is not required to prove intentional conduct. The court stated that "intention is a coefficient of risk" and held that "[w]hen the safety of the workplace is so deliberately compromised that the employer is demanding that the worker face almost certain injury by doing his job, then the law considers that the employer has intended such injury." Nevertheless, the court dismissed the worker's case because the worker had not demonstrated that the employer had required him to act in a manner that injury was substantially certain to occur.

In Helf v. Chevron U.S.A., 203 P.3d 962 (Utah 2009), the Supreme Court of Utah, allowed an action by a worker against her employer on the basis that the workplace supervisors knew she would be injured when they instructed her to neutralize spent toxic sludge, a procedure that created ultrahazardous vapors. The plaintiff alleged that her exposure to the fumes resulted in injuries consisting of "complex partial seizures, headaches, eye irritation, a twitching eyelid, nausea and vomiting, lethargy and weakness of extremities, disorientation, and mucous membrane irritation." The court stated that intent to injure

> requires a specific mental state in which the actor knew or expected that injury would be the consequence of his action. To demonstrate intent, a plaintiff may show that the actor desired the consequences of his actions, or that the actor believed the consequences were virtually certain to result. But a plaintiff may not demonstrate intent by showing merely that some injury was substantially certain to occur at some time.... [T]he employer must know or expect that a specific employee will be injured doing a specific task. In these situations, the knowledge and expectation that injury will occur robs an injury of its accidental character, moving it out of the realm of negligence and into the realm of intent.

Id. at 974. The court then held that the plaintiff's allegations satisfied that standard.

In Cunningham v. Anchor Hocking Corporation, 558 So.2d 93 (Fla. Dist. Ct.App.1990), the court held that the complaint's allegations that the employer had diverted fumes into the workplace and removed manufacturers' warning labels from products used in the workplace could, if proved, constitute claims for "battery, fraud and deceit," thus falling outside the workers' compensation statute. *See also* Birklid v. Boeing Co., 904 P.2d 278 (Wash. 1995) (alleging that the employer had removed chemical labels and denied access to material safety data sheets). In O'Brien v. Ottawa Silica Company, 656 F.Supp. 610 (E.D.Mich.1987), where the employer allegedly withheld medical information of the worker's occupational illness, the court held that the employer's conduct constituted intentional fraud. The plaintiff in *O'Brien* alleged that the employer knew from information supplied by company doctors that the decedent and other workers were developing asbestos-related disease from exposures in the workplace. The plaintiff further alleged that the employer ignored the doctors' recommendations to take precautions to protect the decedent and failed to inform the decedent of the health problems discovered by the doctors. The court held that these facts, if proven, provided a basis for a direct action against the employer for intentional misconduct because injury was "substantially certain to occur."

Many courts have been reluctant to read intentional misconduct into the failure-to-warn circumstances, however. *See, e.g.*, Wilson v. Asten–Hill Mfg., 791 F.2d 30 (3d Cir.1986); Miller v. Ensco, Inc., 692 S.W.2d 615 (Ark.1985); Reed Tool Co. v. Copelin, 689 S.W.2d 404 (Tex.1985). These states, therefore, would prohibit an employee action for intentional misconduct where the employer failed to warn of hazards, failed to provide adequate safety equipment and/or training, or breached workplace safety regulations, whether or not those acts were done knowingly. For example, in DaGraca v. Kowalsky Bros., Inc., 919 A.2d 525 (Conn. App. Ct. 2007), the court held that intentional conduct required knowledge on the part of the employer that the workers' deaths were "substantially certain" to occur, and stated that negligence, gross negligence, and recklessness did not meet that standard. The decedents had been asphyxiated when assigned the job of removing sedimentation from manholes and sealing the sewer pipe intake and outflow openings without safety equipment. The court held that the conduct alleged did not demonstrate knowledge that the workers' deaths were substantially certain to occur. *See also* Lee v. E.I. du Pont de Nemours & Co., 2008 WL 162894 (Ky. App. Ct. 2008) (stating that the defendant's "knowledge and appreciation of the risks involved in working with and exposure to asbestos, and its failure to protect [the plaintiff] from those risks, do not rise to level of intent").

These cases indicate that the traditional distinctions between intent to injure and recklessly endangering the health of workers may become blurred in the toxic tort context. Notwithstanding these developments, however, most states continue to construe the intentional misconduct exception narrowly. Its use by an employee, therefore, as a means of bringing an independent action against the employer may be quite limited, depending upon the jurisdiction.

b. *Aggravation of Injury*

A few states have recognized an exception to the exclusivity of workers' compensation where the employer acted in a manner that aggravated the worker's injury. Under this theory, a tort action could be brought against the employer only for the aggravation of the injury and not for development of the illness in the first place. The chief case applying this theory is Johns–Manville Products Corp. v. Contra Costa Superior Court, 612 P.2d 948 (Cal.1980). The California workers' compensation statute encompassed intentional conduct, and provided for a one-half increase in benefits if the requisite intent could be proved. In *Contra Costa*, the complaint alleged that the employer had conducted health monitoring of its employees and had knowingly concealed adverse health information from an employee. The court held that under these circumstances, the employer could be liable in tort for the aggravation of the employee's condition. *See also* Millison v. E.I. duPont de Nemours & Co., 501 A.2d 505 (N.J.1985) (allowing an exception for aggravation of injury, but requiring the plaintiff to prove a "deliberate corporate strategy" of concealment of health condition).

Applying the same rule, but reaching a different result, the court in Bazzini v. Technicolor, Inc., 2010 WL 186157 (Cal. App. Ct. 2010), held that the plaintiff presented insufficient evidence of fraudulent concealment by the employer to meet the requirements of the aggravation rule. The plaintiff alleged that his exposures to chemicals used to develop film in the workplace caused him to develop a periodic rash of which the employer was aware. The plaintiff later developed cancer. He argued that the employer knew the rashes were a precursor to the cancer, but concealed that information from him. The court disagreed, saying that there was no evidence that the employer had actual knowledge of any connection between the rashes and cancer.

c. Dual Capacity

This exception is extremely limited in toxic tort actions. It has been applied where an employer undertakes a duty to the employee that is independent of and separate from the employer-employee relationship. The duty is one that the employer owes to the general public, rather than to its employees within the employment relationship. *See* Duprey v. Shane, 249 P.2d 8 (Cal.1952) (applying the dual capacity exception where a chiropractor-employer allegedly negligently treated the employee for a work-related injury) (application of doctrine confined by 1982 statute to a narrow class of actions). In Ashdown v. Ameron Int'l Corp., 100 Cal. Rptr.2d 20 (Cal.Ct.App.2000), the court rejected the worker's estate's argument that the company was both his employer and a manufacturer of a hazardous product with a duty to warn about its dangers. Some questions may arise as to whether an employer that engages in health monitoring of its employees may be open to a tort action for serving in the separate capacity of health care provider. So far, application of the dual capacity exception has not extended that far. In general, employers who provide health screening for their employees are still acting as *employers*. They are not, as the case law seems to require, acting on a duty to the general public.

B. INJUNCTIVE RELIEF FOR UNSAFE WORKING CONDITIONS

When a worker seeks equitable relief for remediation of workplace hazards, rather than monetary compensation, the claim falls outside workers' compensation and within the jurisdiction of the courts of equity in the state. A court may reasonably exercise its equitable powers to grant injunctive relief to a person injured in the workplace as a result of ongoing exposures in the workplace. In Shimp v. New Jersey Bell Telephone Co., 368 A.2d 408 (N.J.Super.Ch.1976), the court ordered injunctive relief in favor of an employee who suffered from an allergy to environmental tobacco smoke (ETS). Taking judicial notice of "the toxic nature of cigarette smoke and its well known association with emphysema, lung cancer and heart disease," the court explained that its authority in equity extended to granting relief to the injured employee "by ordering the employer to eliminate any preventable hazardous condition which the court finds to exist." Accordingly, the court ordered the employer to limit smoking to restricted areas, such as the company lunchroom and lounge. *See also* Smith v. Western Electric Co., 643 S.W.2d 10 (Mo.Ct.App.1982).

The equitable relief granted in *Shimp* was in addition to whatever recovery may have been available under the state workers' compensation law. Such relief is complementary to, rather than in conflict with, the workers' compensation system. Notwithstanding the broad equitable powers of the court to grant relief so as to assure a reasonably safe workplace for employees, cases fashioning such a remedy are few. This may reflect a concern for balancing the equities when only one of many employees has complained of an exposure in the workplace. *See* Gordon v. Raven Systems & Research Inc., 462 A.2d 10 (D.C.Ct.App.1983) (holding that the employer is not required to make changes to the workplace merely to accommodate the sensitivities of a single employee).

C. REGULATION UNDER THE OCCUPATIONAL SAFETY AND HEALTH ACT

When Congress enacted the Occupational Safety and Health Act (OSHAct), 29 U.S.C.A. §§ 651–678 (West 2009) in 1970, its concerns were twofold—assuring the personal safety and health of workers and reducing lost production and its related increased costs. The OSHAct implements its goals through several interrelated means. First, the Act provides for research into occupational health and safety with the goal of reducing work hazards through the development of appropriate safety and health standards. Second, the Act contains reporting and recordkeeping requirements to make employers accountable and to provide necessary data. Third, the Act establishes and encourages a variety of programs to carry out the goals of the Act, including authorization to establish specific regulations regarding workplace hazards. Finally, the Act authorizes an administrative structure that includes regulatory and punitive measures to implement the Act's goals. As with CERCLA, the Act does not create any private right of action for personal injuries arising in the workplace. The OSHAct's entire thrust is toward information dissemination, regulation, and enforcement of workplace health and safety measures.

1. Administrative Structure

The OSHAct establishes a tripartite administrative structure for oversight of safety and health matters related to the workplace. The most visible agency created under the Act is the Occupational Safety and Health Administration (OSHA), located within the Department of Labor. OSHAct § 5(a)(2), 29 U.S.C.A. § 654(a)(2) (West 2009). OSHA's primary responsibilities are in the areas of standard setting and enforcement. Thus, OSHA is primarily responsible for inspecting workplaces, promulgating regulatory standards, determining compliance with standards, and proposing appropriate sanctions and remedial action where violations have occurred.

The second agency created under the OSHAct is the National Institute for Occupational Safety and Health (NIOSH). OSHAct § 22, 29 U.S.C.A. § 671 (West 2009). NIOSH is the research arm that is responsible for providing information to OSHA to be used in the development of health and safety standards. In contrast to OSHA, NIOSH is under the auspices of the Centers for Disease Control (CDC) within the Department of Health and Human Services. Some critics have viewed the bifurcation of the research and rulemaking functions authorized under the OSHAct as problematic. One benefit of the separation is to allow the research function to avoid any biases that might be present in OSHA, where economic interests are considered in addition to the health and safety of employees. But the lack of coordination between the two agencies on occupational health and safety issues has given some reason for concern. *See generally* Stephen A. Bokat & Horace A. Thompson III, Occupational Safety and Health Law 695–710 (1988) (discussing NIOSH's statutory authority, its programs, and court oversight).

The third administrative arm created by the OSHAct is the Occupational Safety and Health Review Commission (OSHRC). OSHAct §§ 10(c) & 12, 29 U.S.C.A. §§ 659(c) & 661 (West 2009). OSHRC sits as a quasi-judicial review board to oversee citations that have been issued by OSHA for violations of OSHA standards. In general, OSHRC becomes involved when an employer challenges an OSHA citation. The case is decided by an administrative law judge in the first instance, with subsequent board determination available. The system also provides for court review on the record established below before OSHRC.

2. Occupational Safety and Health Standards

a. *Contents of the Standards*

Section 5(a)(2) of the OSHAct requires that employers comply with any standards promulgated pursuant to the Act and contained in the Code of Federal Regulations. Standards exist for individual substances, including asbestos, lead, and bloodborne pathogens. The process for promulgation of standards is protracted, and it is not uncommon to have the courts involved in resolving legal challenges to proposed standards. These standards establish permissible exposure limits (PELs) for the specific substances and provide for health and safety measures. In general, OSHA may only promulgate a health standard upon a finding that a risk of "material impairment" of employees' health occurs at the current levels of exposure. Industrial Union Department, AFL–CIO v. American Petroleum Institute, 448 U.S. 607 (1980).

Typically, a standard includes requirements and specifications for labels and personal protective equipment. It also includes requirements for employer monitoring of employee exposure to the designated substance. Where the standard suggests employee medical examinations or laboratory screening tests, OSHA cannot compel the examination or test for a specific employee, but may require the employer to make testing available. For example, in the lead standard, specifications for monitoring employee blood lead levels are set forth, as well as a medical removal program that enables an employee with excessive blood lead levels to be removed to a non-lead exposure job while the levels recede without being required to take a reduction in pay. *See* 29 C.F.R. § 1910.1025 (2010).

b.   *Example: Bloodborne Pathogens Rule*

The bloodborne pathogens standard became effective in 1992, primarily as a result of concern for the spread of HIV through contact with human blood in the health care workplace. 29 C.F.R. § 1910.1030 (2009). The standard requires employers with one or more employees at risk of contracting HIV or hepatitis-B virus (HBV) through workplace exposure to develop and submit a written exposure control plan, updated at least annually. The plan must be available to all employees. In implementing the plan, the employer is required to follow universal precautions. This essentially means that all substances regulated under the standard are to be treated as being contaminated with the pathogens, whether or not it is known that the pathogens are present. For example, all needles and sharps used in a hospital are treated as carriers of the viruses, and use and disposal are regulated uniformly and strictly.

To follow universal precautions, employers may implement engineering controls—those that eliminate the hazard altogether—or work practice controls—those that reduce exposure by placing precautions on risky tasks. Thus, needles may no longer be recapped, thereby reducing the risk of exposure by eliminating the risk of skin puncture during that task. The work practice controls mostly address containers, personal protective equipment, and housekeeping, with special attention given to HIV and HBV research laboratories and production facilities.

In addition, the standard makes available to all employees with occupational exposure to HBV a vaccination and to those who have been exposed a post-exposure evaluation. Confidentiality is required of all records kept regarding employees.

The bloodborne pathogens rule provides an example of the kinds of choices OSHA must make in developing a standard. It also demonstrates some of the important policy issues that must be weighed in the process. Concern for worker privacy is crucial, but identification of routes of exposure and collection of information regarding hazards in the workplace are important in advancing the goals of the OSHAct. Sometimes these various policies may conflict sharply. Workers may be reluctant to report exposures and may be unwilling to participate in any medical monitoring made available by the employer out of fear of discrimination. Federal laws governing discrimination in the workplace may provide some relief, but the law surrounding the application of these laws to specific workplace situations is still evolving.

3. General Duty Clause

Distinct from compliance with the OSHA standards is the employers obligation pursuant to the general duty clause of the OSHAct. Section 5 of the Act provides that an employer must keep the workplace free from "recognized hazards" that cause or are likely to cause death or serious physical injury to the employees. This provision was intended to be a catchall to mandate a duty in situations in which the OSHA standards are not applicable. This section has not been interpreted to establish strict liability, and the short clause is open to interpretation at every turn. Thus, OSHRC has interpreted the clause to require that for liability to exist under the general duty clause, the employer must have been able to avoid the violation. *See* National Realty & Construction Co. v. OSHRC, 489 F.2d 1257 (D.C.Cir.1973).

For a hazard to be "recognized" within the meaning of the general duty clause, it must be one of which the employer, or at least the employer's industry, had knowledge at the time of the violation. "Hazard" has been interpreted broadly, and includes those exposures that are not apparent to the human senses. Much controversy has ensued over the interpretation of the degree of certainty that must exist for the requisite causation, with the major disagreement being over whether a probability or possibility test was intended.

Finally, the general duty clause was intended to address serious harms—only those that cause or are likely to cause death or serious physical injury. Mandatory penalties per violation are set forth in the OSHAct, but, again, the Act does not provide a remedy for damages for private persons.

4. Hazard Communication Standard

The OSHA Hazard Communication Standard is different from the standards for specific substances discussed above. For one thing, this standard applies to all chemicals and reaches beyond the workplace to the party that manufactured or imported the chemical. Moreover, the thrust of the standard is on worker autonomy. The theory behind the Hazard Communication Standard is to provide workers with sufficient information to make their own choices regarding the hazards that they face in the occupational setting. This recognition of worker autonomy is a move away from the older concept of the paternalistic employer.

The goal of the Hazard Communication Standard (HCS), 29 C.F.R. § 1910.1200 (2010), is to provide for the evaluation of chemicals used in the workplace and to provide a comprehensive mechanism for the communication of information regarding the hazards from manufacturers to employers and, ultimately, from employers to employees. The standard applies to hazardous chemicals known to exist in the workplace "in such a manner that employees may be exposed under normal conditions of use or in a foreseeable emergency." 29 C.F.R. § 1910.1200(b)(2) (2010). It applies only to chemicals that are known to pose a health hazard or a physical hazard. 29 C.F.R. § 1910.1200(c) (2010). A "health hazard" is determined by "statistically significant evidence based on at least one study conducted in accordance with established scientific principles that acute or chronic health effects may occur in exposed employees." A "physical hazard," on the other hand, is determined by "scientifically valid evidence" that it is (among other things) combustible, explosive, or reactive.

Pursuant to the Hazard Communication Standard, determination of the existence of a hazard is placed primarily on the manufacturers and importers of the chemicals. The manufacturer or importer is required to develop a material safety data sheet (MSDS) for each hazardous chemical containing specific detailed information regarding the chemical and the hazards it presents. The MSDS travels with the chemical to the employer-purchaser's place of business. The manufacturer or importer also must properly label the substance. *See* Martin v. American Cyanamid Co., 5 F.3d 140 (6th Cir.1993).

OSHA has proposed a change in labeling requirements that would coordinate the Hazard Communication Standard's requirements with the United Nations Globally Harmonized System for Classification and Labeling of Chemicals. A public hearing on the proposal was held in March, 2010. The proposed rule would change some of the criteria currently in place in the Hazard Communication Standard, including the definitions of physical and health hazards, labeling requirements, and the presentation of information on the MSDS. *See generally* Greg Hellman, *Revised Labels Required Under Harmonized Labeling Proposal, Hearing Participants Say*, 40 Occup. Safety & Health Rptr (BNA) 198 (Mar. 11, 2010).

The HCS also sets forth duties of employers. An employer is required to develop a written hazard communication program designed to identify hazardous chemicals present in the workplace and to formulate a plan for informing employees of the hazards. This written program must be accessible to all employees. 29 C.F.R. § 1910.1200(e) (2010). The MSDS is an integral part of the hazard communication program, and employers are required to make MSDSs available and obvious to employees while at work. 29 C.F.R. § 1910.1200(g) (2010). The hazardous chemicals should be properly and clearly labeled. The standard contemplates providing information and training on the handling of hazardous substances in specific work operations. Further, the employer is expected to develop methods to determine and manage a release of the hazardous chemical as well as steps employees can take to protect themselves under such circumstances. 29 C.F.R. § 1910.1200(h) (2010).

While this explosion of information made available to the worker regarding workplace exposures is certainly salutary, one might well wonder whether the HCS's goal of worker autonomy has been effectively achieved. The threat of latent disease that may or may not manifest itself years or decades later may have little impact on a worker making an employment decision. Rather, the individual worker's personal economic situation—need for a job, need for job advancement, or overall economic needs—may trump these speculative health concerns. Furthermore, the wealth of information itself may prove overwhelming for many individuals. Assessing and comprehending one's own true risk of ill health effects is a daunting endeavor, one that professional risk analysts find difficult at best. Nevertheless, on balance, the HCS's requirements of evaluation of chemicals in the workplace and disclosure of known hazards are a necessary step toward achieving the OSHAct's goal of protecting workers' health.

5. OSHA Enforcement

OSHA is responsible for workplace inspections, but any penalties assessed against employers deemed to be in violation of applicable standards are assessed by OSHRC. Civil penalties are available on a per violation basis, with more severe penalties reserved for willful violations of the OSHAct. The Government's policy toward civil penalties has vacillated, however, depending upon the political climate. Accordingly, no single clear approach to the use of civil penalties has emerged.

Criminal penalties also are available for willful violations of the OSHAct that result in the death of an employee. For an employer's violations to be "willful," the employer must have known of a standard or provision prohibiting the conduct and "consciously disregarded" it or demonstrated reckless disregard for employee safety. J.A.M. Builders, Inc. v. Herman, 233 F.3d 1350 (11th Cir.2000). A corporate officer may be held criminally liable under the OSHAct as an "employer" for company violations where the officer's role in the company was pervasive. United States v. Cusack, 806 F.Supp. 47 (D.N.J.1992). An employee may not be prosecuted under the OSHAct for aiding and abetting an employer, however. United States v. Doig, 950 F.2d 411 (7th Cir.1991).

In appropriate circumstances, the case would be referred to the Department of Justice for evaluation and a decision whether to prosecute. These criminal cases can become very complicated and implicate multiple federal statutes. For example, in United States v. Atlantic States Cast Iron Pipe Co., 612 F.Supp.2d 453 (D.N.J. 2009), the defendant company and some of its managers were convicted for violating various provisions of the OSHAct, the Clean Water Act, and the Clean Air Act, for offenses ranging from conspiracy to pollute to obstructing an OSHA investigation.

D. STATE CRIMINAL ENFORCEMENT OF WORKPLACE SAFETY

The OSHAct has been interpreted to permit the states to enact their own criminal laws governing workplace health and safety violations. For example, in People v. Pymm, 563 N.E.2d 1 (N.Y.1990), the court held that the OSHAct did not preempt state criminal laws applying to workplace health and safety. *Pymm* involved a hidden mercury reclamation operation set up in the basement of a thermometer plant. The court noted that mercury can be highly toxic, and exposure at chronic low doses can cause permanent neurological damage. Various OSHA inspections revealed that workers at the plant were not adequately protected from the hazards posed by exposure to mercury. In addition, the employer had failed to reveal the basement operation to the inspectors. Once the basement area was located and inspected, mercury levels tested at five times the permissible level under OSHA. The employers were charged under state law with counts of conspiracy, falsifying business records, and first and second degree assault.

The *Pymm* court held that the OSHAct established a minimum standard of workplace safety and that the OSHAct penalties therefore acted as a floor above which the states could act in supplementing them with their own criminal penalties. The court relied on the savings clause contained in the OSHAct in concluding that state criminal laws governing the same conduct as that regulated by the OSHAct were valid as applied. The court stated:

> We do not accept the appellants' argument that Congress' foremost purpose in drafting the [OSH] Act was to ensure uniformity of workplace health and safety standards and that individual State prosecutions stand as an obstacle to the accomplishment of that purpose. The Act's ... provisions ... indicate to us that Congress was willing to accept a multiplicity of regulatory approaches provided that the safety and health of workers were not compromised....
>
> ... In fact, criminal prosecutions under State criminal law would seem to further the goal of ensuring the safety and health of American workers by deterring future instances of criminally culpable employer conduct.

More recently, an Arizona court similarly ruled that OSHA does not preempt state criminal prosecutions for violation of state workplace safety standards. The convictions for negligent homicide, aggravated assault, and other charges were related to the death of one worker and injuries of others who were overcome by toxic sewage gas at the defendant's sewage treatment facility where they worked. Arizona v. Far West Water & Sewer Inc., 228 P.3d 909 (Ariz. App. Ct. 2010).

Thus, state criminal law may provide a separate means of prosecuting employers for certain types of conduct in providing unsafe working conditions for their employees. For a critique of the use of the criminal justice system as a forum for addressing workplace health and safety, see Thea D. Dunmire, *The Problems With Using Common Law Criminal Statutes to Deter Exposure to Chemical Substances in the Workplace*, 17 N. Ky. L. Rev. 53 (1989).

E. EMPLOYMENT DISCRIMINATION

Employees' susceptibility to injuries related to toxic substances in the workplace could lead to impermissible employment discrimination by employers. This was the ruling of the United States Supreme Court in UAW v. Johnson Controls, Inc., 499 U.S. 187 (1991), in which employees of a battery manufacturer alleged that they had been discriminated against in matters of employment on the basis of an employee protection policy directed at the exposure of female workers to lead. There was no dispute that the employer was in compliance with the OSHA standard for lead in the workplace.

The employer's policy was concerned with protecting the developing fetuses of pregnant employees from the potentially harmful effects of chronic low-level exposure to lead in the mothers' jobs. The case contained an overt gender issue: Did the employer's enforcement of its policy preventing women of child-bearing age from working in positions that would necessitate exposure to lead, a known teratogenic substance, violate Title VII of the federal anti-discrimination laws? The Court answered with a resounding "yes." Because the fetal protection policy was discriminatory on its face, the Court applied the "bona fide occupational qualification" (BFOQ) test to determine whether the discrimination was justifiable. The BFOQ test required that to use gender or pregnancy as a basis for discrimination, the employer must be able to show that gender or pregnancy actually interferes with the employee's ability to perform the job. This test plainly was not met.

The issue that was not completely resolved by *Johnson Controls*, however, was whether in the absence of the discriminatory policy the employer would find itself subject to increased tort liability for birth defects to employees' offspring. If so, arguably the employer would experience substantial cost increases. While the Court stated that such concerns are not a defense to a Title VII discrimination claim, the Court noted that where an employer has not acted negligently—having, presumably, complied with both OSHA and Title VII and given employees appropriate warning regarding the hazards to which they and their developing fetuses may be exposed—imposition of tort liability would be unlikely. *Cf.* Widera v. Ettco Wire & Cable Corp., 611 N.Y.S.2d 569 (N.Y. App.Div.1994) (in a case not involving discrimination issues, holding appropriate the dismissal of an action brought by an infant allegedly injured by in utero exposure to workplace chemicals carried into the home on the parent's work clothes because the employer owed no duty to the infant). Nevertheless, significant questions remain concerning the possibility and projected impact of increased tort liability. Among the many messages sent by the Supreme Court in *Johnson Controls* are that employer self-protection from tort liability cannot come at the cost of impermissible discrimination and that worker autonomy is to be respected in decisions relating to health and safety in the workplace, provided that all relevant information is made available.

Other discrimination issues have emerged as a result of employee exposure to toxic substances in the workplace. Concerns have been expressed as to whether information obtained by employers through health or genetic screening and monitoring may be used in personnel decisions, with respect to both hiring and retention. Health concerns may involve the extent to which a worker may begin to manifest early signs and symptoms of latent disease related to workplace exposures. Another kind of health concern is the existence of communicable disease in the worker, an issue that has raised much interest because of the spread of HIV and the risk of exposure in some workplaces, such as health care settings and medical laboratories.

Genetic concerns may include a worker's genetic predisposition to developing certain illnesses or whether a worker has a genetically predisposed sensitivity to a particular substance in the workplace that could cause health problems. For an early overview of the complex subject of genetic screening and monitoring in the workplace, including the legal issues raised, see generally United States Congress, Office of Technology Assessment, Genetic Monitoring and Screening in the Workplace (1990). Genetic screening, which has become easily available now, is a tempting tool for employers seeking to reduce the costs—in increased insurance benefits and lost productivity—of some workers.

In addition to Title VII, Congress has enacted several anti-discrimination statutes that reach health and genetic discrimination. The Federal Rehabilitation Act, 29 U.S.C.A. §§ 701–796 (West 2010), applies to public employees, whereas the Americans With Disabilities Act (ADA), 42 U.S.C.A. §§ 12101–12213 (West 2010), applies to private employment situations. Both statutes make it illegal to discriminate against an individual otherwise qualified for the job on the basis of a disability. More recently, Congress enacted the Genetic Information Nondiscrimination Act of 2008, Pub. L. No. 110–233, 122 Stat. 881 (2008). For an analysis of this new act, see Jessica L. Roberts, *Preempting Discrimination: Lessons From the Genetic Information Nondiscrimination Act*, 63 Vand. L. Rev. 439 (2010).

CHAPTER SIX

OTHER SPECIAL DEFENDANTS

A. GOVERNMENTAL ENTITIES

1. Sovereign Immunity Generally

Sometimes injured persons will seek to bring claims against a governmental entity on the basis of the government's conduct. The conduct of which the plaintiff complains may be any kind of activity for which a private party could be liable. In the absence of a statute to the contrary, sovereign immunity generally protects governmental entities from many kinds of actions, including tort actions. Where the governmental entity has waived its sovereign immunity, the statutes generally are riddled with exceptions.

In addition to sovereign immunity other restrictions on suits against the government may also exist, either within the waiving statute or elsewhere. For example, states typically have notice of claim provisions for actions against public entities that require the filing of a written notice with the public entity within a certain period of time following accrual of the cause of action. The time period is typically rather short. *See* N.J. Stat. Ann. § 59:8–8 (West 2010) (ninety days). Furthermore, shortened statutes of limitations may apply to tort actions against governmental entities. *Compare* N.Y Civ. Prac. L. & R. 214 (McKinney 2010) (three-year limitations period for tort actions) *with* N.Y. Gen. Mun. Law § 50–i(1) (McKinney 2010) (one-year and ninety-days limitations period for tort claims against public entities). Determination of when a cause of action accrues for notice of claim purposes will be governed by the case law interpreting the statutes of limitations generally. *See* Kenney v. Scientific, Inc., 497 A.2d 1310 (N.J.Super. Law Div. 1985) (applying the state's discovery rule to accrual for determination of the timeliness of the notice of claim). *See generally* Chapter Seven, Sec. B *infra*.

The result has been that toxic tort plaintiffs who bring suit against governmental entities may encounter substantial limitations on their ability to bring suit against a public entity.

2. State Tort Claims Acts

Some examples of state rules waiving sovereign immunity—and providing substantial exceptions— are instructive. Kenney v. Scientific, Inc., 497 A.2d 1310 (N.J.Super. Law Div.1985), a case construing the New Jersey Tort Claims Act, N.J. Stat. Ann. § 59:1–1 to 1–7 (West 2010), offers an example of the myriad issues that can arise when a plaintiff sues the government on a toxic tort claim. The New Jersey act illustrates the problems courts have with the exceptions-within-exceptions approach of many tort claims acts. The *Kenney* action was brought by residents in the vicinity of two landfills—one privately owned and one owned and operated by the township—against the owners and operators of the landfills, numerous generators (including another township) of waste deposited at the landfills, the transporters of the waste, and the State of New Jersey (for licensing the landfills and failing to properly inspect, regulate, and supervise them). As with most tort claims acts, the New Jersey act retains immunity for strict liability claims; thus, the *Kenney* plaintiffs alleged claims for negligence and nuisance, as well as an assortment of other theories.

The New Jersey Tort Claims Act applies to all public entities, including the state, counties, municipalities, and public agencies. N.J. Stat. Ann. § 59:1–3 (West 2010). While stating a general rule of sovereign immunity, the Act allows a public entity to be liable "for injury proximately caused by an act or omission of a public employee within the scope of his employment" in the same manner that a private person would be liable. *See* N.J. Stat. Ann. § 59:2–2 (West 2010). The Act contains a variety of exceptions to this liability. Among the exceptions are matters that related to the plaintiffs' claims in *Kenney*. First, no public entity may be liable for licensing a landfill or licensing a hauler of waste. Nor may the public entity be liable for improper inspection, regulation, or supervision of the landfill. Thus, in *Kenney* neither the state nor the township could be liable under these theories.

The *Kenney* court was more concerned about a separate limitation that applied to actions arising from dangerous conditions of public property, which theory clearly formed the basis for the plaintiffs' allegations. Under the Act, the public entity may be held liable upon a showing (1) that the property was in a dangerous condition at the time of the plaintiff's injury, (2) that the condition was the proximate cause of the injury, and (3) that the injury was reasonably foreseeable. In addition, one of the following must be shown: (1) a negligent or wrongful act or omission by a public employee; or (2) actual or constructive notice of the dangerous condition and sufficient time to protect against the injury. Moreover, the entity's measures to protect persons against the condition, or its failure to take measures, would lead to liability only if "palpably unreasonable." N.J. Stat. Ann. § 59:4–2 (West 2010).

With respect to the state, the court dismissed the claims because the allegations did not arise from a condition of state property. But with respect to the township, the court found a question of fact on the reasonableness of the township's activities at its landfill.

Another instructive example is the ongoing and massive litigation brought by workers at the World Trade Center following the attacks of September 11, 2001, involving respiratory and other health problems the workers—many of whom were firefighters and police personnel—claimed were caused by exposure to toxic substances in the aftermath of the collapse of the towers. The plain-

tiffs brought suit against the city and the Port
Authority of New York and New Jersey, which was
the entity that operated the World Trade Center.
The state of New York has broadly waived its
sovereign immunity in the Court of Claims Act,
N.Y. Ct. Cl. Act §§ 1–12 (McKinney 2010), but
significant exceptions have developed in the case
law. Thus, for example, public entities are granted
immunity for acts conducted while providing a
"public function," such as fire and police protection, unless the public entity had a "special relationship" with the plaintiff. Accordingly, in Pelaez
v. Seide, 810 N.E.2d 393 (N.Y. 2004), the New York
Court of Appeals held that the city and a nearby
county could not be held liable for injuries to children from exposure to lead paint. The public entities had operated programs to address the lead
paint health problem. The *Pelaez* court stated that
no special relationship existed because the public
entities had no power to prevent the injuries from
occurring.

In the World Trade Center litigation, the district
court refused to dismiss the claims against the city
on these grounds because too many fact questions
existed. *See* In re World Trade Ctr. Disaster Site
Litig., 456 F.Supp.2d 520 (S.D.N.Y. 2006). Among
other things, there was a question whether the city
had entered into a special relationship with the
plaintiffs by assuming control of the disaster site
and by replacing EPA as the primary authority over
the indoor air environment.

Separate immunity statutes were also invoked in the World Trade Center litigation. The State Defense Emergency Act (SDEA) provides a grant of immunity for actions taken "in good faith carrying out, complying with or attempting to comply with any law, any rule, regulation or order duly promulgated or issued pursuant to [the SDEA]" and "relating to civil defense." N.Y. Unconsol. Law § 9193(1) (McKinney 2010). The SDEA includes the following within the definition of "civil defense": "measures to be taken following attack ... [;] ... decontamination procedures ... [and] essential debris clearance." But in general, the activities giving rise to immunity are considered actions that must be taken in immediate response to an emergency, rather than ongoing activities. In re World Trade Ctr. Disaster Site Litig., 456 F.Supp.2d 520 (S.D.N.Y. 2006).

Another statutory immunity provision invoked in the World Trade Center litigation is the Disaster Act, which provides that a "political subdivision shall not be liable for any claim based upon the exercise or performance or the failure to exercise or perform a discretionary function or duty on the part of any officer or employee in carrying out the provisions of this section." N.Y. Exec. Law § 25 (McKinney 2010). One question that has arisen in the context of this litigation is whether the Act immunizes a public entity from liability for damages resulting from violations of the state Labor Law or Industrial Code. The plaintiffs alleged such violations. In Daly v. Port Authority of New York & New Jersey, 793 N.Y.S.2d 712 (N.Y. Sup. Ct. 2005), another case based upon the circumstances at the World Trade Center, the court said that public entities do not have the discretion to violate applicable statutes.

These examples demonstrate the complexity of the issues related to state sovereign immunity. The World Trade Center issues show the difficulty courts have with applying immunity provisions developed in a completely different context to the aftermath of a massive toxic release. For a discussion of all aspects of the World Trade Center exposures, see Jean Macchiaroli Eggen, *Toxic Torts at Ground Zero*, 39 Ariz. St. L.J. 383 (2007).

3. Federal Tort Claims Act

The United States Government has waived its sovereign immunity for tort claims in limited circumstances. The Federal Tort Claims Act, 28 U.S.C.A. § 1346(b) (West 2010), provides that the federal district courts shall have exclusive jurisdiction over claims for money damages against the United States alleging personal injury, wrongful death, or property damage as a result of a negligent act or omission by a Government employee within the scope of employment. Although the case law interpreting the Federal Tort Claims Act generally has developed outside of the context of toxic torts, several significant toxic tort cases have involved interpreting the Act.

a. Discretionary Function Exception

By far the most sweeping and problematic exception to the United States' waiver of immunity for tort claims is the discretionary function exception. This exception provides that the United States may not be held liable for any claim "based upon the exercise or performance or the failure to exercise or perform a discretionary function or duty on the part of a federal agency or an employee of the Government, whether or not the discretion involved be abused." 28 U.S.C.A. § 2680(a) (West 2010). What constitutes a discretionary function is not easy to ascertain.

In Berkovitz v. United States, 486 U.S. 531 (1988), the United States Supreme Court demonstrated the depth of analysis that may be required to determine whether the conduct that was alleged was a matter of protected governmental discretion. *Berkovitz* was an action for personal injuries suffered by an infant allegedly as a result of ingesting a dose of an oral polio vaccine. The plaintiffs claimed that the Division of Biologic Standards (DBS), an agency within the National Institutes of Health, had improperly licensed the vaccine. They claimed further that the Bureau of Biologics of the Food and Drug Administration had improperly released the specific lot of vaccine from which the child's dose came.

For conduct to fall within the discretionary function exception it must involve judgment or choice on the part of the actor. Dalehite v. United States,

346 U.S. 15 (1953). Moreover, the conduct must be of the sort that the discretionary function exception was enacted to protect, so as to "prevent judicial 'second-guessing' of legislative and administrative decisions." United States v. Varig Airlines, 467 U.S. 797 (1984). While these principles may seem somewhat vague, it is clear from the *Berkovitz* decision that the discretionary function exception will *not* apply "when a federal statute, regulation, or policy specifically prescribes a course of action for an employee to follow." The Court also made clear that the discretionary function exception does not apply automatically to all agency activities.

Beyond these general guidelines, courts must conduct close and specific scrutiny of the agency conduct forming the basis of the complaint. In *Berkovitz*, the Court first examined the required duties of DBS with respect to licensing vaccines. It concluded that more specificity was needed as to the plaintiffs' claim. If the plaintiffs were claiming that the vaccine had been licensed without DBS first making its required determination as to whether the vaccine complied with regulatory standards, then the claim would not involve a discretionary function, but rather a mandatory function, and would be actionable. If, on the other hand, the plaintiffs were claiming that DBS had made the determination of compliance incorrectly, and if that determination properly consisted of policy judgments, then the discretionary function exception would shield the conduct.

With respect to the release of the vaccine lot, the Court conducted a different analysis. First, the Court stated that any claims challenging the Bureau of Biologics' right to determine the appropriate manner of release of vaccine lots would be construed to arise from a discretionary function. Ultimately, however, the *Berkovitz* plaintiffs' claims were held not to fall within the exception because the Bureau had chosen to put into place its own *mandatory* policy for lot release. Because Government employees had no discretion to deviate from the mandatory policy, the conduct could form the basis of an action against the Government. Thus, although the establishment of the policy on lot inspection was discretionary in the first instance, once the Bureau put into effect a mandatory policy that all employees were required to follow, the agency action in releasing the lot of vaccine could not be a protected discretionary function.

Berkovitz is a complex case with important lessons for attorneys. It instructs courts to undertake focused and detailed analysis of each aspect of the conduct alleged in the complaint before ruling on the applicability of the discretionary function exception. The lesson of the Bureau of Biologics' internal policy is that regulatory activity that first appears as discretionary may be transformed into nondiscretionary conduct. After *Berkovitz*, however, agencies may be discouraged from putting into place their own stringent safety policies for fear of opening the door to liability. In C.R.S. by D.B.S. v. United States, 820 F.Supp. 449 (D.Minn.1993), a serviceman alleged that he had contracted HIV as a result of a blood transfusion at a military hospital. The military had followed existing blood guidelines issued by the American Association of Blood Banks and by the FDA. The court held that the Government could not be held liable for failing to develop more stringent guidelines. This result is correct. But *Berkovitz* may inhibit agencies from taking extra safety measures when they have good reason to do so.

The Tenth Circuit applied the rule of *Berkovitz* to shield the United States in Aragon v. United States, 146 F.3d 819 (10th Cir.1998), where landowners residing in the vicinity of a former Air Force base brought negligence claims against the United States for contamination of their water wells. During the time the Air Force base had been in operation, the military washed aircraft with trichloroethylene (TCE), a toxic organic solvent, to remove radioactive debris and dust from planes that had flown over nuclear detonation sites. The court first noted that neither the relevant executive order nor the Air Force manual prescribed a specific, mandatory course of conduct regarding wastewater disposal from washdown operations at the base. The court then held that all Air Force base operational decisions, including those involving the disposal of industrial waste, were grounded in policy because of the relationship of the decisions to military exigencies at a particular point in time. Therefore, the court ruled that the discretionary function exception to the FTCA applied to immunize the United

States against the plaintiffs' claims. *See also* Andrews v. United States, 121 F.3d 1430 (11th Cir. 1997) (applying the discretionary function exception to the U.S. Navy's hiring of a contractor to remove household and industrial waste from a military base). *Aragon* demonstrates the application of *Berkovitz* to an entirely different category of cases. Although the court closely scrutinized the documents referencing the Air Force's handling of its industrial wastes, the court seemed to grant much latitude to military decision making as a discretionary activity. Similarly, in Oxendine v. United States, 2009 WL 3757517 (D.S.C. 2009) (slip op.), another case involving TCE releases from a different Air Force base, the court held that in the absence of a statute or regulation establishing mandatory rules for TCE, the military has discretion to conduct the day-to-day operations of its facility in the advancement of policy. Decisions as to how to conduct military operations were deemed to involve policy analysis.

In a case that did not directly implicate military operations, the court in Shea Homes Ltd. Partnership v. United States, 397 F.Supp.2d 1194 (N.D. Cal. 2005), held that the discretionary function exception shielded the Government from tort claims related to its efforts to abate the release of methane gas from a former Air Force landfill site. The U.S. Army Corps of Engineers had taken various steps over several years to abate the release of methane, but, the court ruled, none of those steps was mandated. Moreover, the court held that California state regulations requiring a facility's operator to take "necessary" steps to protect public health when methane gas reaches certain levels in the air did not mandate any specific action, leaving it up to the discretion of the operator.

In contrast, the Ninth Circuit reinstated a negligence suit against the United States in Whisnant v. United States, 400 F.3d 1177 (9th Cir.2005), where an employee of a private company alleged injuries from exposure to toxic mold while making weekly deliveries at a naval base. Using a *Berkovitz* distinction, the court stated that while the Government may have been immune from actions based upon its choice of safety procedures, it was not immune for negligence claims arising from implementation of its chosen procedures. The court further held that removing known health and safety hazards was a matter of safety, not policy, so violations would not be protected by the exception.

In a major decision with far-reaching implications, a federal court held in 2009 that local residents near New Orleans could maintain an action against the United States for damages in the aftermath of Hurricane Katrina. In re Katrina Canal Breaches Consol. Litig., 647 F.Supp.2d 644 (E.D. La. 2009). The action was based upon alleged wrongful conduct by the U.S. Army Corps of Engineers in maintaining and operating the Mississippi River Gulf Outlet (MRGO), a navigational channel designed to provide a shorter commercial shipping route between New Orleans and the Gulf of Mexico. A characteristic of the MRGO was its changing configuration, something the Army Corps was aware of from the very beginning. As a result, with the natural widening of the channel, significant degradation of the abutting levees and the environment occurred, which contributed to the detrimental effects of the hurricane. The court characterized the Army Corps' approach to the maintenance and operation of the MRGO as "myopic," stating that the Army Corps "simply chose to ignore the effects of the channel; it only examined the requirements to keep the channel open regardless of its effects on the environment and the surrounding communities." Thus, the court reasoned, "once the Corps exercised its discretion to create a navigational channel, it was obligated to make sure that the channel did not destroy the environment surrounding it thereby creating a hazard to life and property." This obligation included notifying Congress of the potential for catastrophic loss of life and property so that sufficient funds could be appropriated. Accordingly, the court concluded that the "on-going engineering decision to let a navigational channel's contours run amuck" was not the kind of decision that the discretionary function exception was intended to protect.

b. *Feres Doctrine and Military Service*

Another exception to the Federal Tort Claims Act that has figured prominently in toxic tort litigation is the *Feres* doctrine. The *Feres* doctrine played a significant role in the Agent Orange litigation. When Vietnam veterans and their families commenced the federal class action for personal injuries arising from exposure to the herbicide known as "Agent Orange" during the Vietnam war, they named manufacturers of the herbicide as defendants, but not the United States Government. An important reason for omitting the Government from the suit was the fact that the veterans' action fell well within a recognized exception to the Act. In Feres v. United States, 340 U.S. 135 (1950), the Supreme Court held that armed forces members cannot bring tort actions against the Government for harms that "arise out of or are in the course of activity incident to service." Policy considerations support this rule. First, a compensation mechanism for injured members of the armed forces was available through the Veterans' Administration. Second, suits against the Government, if allowed, were seen as detrimental to military discipline. Third, the relationship between the Government and the armed services personnel is uniquely federal.

An issue of law that arose in the Agent Orange litigation related to the fact that the defendants sought to implead the Government, claiming that the Government should be liable to the defendants for any damages the defendants may be ordered to pay to the plaintiffs. The court held that under the rule of Stencel Aero Engineering Corp. v. United States, 431 U.S. 666 (1977), which extended the *Feres* doctrine, the Government could not be required to indemnify defendants in an action in which the plaintiffs could not have sued the Government directly. Thus, because the members of the plaintiff class who were members of the armed forces were not allowed to sue the Government directly, *Stencel* prevented the defendants from impleading the Government with respect to those claims. This applied as well to the derivative claims of family members.

With respect to the civilian family members' claims of related miscarriages and fetal deformations, however, the court held that neither the rationale behind *Stencel* nor the policies underlying *Feres* applied, and the Government could be held liable as a third-party defendant. *See* In re "Agent Orange" Prod. Liab. Litig., 580 F.Supp. 1242 (E.D.N.Y.1984). These independent claims of family members ultimately failed on several grounds, including causation and the discretionary function exception. *See* Adams v. United States, 818 F.2d 201 (2d Cir.1987); In re "Agent Orange" Prod. Liab. Litig., 603 F.Supp. 239 (E.D.N.Y.1985). More recently, however, the federal courts have taken a restrictive approach to the issue of civilian family members. Joining the position of other federal appeals courts, the Fourth Circuit held that children who claimed severe birth defects caused by their servicemen-fathers' exposure to toxic chemicals during the Persian Gulf War were barred from suing the United States. Minns v. United States, 155 F.3d 445 (4th Cir.1998). The *Feres* doctrine applied because the claims by the children and their mothers were "based on essentially the same facts as the potential serviceman's cause of action."

B. GOVERNMENT CONTRACTORS

The Agent Orange litigation involved a further issue related to the operation of the Federal Tort

Claims Act. The herbicide products manufactured by the defendants were ordered by the Government for military use. Thus, these Government contractors argued that because they manufactured the herbicide to Government specifications, they should be protected. *See* In re "Agent Orange" Prod. Liab. Litig., 818 F.2d 187 (2d Cir.1987) (actions by plaintiffs who opted out of the Agent Orange class action).

Policy reasons favor allowing Government contractors to be immune from suits seeking compensation for injuries arising out of contracts with the Government, at least in some circumstances. Liability imposed upon Government contractors could impair the military procurement process, which has its own special concerns for military efficiency, avoidance of delay, and cost containment. Because Government contractors manufacture their products to Government specifications for uses set by the Government, the Government's control over the product would seem to work in favor of immunity for the contractor. On the other hand, courts demand some assurance that the Government was at least aware of the hazards of the product that gave rise to the plaintiffs' claims against the contractor.

The accepted elements of the Government contractor defense consist of the following:

1. That the Government established the relevant specifications;

2. That the contractor met the Government's specifications in all material respects; and

3.   That the contractor warned the Government of all relevant hazards.

See Boyle v. United Technologies Corp., 487 U.S. 500 (1988). In *Boyle*, the Supreme Court held that federal common law governs the Government contractor defense. The Court determined that the issues raised by the Government contractor defense were unique federal interests warranting creation of federal common law. The Court reasoned that because the Government is insulated from liability for its choice of the design of military products due to the discretionary function exception, allowing the contractors to share the immunity was reasonable.

In the Agent Orange litigation, the Second Circuit allowed the defendant contractors to assert the Government contractor defense, finding that they met the first two elements and that no hazards existed to be communicated to the Government. In re "Agent Orange" Prod. Liab. Litig., 818 F.2d 187 (2d Cir.1987). The information regarding the hazards of the herbicide is now dated. Reaffirming the earlier view of the defense in the context of the Agent Orange litigation, the Fifth Circuit, in Miller v. Diamond Shamrock Co., 275 F.3d 414 (5th Cir. 2001), held that the contractor need only warn the Government of hazards of which the contractor had actual knowledge at the time.

Another aspect of the *Boyle* decision held that the government contractor defense could only be used by the contractor if the Government itself was immune under the discretionary function exception to the FTCA. In a more recent action involving the acts underlying the original Agent Orange litigation, the Second Circuit held that the Government's choice to use the herbicide in the Vietnam War was discretionary because it involved a "trade-off between greater safety and greater combat effectiveness." In re "Agent Orange" Prod. Liab. Litig., 517 F.3d 76 (2d Cir. 2008). The case involved plaintiffs who would otherwise have been members of the earlier class settlement, but whose illnesses did not manifest until after the settlement fund expired.

What constitutes the approval of "reasonably precise specifications" by the Government, in the words of the Supreme Court in *Boyle*? One of the arguments raised by the plaintiffs in the 2008 Agent Orange case was that the Government had merely "rubber-stamped" the specifications set by the contractors. The court rejected this argument, saying that *Boyle* contemplated that the Government would rely on the contractors' expertise in setting the specifications for the ordered product. In In re FEMA Trailer Formaldehyde Prods. Liab. Litig., 2009 WL 3241579 (E.D.La. 2009) (slip op.), part of the mass litigation claiming personal injuries from exposure to substances in the trailers provided to residents of the Gulf Coast following Hurricanes Katrina and Rita, the court ruled that the government contractor defense was "seemingly unavailable" to one of the defendant contractors because the Government had left major decisions on installation of the trailers to the full discretion of the contractor.

C. SUCCESSORS AND PREDECESSORS

1. Successor Corporations

Because of the long latency periods following toxic exposures, it is not uncommon for culpable parties to disappear, become insolvent, or change hands. The traditional rule is that successor corporations do not assume the liabilities of their predecessors, including liabilities in tort, unless one of the following is present:

1. express or implied agreement;

2. de facto consolidation or merger of the selling corporation and the purchasing corporation;

3. the purchasing corporation is a mere corporate continuation of the selling corporation; or

4. fraud or other intent to avoid responsibility for the liabilities.

This rather narrow set of rules developed out of concern for commercial creditors and shareholders and to address various tax and contract law issues. Accordingly, these exceptions to the traditional rule of nonliability generally have been applied quite narrowly. This traditional rule is also embodied in Restatement (Third) of Torts: Products Liability § 12 (1998).

Thus, de facto merger has been interpreted to apply when the stockholders of the selling corporation and those of the purchasing corporation are identical. The "mere continuation" exception requires that the plaintiff be able to show "that there is continuity in management, shareholders, personnel, physical location, assets and general business operation between selling and purchasing corporations following the asset acquisition." Ramirez v. Amsted Industries, 431 A.2d 811 (N.J.1981). Continuation of the general business of the selling corporation, without these other factors, would not trigger the exception.

In the era of increasing product liability actions, the traditional rule has been criticized as too narrow. *See generally* Ramirez v. Amsted Industries, 431 A.2d 811 (N.J.1981). Some courts have created a separate exception to the rule of nonliability for continuation of the same product line. According to this exception, if the successor corporation continues to manufacture the same product line using the same design, personnel, and location, it may be liable for product liability claims arising out of a product that was manufactured by the predecessor. In Ray v. Alad Corp., 560 P.2d 3 (Cal.1977), the court characterized the rule as follows: "[A] party which acquires a manufacturing business and continues the output of its line of products under the circumstances here presented assumes strict tort liability for defects in units of the same product line previously manufactured and distributed by the entity from which the business was acquired." Thus, this exception will apply notwithstanding the fact that the successor did not expressly assume the liabilities of its predecessor nor did it actually manufacture the product that caused the plaintiff's injury. For courts that recognize the product line exception, the following factors must be met: (1) all remedies for plaintiffs against the original manufacturer have been destroyed as a result of the successor's acquisition of the business; (2) the successor continues to manufacture essentially the same product; (3) the successor is in a position to spread the risks; and (4) the successor benefits from the original manufacturer's goodwill associated with the product line.

The policy underlying this extension of liability was that in a product line continuation situation, the successor may be credited with the skill and experience of its predecessor and is in a superior position to the consumer to bear the costs and assess the risks. Defendants have criticized this exception for creating an impediment to business transactions because potential purchasers would be uncertain about the number of liabilities that could arise. Nevertheless, courts that have adopted the exception have observed that the unknown, potential liabilities should either be handled as part of the acquisition through price reduction or partial indemnification agreements, or be dealt with through insurance. *See* Ramirez v. Amsted Industries, 431 A.2d 811 (N.J.1981).

The *Third Restatement* rejects the product line exception, as do any number of courts. *See* Restatement (Third) of Torts: Products Liability § 12, cmt. g (1998). In Tabor v. Metal Ware Corp., 168 P.3d 814 (Utah 2007), the Utah Supreme Court rejected the product line exception and embraced the traditional rule of non-liability, allowing only the four

traditional exceptions. The court stated that it believed the traditional exceptions sufficiently protected consumers, but that if an extension is warranted,
it is the role of the legislature to do so.

2. Predecessors in Title

A different set of problems arises when a party
attempts to hold a distant predecessor strictly liable
for contamination of the property. In T & E Industries, Inc. v. Safety Light Corp., 587 A.2d 1249
(N.J.1991), the plaintiff, T & E, was the current
owner of a site contaminated by radium tailings.
Radium was processed at the site for many years by
United States Radium Corporation (USRC), which
owned the property until 1943. USRC's immediate
successor was unaware of the hazards associated
with the radium tailings and constructed a portion
of its plant over the tailings. The property was
subsequently owned by a series of parties and was
eventually purchased by T & E, an electronic component manufacturer, in 1974. In 1979, T & E was
ordered to decontaminate or abandon the site, pursuant to a 1978 federal law governing mill tailings.
The property could not be sold until cleanup occurred. T & E then sought to hold USRC liable on
the basis of strict liability for abnormally dangerous
activities.

While the traditional rule of caveat emptor usually applied in a situation such as this, the *T & E*
court was convinced that this case fell within an
exception. The exception, as set forth in the Re-

statement (Second) of Torts § 353, as well as case law, allows a seller to be liable for affirmative concealment or passive failure to disclose a condition of the property posing an unreasonable risk to persons. Here, the distant seller knew of the risk and was in a position superior to purchasers of the property to assess the scope of the risk and prevent future harms, in the court's view. The exception was not intended to prevent sellers and purchasers from entering into real property transactions, provided that the hazards are disclosed and the purchaser voluntarily assumes the risk.

The *T & E* case is representative of several lines of cases that have moved away from the traditional rule of caveat emptor. In this instance, the plaintiff-buyer was a commercial entity. This trend toward minimizing the impact of caveat emptor is indicative of an interest in assuring that a responsible entity may be held accountable, rather than innocent parties.

D. INSURERS

Insurance companies are significant participants in toxic tort litigation. As defendants seek to interpret their liability insurance agreements as expansively as possible, so as to be covered for the activities involved in the underlying lawsuit, their insurers seek to both limit coverage and shift liability to other parties and insurers related to the case. Thus, where an asbestos worker suffering from asbestos-related disease files suit against twenty manufacturers of asbestos products, each insurer of a defendant manufacturer will attempt to shift liability for the full amount of damages onto the other defendants. Moreover, where a single defendant was insured by multiple companies, seriatim, over the period of time from first exposure to manifestation of the illness, each insurer will seek to impose liability for the full amount of the damages on the others. These issues implicate both the duty to defend the lawsuit and the duty to indemnify.

Insurance issues in toxic torts typically arise as matters of interpreting the provisions of comprehensive (or commercial) general liability (CGL) policies. As a matter of established law, the duty to defend the insured is broader than the duty to indemnify, although courts may become involved in both aspects. While discussion of all the issues raised by CGL policies in the context of toxic tort litigation is far beyond the scope of this book, a brief overview of some of the issues is useful here. For a general compilation of coverage issues in toxic tort litigation, a good starting point is Medaglia & von Mehren, *Beyond Asbestos and Environmental Litigation: Coverage Disputes in the Twenty–First Century,* 33 Tort & Ins. L.J. 1023 (1998).

1. Coverage Questions

a. *Occurrence*

Coverage questions have arisen in situations in which an action has been brought against the insured for personal injury or property damage associated with the insured's use or disposal of hazardous substances. The standard CGL policy describes the trigger for coverage in terms of an "occurrence" (changed from the earlier term "accident"). Occurrence is defined to include both isolated accidental releases and continuous exposures. The occurrence must not be expected or intended. For an occurrence to be intended, the harm must have been intentional, not merely the act. Thus, the intentional disposal of hazardous waste at a facility is covered, provided that the insured did not intend that it migrate into the drinking water supply of a nearby community, thus causing the lawsuit for which coverage is sought. But coverage may be precluded where the insured was aware of the likelihood of harm that may result from its activities, as where the insured had reason to know that the drinking water supply was contaminated from the site, yet continued to dispose of wastes at the site. *See* American Mutual Liability Insurance Co. v. Neville Chemical Co., 650 F.Supp. 929 (W.D.Pa. 1987).

Product liability suits may also raise questions about what constitutes an "occurrence." In In re Silicone Implant Insurance Coverage Litig., 667 N.W.2d 405 (Minn.2003), the Minnesota Supreme Court held that an occurrence was triggered when a woman received the implant. Applying an injury-in-fact rule, the court stated that "bodily damage occurs at the time of implant."

b.   Latent Illness

As the Minnesota case demonstrates, a major coverage issue in toxic tort actions involves identifying the insurer or insurers who are required to indemnify the insured when a plaintiff recovers for personal injuries that are manifested years or decades after exposure. The typical CGL policy requires that the bodily injury have occurred within the policy period. Whether a particular insurer will be responsible depends on the trigger of coverage used. The "trigger" is some event within the period of time that the policy was in effect that forms the basis for coverage.

Time of exposure is one such trigger. The theory underlying this trigger is that in many circumstances it can be assumed that the plaintiff suffered some form of bodily harm at the time of exposure, even if the disease did not manifest observable symptoms until much later. This is the basic theory behind In re Silicone Implant Insurance Coverage Litig., 667 N.W.2d 405 (Minn. 2003). In Insurance Company of North America v. Forty–Eight Insulations, Inc., 657 F.2d 814 (6th Cir.1981), the court held that exposure to asbestos fibers during the policy period can be deemed to immediately initiate the disease process, thus causing the requisite bodily injury at the time of exposure. There seems to be some difference of interpretation as to whether the existing scientific literature must support the presumption of injury at the time of exposure—as with asbestos—or whether the exposure itself creates the presumption of sub-clinical injury. In ongoing-exposure cases, such as workplace exposures, at least some courts have identified the date of last exposure as the trigger. *See* IBM v. Liberty Mutual Insurance Co., 363 F.3d 137 (2d Cir.2004) (applying New York law).

In contrast, some courts have applied a discovery trigger. Under this rule, the bodily injury is held to occur at the time the illness manifests itself in objective symptoms. *See* Eagle–Picher Industries, Inc. v. Liberty Mutual Insurance Co., 829 F.2d 227 (1st Cir.1987) (asbestos). The discovery rule is consistent with the transformation in statutory limitations periods for personal injury actions arising from toxic exposures. *See* Chapter Seven, Sec. B, *infra*. The discovery rule may be more difficult for an insurer to take into account than the exposure rule, as the insured's activities and the risks that are being insured at the time of manifestation of the disease may not have been the same kinds of activities that gave rise to the claim. Thus, predicting potential liabilities becomes more difficult as time goes on.

In Zurich Insurance Co. v. Northbrook Excess & Surplus Insurance Co., 494 N.E.2d 634 (Ill.App.Ct. 1986), the court took a compromise position and applied a "split trigger." This test resulted in coverage by both the carrier that insured the loss at the time of exposure and the insurance carrier at the time of discovery of the illness.

The broadest interpretation of the bodily injury requirement, however, is the multiple or continuous trigger, which finds coverage by any policy in effect during the entire time from first exposure to manifestation of disease. *See* Keene Corp. v. Insurance Co. of North America, 667 F.2d 1034 (D.C.Cir. 1981). The theory behind this trigger is that in latent disease cases the bodily injury is continuous throughout the period from the initial exposure to the manifestation of illness. This trigger is beneficial to the insured because it provides the most coverage. With many insurance carriers often covering the risk, the insured may seek to be indemnified by as many as necessary (each up to the policy limits, of course) to reimburse the loss. Thus, in Associated Aviation Underwriters v. Wood, 98 P.3d 572 (Ariz.Ct.App.2004), the court, applying a continuous trigger theory, held that the insurer was required to provide coverage if at any time during the policy period the claimants were exposed to TCE in their drinking water, had TCE-related illness developing in their bodies, or manifested the symptoms of TCE-related illness. Thus, the trigger included the existence of cellular damage, which is sometimes a controversial issue in toxic tort coverage disputes.

When claims involve multiple insurers and a continuous trigger, apportionment of payments among the insurers becomes an issue. Instead of imposing joint and several liability, many states have adopted some version of the "pro rata allocation" approach. For example, the Massachusetts Supreme Judicial Court addressed this issue in Boston Gas Co. v. Century Indemnity Co., 910 N.E.2d 290 (Mass.

2009), in the context of an action alleging environmental contamination beginning early in the Twentieth Century and running until its discovery in 1995. The court held that the fairest way to handle the multiple insurer issue here was to hold each insurer liable only for a pro rata share of the cost of cleaning up the site. The court said that unless it were possible to accurately assess the losses during a particular insurer's policy coverage, the pro rata share should be determined by employing a "time-on-the-risk" method for each insurer. *Cf.* Viking Pump Inc. v. Century Indemnity Co., 2009 WL 3297559 (Del. Ch. 2009) (holding that certain provisions in many CGL policies allow the insured to obtain "all sums" coverage from an insurer of its choice, even where state law would otherwise impose a pro rata allocation).

c. *Property Damage*

The CGL policy also typically covers property damage liability, defined as injury to or destruction of tangible property during the policy period. Sometimes defining property damage is not so easy. This was the case with the surge of litigation involving abatement of asbestos in buildings. In claims brought by building owners for recovery of the costs of inspecting the buildings and remediating the conditions of deteriorating asbestos, insurers have argued that no physical injury or destruction of property occurred and that therefore the loss is not covered. Thus, in Great Northern Insurance Company v. Benjamin Franklin Federal Savings & Loan

Assn, 793 F.Supp. 259 (D.Or.1990), the court held that the costs of asbestos remediation were not covered under a policy covering "direct physical loss." In contrast, in United States Fidelity & Guaranty Co. v. Wilkin Insulation Co., 578 N.E.2d 926 (Ill.1991), the court held that the presence of asbestos in the building constituted property damage within the meaning of the insurance policies. The insurers argued that any harm was mere intangible economic harm as evidenced by diminished property values. The court rejected this argument, stating that because the ill health effects of asbestos are known, and because building owners are required by law to remove the asbestos due to its potential toxic effects, its presence constitutes true property damage. *Cf.* Pirie v. Federal Insurance Co., 696 N.E.2d 553 (Mass.App.Ct.1998) (holding that the costs of removal of lead paint, pursuant to a state agency's order, do not constitute "physical loss" covered by the policy, but rather constitute an "internal defect" that "does not rise to the level of a physical loss").

The trigger of coverage in a property damage case may differ from the trigger in a personal injury case. Courts tend to look at this issue on a case-by-case basis. The result may depend on the continuing nature of the damage. *See generally* M. Stuart Madden & Gerald W. Boston, Law of Environmental and Toxic Torts 865–903 (3d ed. 2005) (discussing various issues of coverage within the context of environmental and toxic torts).

2. Payments for Multiple Occurrences

Many toxic tort actions claim injury occurring over a period of time. This is true whether the action arises from a workplace exposure, such as asbestos, a consumer product, such as a prescription drug, or contamination of water or land. A New York appellate court was called upon to address this issue in Hiraldo v. Allstate Insurance Co., 778 N.Y.S.2d 50 (App.Div.2004). The court held that continuous exposure to lead paint was a single occurrence and limited coverage to one annual policy limit. The policy in question was explicit enough to unambiguously govern. But this could be a slippery problem where the policy language is vaguer.

Another problem related to multiple occurrences involves multiple claimants for injuries arising from the same course of conduct. Where a policy contains a monetary limit for each occurrence, this issue could become significant. This was the case in American Red Cross v. Travelers Indem. Co., 816 F.Supp. 755 (D.D.C.1993), in which the insured was seeking to be indemnified for claims made against it by covered persons who claimed to have received HIV-contaminated blood products. The insurer argued that all the claims constituted a single occurrence within the contemplation of the policy and were subject to the single occurrence cap. The court held, however, that the claims were separate because separate acts or omissions occurred and the injuries were due to separate causes. Thus, the insured was entitled to multiple payments, rather than one payment, with the cap applying separately to each one. As this case demonstrates, the court will look beyond the absolute number of claims for which the insured seeks to be indemnified and determine whether the overall circumstances and causation constitute a single occurrence or multiple occurrences.

3. Pollution Exclusion Clauses

Pollution exclusion clauses have appeared in CGL policies for several decades. The exclusion has been applied to both land-related liabilities and product-based liabilities. As a historical matter, the wording of the exclusion has changed over time, apparently to clarify the intent of the clause as a result of substantial litigation throughout the 1970s. Initially, the pollution exclusion clauses exempted releases into land, air, or water of categories of toxic substances, but the exclusion did not apply to "sudden and accidental" releases. These older policy provisions are important for toxic tort litigation because often courts are called upon to construe the provisions of a policy that was in effect at a much earlier date.

What constituted a "sudden and accidental" release occupied much of the case law, and revision of the CGL policy in the mid-1980s predictably gave rise to new language for the pollution exclusion clause. The clause excluded bodily injury or property damage "arising out of the actual, alleged or threatened discharge, dispersal, release or escape of pollutants." The new pollution exclusion deleted the "sudden and accidental" exception that had appeared in the older exclusion clause and removed the phrase that required the discharge to be "into the land, the atmosphere or any watercourse or body of water." The exclusion by its terms also applies to governmental cleanup liabilities.

Predictably, much litigation has ensued over the policy language, and courts differ broadly in their interpretations of the pollution exclusion clause in cases that do not fit the traditional model of environmental pollution. Indoor releases are one example. In NGM Insurance Co. v. Carolina's Power Wash & Painting, LLC, 2010 WL 146482 (D.S.C. 2010), the court, applying South Carolina law, held that the absolute pollution exclusion clause did not apply to an action in which the insured was alleged to have exposed persons to paint fumes while the insured was painting the interior of a building. *See also* Belt Painting Corp. v. TIG Insurance Co., 795 N.E.2d 15 (N.Y. 2003) (paint and solvent fumes). In contrast, in Reed v. Auto–Owners Insurance Co., 667 S.E.2d 90 (Ga. 2008), the Georgia Supreme Court held that the release of carbon monoxide from a faulty heater inside a home fell within the pollution exclusion clause and excluded coverage.

Lead paint is another example of litigation that does not fall within traditional notions of pollution. A majority of jurisdictions addressing the lead paint issue in this context has held that a reasonable interpretation of the pollution exclusion clause would lead to the conclusion that it should not exclude such claims. In Sphere Drake Insurance Co. v. Y.L. Realty Co., 990 F.Supp. 240 (S.D.N.Y.1997), the court stated that the ordinary policyholder would understand the exclusion as applying to industrial and environmental pollution, but not to lead paint flaking over time inside a residence. Where courts have determined that the language of the pollution exclusion clause is ambiguous, they have construed the clause strictly against the insurer, pursuant to long-standing rules of construction. *See, e.g.,* Insurance Co. of Illinois v. Stringfield, 685 N.E.2d 980 (Ill.App.1997); Sullins v. Allstate Insurance Co., 667 A.2d 617 (Md.1995); Atlantic Mutual Insurance Co. v. McFadden, 595 N.E.2d 762 (Mass. 1992). The court in Byrd v. Blumenreich, 722 A.2d 598 (N.J.Super.Ct.1999) stated that the language of the typical pollution exclusion clause was "not ordinarily understood to apply to the imperceptible chipping or flaking of lead paint which is attributable, not to an active or physical event, but rather to an involuntary effect occurring over a considerable period of years." *Accord* Herald Square Loft Corp. v. Merrimack Mutual Fire Insurance Co., 344 F.Supp.2d 915 (S.D.N.Y.2004).

Insurers often include separate, specific exclusions relating to mold and lead in the CGL policies. These clauses have generated their own problems of interpretation, and some of the distinctions seem forced. *Compare* Alea London Ltd. v. Rudley, 2004 WL 1563002 (E.D.Pa.2004) (holding that property damage caused directly by mold caused by a leaking washing machine was excluded by the mold exclusion in policy) *with* Home Insurance Co. v. McClain, 2000 WL 144115 (Tex.Ct.App.2000) (holding that mold damage caused by a roof leak was not precluded by the mold exclusion). Mold claims have also been problematic when, in the absence of a mold exclusion, an insurer has raised the pollution exclusion as a defense. Because mold occurs naturally in the environment, some courts have held that the pollution exclusion does not apply. Thus, in Keggi v. Northbrook Property & Casualty Insurance Co., 13 P.3d 785 (Ariz.Ct.App.2000), the court held that mold did not fit the plain-language definition of a pollutant.

These brief examples demonstrate that new issues uncontemplated by the drafters of the CGL policies will continue to arise, thus requiring careful interpretation of the policy language. In addition, although the language of the pollution exclusion clause has changed, courts may be called upon to interpret both the old and new versions in the context of toxic tort actions. When the plaintiff alleges latent illness from an exposure that occurred years earlier, multiple insurers and policies could be implicated, depending upon the trigger of coverage used. Accordingly, the opportunity for numerous complex issues of coverage often presents itself in toxic tort litigation.

E.   INDETERMINATE DEFENDANTS

One of the unique characteristics of toxic torts is the frequency with which plaintiffs are unable to identify the precise defendant or defendants that caused their injuries. The realities of toxic causation account for this difficulty. The problem of indeterminacy may arise from a variety of directions. For example, an asbestos plaintiff may have been exposed to numerous asbestos-containing products during the course of employment, but may not be able to identify the precise manufacturers of the products after a lapse of many years. Or, persons claiming injury from groundwater contamination from a local waste disposal site may be unable to determine which specific substance deposited at the site caused their injuries. Moreover, dozens or even hundreds of waste generators may have deposited similar hazardous substances at the site, making precise identification impossible.

The problem of indeterminate defendants has arisen most frequently in the DES cases, however. Diethylstilbestrol (DES) was a prescription medication given to many women from 1947 until 1971 to prevent miscarriages and for a variety of other conditions. DES has been associated with the development of adenocarcinoma of the vagina and other ailments in offspring who had been exposed to the DES in utero while their mothers were ingesting the drug. The manifestation of the physical problems in the offspring generally have occurred during adolescence and into early adulthood.

The DES indeterminacy issue resulted from the unique circumstances surrounding the marketing of the drug during the decades when it was in production. First, DES essentially was produced in "generic" form, with no distinctions made between the products of separate drug companies. The design and formula of the drug were identical among manufacturers. Second, approximately 300 companies participated in the manufacture or marketing of DES during the period. The market has been characterized as a "fluid" one in which companies passed in and out of the market on an irregular basis, making it difficult for a plaintiff to pinpoint the probable group of manufacturers who may have produced the drug ingested by his or her mother. Finally, because of the lapse in time between exposure and manifestation—in conjunction with the protracted time period during which the drug was developed and eventually marketed—many crucial records on the production of DES have been lost by the companies, making it difficult to determine the type of DES manufactured by them. The plaintiffs' own records often have been incomplete as well. *See generally* Collins v. Eli Lilly Co., 342 N.W.2d 37 (Wis.1984) (describing the background circumstances relevant to the marketing and FDA approval of DES).

Plaintiffs in DES cases have argued for the application of a variety of legal doctrines to overcome the problems created by the indeterminate defendant problem. In general, however, courts have been reluctant to apply either traditional or innovative theories of collective liability to relieve the DES plaintiff's burden in this situation. *See generally* Burnside v. Abbott Laboratories, 505 A.2d 973 (Pa.Super.1985) (stating the standard rule that where the plaintiff is unable to identify the defendant or defendants responsible for the injury, the action must be dismissed). Thus, most jurisdictions have rejected indeterminate claims for failure to identify the defendant.

1. Alternative Liability

Some DES plaintiffs have argued for the application of the rule of alternative liability established by Summers v. Tice, 199 P.2d 1 (Cal.1948). *Summers* involved a hunting accident in which two hunters discharged their firearms simultaneously, injuring the plaintiff. The plaintiff was unable to identify which hunter's bullet caused the injury and named both as defendants in the lawsuit. The court allowed the action to proceed, announcing the following rule adopting Section 433B(3) of the Restatement (Second) of Torts:

> Where the conduct of two or more actors is tortious, and it is proved that harm has been caused to the plaintiff by only one of them, but there is uncertainty as to which one of them has caused it, the burden is upon each such actor to prove that he has not caused the harm.

Thus, it is incumbent upon a defendant to exculpate itself by showing that its activities could not have caused the injury to the plaintiff. The rule of alternative liability is supported by the fact that the defendants, even though acting independently, are in a superior position to sort out the facts and circumstances of the incident alleged and identify the specific cause.

In general, courts have rejected application of alternative liability to DES cases. *See* Collins v. Eli Lilly Co., 342 N.W.2d 37 (Wis.1984). A primary reason for rejection of this theory in the context of DES is the fact that the DES manufacturers were not necessarily in any better position than the plaintiffs to identify the specific manufacturer or manufacturers whose DES caused the injury alleged. A second reason points to the assumption underlying the alternative liability theory that all negligent parties will be brought before the court. This is not the case in DES litigation, reducing the likelihood that the responsible party will be held liable to the plaintiff.

Nevertheless, at least one court has applied the alternative liability theory in DES litigation. In Abel v. Eli Lilly & Co., 343 N.W.2d 164 (Mich.1984), the court required that the plaintiffs bring all potential tortfeasors before the court. Once this was done, the plaintiffs were required to prove: (1) that all defendants manufactured or distributed the DES involved; (2) that the plaintiffs' mothers ingested DES; (3) that the DES ingested was marketed in Michigan; and (4) that the drug ingested caused the type of injury suffered by the plaintiffs. A defendant could then exculpate itself by showing that it could not have manufactured or distributed the DES ingested by the plaintiffs' mothers.

2. Concerted Action and Civil Conspiracy

DES plaintiffs have attempted unsuccessfully to apply the theory of concerted action in indeterminate defendant cases. Concerted action requires a common plan or design among the defendants, and DES plaintiffs have argued that the collaboration among the various manufacturers of DES to obtain FDA approval for the drug and to subsequently market the drug constituted the requisite common design. *See* Restatement (Second) of Torts § 876 (1979). Plaintiffs have alleged that there was a tacit understanding among DES manufacturers to improperly test the drug or warn of its hazards. Courts generally have held that plaintiffs have not adequately proved this alleged tacit understanding. Although the manufacturers acted in a parallel fashion, their actions did not rise to the level of concerted action. *See generally* Tigue v. E.R. Squibb & Sons, Inc., 518 N.Y.S.2d 891 (N.Y.1987).

Likewise, a theory of civil conspiracy has been rejected by most courts addressing the indeterminate defendant dilemma in DES actions. The civil conspiracy theory requires the plaintiff to prove that the defendants "combined" to market DES for use in pregnancy knowing that the drug was unsafe. As with concerted action, the parallel behavior of DES manufacturers cannot support the allegation that the defendants conspired. *See* Collins v. Eli Lilly Co., 342 N.W.2d 37 (Wis.1984).

3. Enterprise Liability

The concept of enterprise liability, also known as industry-wide liability, was enunciated in Hall v. E.I. duPont de Nemours & Co., 345 F.Supp. 353 (E.D.N.Y.1972). *Hall* involved plaintiffs who were injured by blasting caps manufactured by defendants pursuant to safety standards developed by the industry. The court held that because the defendants jointly controlled the risk posed by the blasting caps, liability could be imposed on the basis of the industry's culpable conduct. Thus, each defendant contributing to the development of the industry safety standard could be held liable. In DES cases, however, the industry-wide control over the safety standard was not present. Rather, the FDA was responsible for setting the standard; the manufacturers' participation in the FDA approval process was not tantamount to industry control over safety standards. *See* Collins v. Eli Lilly Co., 342 N.W.2d 37 (Wis.1984). *But see* Naomi Scheiner, Note, *DES and A Proposed Theory of Enterprise Liability*, 46 Fordham L. Rev. 963 (1978) (proposing that enterprise liability is the best solution to the causation problems in DES cases).

4. Market Share Liability

As a result of the inadequacy of existing collective liability theories to satisfactorily address concerns raised in the DES cases, some courts have turned to a theory of market share liability. The landmark case of market share liability was Sindell v. Abbott Laboratories, 607 P.2d 924 (Cal.1980). This theory apportions liability among defendants according to the relative participation of each defendant in the marketing of DES. The first requirement of *Sindell* was that the plaintiff join in the lawsuit defendants representing a "substantial share" of the market in the geographical area relevant to the action. If the plaintiff proves a prima facie case, with the exception of identification of the specific defendant causing the injury, the burden then shifts to the defendants. A defendant can only exculpate itself from liability by demonstrating that it could not have manufactured or distributed the DES alleged to have caused the plaintiff's injuries. Those defendants remaining in the lawsuit would be liable for a percentage of the damages that approximates their respective shares of the DES market. The liable defendants will be held severally liable only, and defendants may not be held strictly liable. Brown v. Superior Court, 751 P.2d 470 (Cal.1988). The rationale behind this approach is that the market share is a reflection of the likelihood that a particular defendant caused the injuries alleged.

While some version of *Sindell* market share liability has been adopted in a few states, it has not found general acceptance in DES actions, primarily due to the numerous problems associated with the approach. First, defining the relevant market and determining the respective market shares has proven problematic, particularly in the context of DES where records of the manufacturers' participation in the market may be scant. Second, some critics cite the inequity of the fact that under a market share theory, a non-negligent major participant in the market could end up bearing a substantial share of the liability. In contrast, a small-share, negligent defendant could escape significant liability. Finally, some have expressed concern that the widespread adoption of market share liability would deter the development of new products because manufacturers participating in the market would be required to pay some share of the judgment regardless of their innocence or degree of culpability. *See generally* Sutowski v. Eli Lilly & Co., 696 N.E.2d 187 (Ohio 1998) (stating on a certified question from federal district court that Ohio does not recognize market share liability in the context of DES litigation).

As a result of such concerns, courts that have adopted market share liability have usually attempted to improve upon it by developing some variation of the approach. Thus, in Collins v. Eli Lilly Co., 342 N.W.2d 37 (Wis.1984), the court applied a risk contribution theory of liability. The *Collins* court devised an approach by which the plaintiff need only name as a defendant one member of the class of defendants who could have caused the injury, rather than a broader share of the market. As with *Sindell*, the defendant or defendants named could exculpate themselves by showing that the DES they manufactured could not have caused the plaintiff's injury. The major departure from *Sindell* came with determining the shares of liability. The *Collins* court employed market share as only one factor in a multi-factored consideration focusing on the degree to which the defendant created or participated in the risk that ultimately caused the plaintiff's injury. The factors were: (1) the degree to which the defendant took a role in gaining FDA approval of DES; (2) the defendant's market share; (3) whether the defendant took a leadership role or acted passively; (4) whether the defendant issued warnings on the hazards of DES; (5) whether the defendant continued to produce DES after learning of the hazards; and (6) whether the defendant took any steps to reduce the risk of harm. Thus, the test proposed by the court focused on the level of control that the defendant had over the risk as well as steps that the defendant may have taken to mitigate the hazard.

The New York Court of Appeals took a different approach in adopting market share liability. In Hymowitz v. Eli Lilly & Co., 539 N.E.2d 1069 (N.Y. 1989), the court allowed the plaintiff to name defendants representing a substantial share of the *national* DES market. Liability was based upon the particular defendant's share of the market. In a significant departure from *Sindell*, the defendants would not be allowed to exculpate themselves unless they did not market DES for use during pregnancy. This variation from *Sindell* is significant because a defendant who marketed DES for use during pregnancy but whose product could not have been ingested by the plaintiff's mother because it was not marketed in the relevant geographical area could still be held liable.

5.   Market Share Beyond DES Cases

Market share liability, where adopted, generally has been limited to DES cases because of the unique set of circumstances presented. *See* Hymowitz v. Eli Lilly & Co., 539 N.E.2d 1069 (N.Y.1989) (expressly limiting market share liability in New

York to DES cases). Courts considering other kinds of toxic tort claims have been split on the merits of adopting market share liability. But in general, courts have approached the market share theory circumspectly.

In a major case, Shackil v. Lederle Laboratories, 561 A.2d 511 (N.J.1989), the New Jersey Supreme Court refused to apply market share liability in suits alleging defective DPT vaccines. The court contrasted the DES cases, noting that the generic production of the product that characterized the marketing of DES was not present with respect to DPT vaccine. This was particularly true with respect to the plaintiff's allegation that the particular batch of vaccine from which the plaintiff's dose came was defective. Moreover, the court stated that "the imposition of a theory of collective liability in this case would frustrate overarching public policy and public-health considerations by threatening the continued availability of needed drugs and impairing the prospects of the development of safer vaccines." *But cf.* Morris v. Parke, Davis & Co., 667 F.Supp. 1332 (C.D.Cal.1987) (applying market share liability in a DPT case where manufacturing defects were alleged to be characteristic of an entire industry).

Likewise, most courts that have addressed the issue have rejected market share in asbestos personal injury cases. For example, Celotex Corp. v. Copeland, 471 So.2d 533 (Fla.1985) presented the not uncommon situation in which a worker was able to identify some, but not all, of the manufacturers of the asbestos-containing products to which he had been exposed. Rejecting market share liability, the court found that the types, amounts, and relative toxicity of the asbestos in different products vary, thus distinguishing the products from the generic DES. Due to the magnitude of asbestos litigation, it may well be that any application of a collective liability theory would best be left to the legislature.

In case after case involving exposure to toxic substances, courts have rejected a market share theory where plaintiffs have been unable to identify the specific defendant whose substance caused the injury. In Matter of New York State Silicone Breast Implant Litigation, 631 N.Y.S.2d 491 (N.Y.Sup.Ct. 1995), a trial court refused to allow a market share theory because, unlike DES, breast implants are not fungible and manufacturers can be identified. Bly v. Tri–Continental Industries, Inc., 663 A.2d 1232 (D.C.App.Ct.1995) involved exposure to gasoline fumes containing benzene over a period of twenty to thirty years. The court rejected a market share liability theory because no proof existed to show that the allegedly harmful products were made using the same formula and "an approximation of liability according to market share . . . could not be achieved." Additionally the plaintiffs had not demonstrated their inability to trace the products to a specific producer. Likewise, in Sanderson v. International Flavors & Fragrances, Inc., 950 F.Supp. 981 (C.D.Cal.1996), the court disallowed a market share theory in a matter involving injuries alleged to have been caused by aldehydes in perfume products. The court found it significant that the plaintiff did not allege that the various (seven) products were identical, that the experts acknowledged that different aldehydes had different health effects, and that the plaintiff did not "target a single product made by many manufacturers."

There are a few cases beyond DES in which some courts have ventured to apply a market share theory. These cases are not without controversy, however. A California appellate court has applied the market share liability theory in an asbestos case arising out of a plaintiff's exposure to asbestos fibers in brake pads. In Wheeler v. Raybestos–Manhattan, 11 Cal.Rptr.2d 109 (Cal.Ct.App.1992), the court held that market share liability may be applied where the products of the manufacturers were not fungible. In *Wheeler*, the asbestos-containing brake pads of the manufacturers were not "absolutely interchangeable." The court stated, however, that for the purpose of applying *Sindell*, it was sufficient that the brake pads contained "roughly comparable quantities of the single asbestos fiber, chrysotile." *But see* Goldman v. Johns–Manville Sales Corp., 514 N.E.2d 691 (Ohio 1987) (holding that the market share liability theory was not appropriate because the products were not interchangeable due to varying asbestos contents in the products of the various manufacturers).

Some acceptance of the market share theory has appeared in cases alleging HIV-contaminated blood products. In Ray v. Cutter Laboratories, 754 F.Supp. 193 (M.D.Fla.1991), the court held that market share liability applied to negligence claims brought by hemophiliacs who contracted the virus from a blood clotting product derived from the plasma of thousands of blood donors. The plaintiffs had been unable to identify which batch or batches of the blood product caused their diseases. The latency period between exposure to the blood and discovery of the illness aggravated the situation. Thus, the court held that market share liability was appropriate. In Smith v. Cutter Biological, Inc., 823 P.2d 717 (Haw.1991), another case involving a blood clotting product, the court not only adopted market share liability, but applied the national market approach of *Hymowitz*. The court noted that the clotting product was not generic in the sense of DES; that is, the clotting product was only as safe as the blood of the individual donors that comprised a particular batch. Accordingly, the blood clotting product "is only harmful if the donor was infected; DES is inherently harmful." Nevertheless, the court found that fairness dictated application of market share liability.

In contrast, the court in Doe v. Cutter Biological, Inc., 852 F.Supp. 909 (D.Idaho 1994), refused to apply a market share concept in a clotting-factor case. The court distinguished the clotting factor from DES on the ground that the clotting factor product is not a fungible product. Moreover, the court determined that the clotting factor product could have been traced to the specific producer if the plaintiff had kept records. Thus, the court held that a market share theory was inappropriate in this type of case.

In the clotting factor cases, it is clear that the plaintiffs were in no position to sort out the complex donation and manufacturing scheme that characterized the production of the clotting factor products. Thus, the defendants were in a better position to determine the circumstances under which the product became contaminated and to control the situation in the first instance. This may help to account for some courts' willingness to allow market share liability in these cases.

Another category of litigation in which market share liability has been seriously considered is lead paint litigation. Judicial resistance toward applying a market share theory in the context of lead paint litigation is typified by Skipworth v. Lead Industries Association, Inc., 690 A.2d 169 (Pa.1997). This case involved exposure to lead paint in a residential home that had been built circa 1870. The Pennsylvania Supreme Court distinguished lead paint products from DES because each paint of each manufacturer had a different chemical formulation, and the relevant time period stretched as long as one hundred years. The court examined evidence regarding the potentially different toxicity of paints containing different chemical formulas, resulting in different levels of bioavailability of the lead. The court concluded that these differences in bioavailability would render impossible the task of approximating a particular defendant's responsibility for injuries associated with its paint. Because the market share theory is based on the premise that each manufacturer's ultimate liability would approximate its responsibility for the injuries caused by its own product, these unique circumstances would make the market share theory inappropriate in lead paint litigation. Notably, Pennsylvania has not adopted a market share theory for DES cases, so its restrictive approach in the context of lead paint is not surprising.

In contrast, Wisconsin extended the risk-contribution theory of collective liability—which it had adopted for DES in Collins v. Eli Lilly Co., 342 N.W.2d 37 (Wis.1984)—to lead paint litigation. In Thomas v. Mallett, 701 N.W.2d 523 (Wis. 2005), the Wisconsin Supreme Court said that although the chemical formulas of the manufacturers' paints were not identical, they were "functionally interchangeable," and they all contained lead.

One court has suggested that lead paint plaintiffs may be able to make an argument for some version of collective liability on a public nuisance theory, rather than a product liability theory. *See* Rhode Island v. Lead Indus. Association, 2005 WL 1331196 (R.I. Super. 2005). The court stated that the state need only prove that each defendant's conduct was a proximate cause of the public nuisance alleged so as to allow recovery for the "collective presence" of lead pigment in buildings throughout the state. The fate of this theory was decided when the Rhode Island Supreme Court rejected public nuisance as a viable theory in State v. Lead Indus. Association, 951 A.2d 428 (R.I. 2008), stating that the interference was not a "public" one just because many people in the community claimed harm. But the lower court expressed an interesting notion of collective liability within public nuisance; it requires the right case for further exploration.

The cases suggest that if a court perceives the circumstances to be right, market share may well apply beyond DES. But for the most part, courts have been reluctant to shake the traditional tort tree to fashion remedies for the indeterminate defendant problem.

6. "Commingled Product" Market Share Liability

In In re Methyl Tertiary Butyl Ether (MTBE) Prods. Liab. Litig., 379 F.Supp.2d 348 (S.D.N.Y. 2005), the court held that some of the plaintiffs could rely on a "commingled product theory" of liability. Plaintiffs from many states sought relief from groundwater contamination, or the threat of contamination, by MTBE, a gasoline additive. The defendants sought dismissal of the actions on the ground that the plaintiffs could not identify which defendant's product caused their particular harm. The court analyzed the approaches to collective liability in the states involved and ruled that various forms of collective liability would apply, to the extent that those approaches were recognized in the individual states.

The court expressed the opinion that MTBE presented circumstances similar to DES, which had given rise to the market share liability theory.

Thus, the court observed that gasoline containing MTBE "is an indiscrete liquid commodity that mixes with other products during transport, and might not vary in appearance from batch to batch," similar to DES. Moreover, the plaintiffs alleged that "when it is released into the environment, it lacks even a chemical signature that would enable identification." Finally, the plaintiffs alleged that even the smallest amount of MTBE could cause the harm alleged, so that the concentration of MTBE in a particular defendant's gasoline was irrelevant.

For some of the plaintiffs, the court determined that the relevant states would accept a "commingled product" theory, which the court articulated as follows:

> When a plaintiff can prove that certain gaseous or liquid products (e.g., gasoline, liquid propane, alcohol) of many suppliers were present in a completely commingled or blended state at the time and place that the risk of harm occurred, and the commingled product caused a single indivisible injury, then each of the products should be deemed to have caused the harm . . . . Under this theory, each refiner actually caused the injury. Thus, if a defendant's indistinct product was present in the area of contamination and was commingled with the products of other suppliers, all of the suppliers can be held liable for any harm arising from an incident of contamination.

Id. at 377–78. The plaintiffs would only have to name those defendants that in "good faith" they believe may have caused their injury. A defendant could exculpate itself by showing that its product was absent from the location at the relevant time. Liability would be several-only, according to each defendant's share of the market at the time the risk was created.

CHAPTER SEVEN

DEFENSES

The earlier chapters have addressed defenses only insofar as they relate directly to substantively negating a specific cause of action that the plaintiff has alleged (e.g. state-of-the-art defense in failure-to-warn product liability claims) or to limit claims against a particular category of defendant (e.g. sovereign immunity and public entities). This chapter discusses other defenses that may be asserted to bar a claim.

A. PREEMPTION

The interface between private law and public law is one of the fundamental characteristics of toxic torts. Much of the conduct alleged in private toxic tort actions is regulated to some degree by public law mechanisms, embodied in statutes or regulations. To a great extent, private rights of action exist independently from the regulatory schemes. But occasionally, and increasingly, there is overlap between duties defined by public law, particularly federal statutes, and those defined by state common law. When this overlap is contradictory or creates sufficiently ambiguous obligations, the defendant may be able to assert a defense that the public law obligation preempts the operation of the common law.

When the preemption defense is asserted, the court is called upon to determine whether Congress intended to allow the common law to operate in the same area of the law, or whether incompatible common law standards are precluded. Where the statute in question contains a preemption provision that addresses this issue, the determination may be easy if the provision is clear. Where the statute is ambiguous or silent, however, the court must construe the statutory language or infer the legislative intent, a task that is much more difficult.

Courts have taken two basic approaches to preemption—express preemption and implied preemption. As a general rule, there is a presumption against preemption. Express preemption derives from language contained directly in the statute that evidences the intent of Congress to preempt state law. Sometimes statutes will contain saving clauses that expressly retain all rights under the common law, and the court's task may be relatively simple. *See, e.g.,* CERCLA § 310(h) (providing that CERCLA "does not affect or otherwise impair the rights of any person under Federal, State, or common law" except under limited circumstances). Where the express language of the statute indicates an intent to preempt state law, the language may be ambiguous or unclear as to the scope of preemption. Where the statute is silent, the court must determine whether (1) the legislature intended to "occupy the field" with legislation that was so sweeping that no room was left for the state law or (2) the state law actually conflicts with the federal statutory scheme. A court may find an "actual conflict" where it is impossible to comply with both the state law and the federal statutory requirements or where the state law acts as an obstacle to the fulfillment of the statutory objectives. The exact parameters of express preemption and implied preemption are not clear, particularly in the context of product liability actions. For an overview of the cases and standards, see Jean Macchiaroli Eggen, *The Mature Product Preemption Doctrine: The Unitary Standard and the Paradox of Consumer Protection*, 60 Case W. Res. L. Rev. 95 (2009).

1. Federal Environmental Cases

Several important cases have addressed the existence of private rights of action in areas that overlapped with statutory provisions of the federal environmental laws. The United States Supreme Court has read the federal environmental statutes expansively to preempt such claims. Thus, in Milwaukee v. Illinois, 451 U.S. 304 (1981), the Court held that the plaintiff-respondent, the State of Illinois, had no claim under the federal common law against the City of Milwaukee and other public entities for endangering the health of its citizens through improper treatment and disposal of sewage into Lake Michigan. Rather, the Federal Water Pollution Control Act (Clean Water Act) provisions covering discharge permits preempted the pre-existing federal common law providing a cause of action for abatement of the nuisance. The Court held that Congress, in enacting the Clean Water Act, 33 U.S.C.A. §§ 1251–1387 (West 2010), occupied the field with a comprehensive program of water pollution regulation. *See also* Middlesex County Sewerage Authority v. National Sea Clammers Association, 453 U.S. 1 (1981) (preemption of the federal common law of nuisance by the comprehensive provisions of Clean Water Act and Marine Protection, Research, and Sanctuaries Act of 1972). The *Milwaukee* Court left open the issue of whether actions under state law survived. In International Paper Co. v. Ouellette, 479 U.S. 481 (1987), the Court held that a state-law claim involving interstate water pollution was expressly preserved by the Clean Water Act's savings clauses.

2. Product Liability: Express Preemption

The United States Supreme Court has been very active in the area of product preemption, with many cases arising from toxic or related tort actions. The seminal case in matters related to express preemption and toxic torts is Cipollone v. Liggett Group, Inc., 505 U.S. 504 (1992). Although the *Cipollone* case dealt directly and narrowly with the impact of various cigarette labeling acts on state tort law, the decision has proved to be far-reaching in its doctrinal scope. Indeed, *Cipollone*'s significance not only touches all aspects of tobacco litigation—from smoker suits to environmental tobacco smoke suits to challenges to cigarette advertising—but also influences tort litigation involving products other than tobacco.

a. *Cipollone and the Cigarette Labeling Acts*

The *Cipollone* case involved a decedent whose representatives claimed that she developed lung cancer as a result of smoking cigarettes manufactured by the defendant-respondent company. She began smoking in 1942 and smoked until her death in 1984. The action stated claims based upon strict product liability, negligence, express warranty, and fraudulent misrepresentation, all under state law. The respondents raised the preemption defense, arguing that the petitioner's claims were precluded by federal acts regulating cigarette labeling and advertising.

One of the requirements of the original 1965 cigarette labeling act was that all packages of cigarettes bear the label "CAUTION: CIGARETTE SMOKING MAY BE HAZARDOUS TO YOUR HEALTH." The Act contained an express preemption provision prohibiting other state cigarette labeling requirements, but not affecting state common-law actions: "No statement relating to smoking and health shall be required in the advertising of cigarettes." The Court interpreted "statement" to mean state positive-law enactments relating to the labeling of cigarette packages. In 1969, however, both the warning and the preemption provision changed. Congress modified the label to state: "WARNING: THE SURGEON GENERAL HAS DETERMINED THAT CIGA-

RETTE SMOKING IS DANGEROUS TO YOUR HEALTH." The preemption provision changed from a prohibition of "statements" to a proscription of any "requirements or prohibitions imposed under state law with respect to the advertising or promotion" of cigarettes. The Supreme Court interpreted this new provision to encompass obligations imposed under the common law in addition to any regulations or labeling requirements under state statutes.

The Court then determined the effect that the 1969 preemption provision had on the petitioners' specific claims. Timing was significant in this case, as the decedent began smoking well before the original Act was enacted, but continued smoking thereafter. The Court examined each claim individually. First, the Court held preempted any failure to warn claims with respect to the period *after 1969*, the date when the language of the preemption provision changed. In a significant distinction, the Court stated that preemption would not apply to claims that derive solely from the manufacturers' testing or research or other such activities unrelated to the advertising or promotion of cigarettes.

Second, the claim for breach of express warranty was not preempted. The Court characterized express warranties as requirements imposed by a private party, and not requirements imposed under state law. Accordingly, any express warranty claims would not fit within the language of the preemption provision of either the 1965 Act or the 1969 Act. It mattered not that the express warranties claimed may have been based on advertising rather than made in documentary form.

Third, the Court held that some of the fraudulent misrepresentation claims were preempted, while others survived. The Court held preempted any claims that the manufacturers advertised the cigarettes in a manner so as to neutralize the health warnings because it viewed such claims as an aspect of failure to warn. In contrast, however, the petitioners' allegations that the manufacturers concealed material information regarding the health effects of their cigarettes generally were not preempted. The Court reasoned that the relevant duty underlying this category of claims was a general duty not to deceive rather than any duty associated solely with smoking and health, thus taking the claims outside of the preemption provision.

Finally, the Court held that the claims for conspiracy to misrepresent or to conceal material facts were not preempted. The basis for these claims was the same as for the intentional fraud claims; thus, they should be treated the same for preemption purposes.

As the Court's analysis of the misrepresentation claims demonstrates, the use of broad or vague language in a preemption provision that has been interpreted to include within its preemptive scope state tort-law claims does not necessarily lead to preemption of *every* state common-law claim. Read in the light of the presumption against preemption, across-the-board preemption of all common-law claims clearly would be disfavored. Rather, *Cipollone* makes clear that the plaintiff's specific claims and underlying allegations must be carefully compared to the intended scope of the particular federal statute's preemption provision. The plaintiff's characterization of a claim in the complaint will not necessarily control. For example, a plaintiff may characterize a claim as failure to warn, but the claim may in fact be one for negligent research and testing (which ultimately led to an inadequate warning of the hazards of the product). Under *Cipollone*, the claims based on testing and research would stand, while the specific warning claims (post–1969) would be preempted.

Several aspects of the *Cipollone* decision have been relied upon by plaintiffs' attorneys in subsequent tobacco litigation. Not long after *Cipollone*, a class action was filed in federal district court in Louisiana, alleging claims against the major cigarette manufacturers for nicotine addiction on behalf of a potential class of sixty million American smokers. The claims in Castano v. American Tobacco Co., 870 F.Supp. 1425 (E.D.La.1994) focused on the research and testing practices of the cigarette industry to the extent that nicotine was a known addictive substance. On a motion for summary judgment seeking to dismiss the claims on preemption grounds, the defendants argued that all of the class claims were essentially warning claims regardless of the words used to characterize them. The district court disagreed and, applying *Cipollone*, denied the motion. The *Castano* complaint also contained implied warranty claims, a category of claims not addressed in *Cipollone*. The court allowed the implied warranty claims, holding that those claims did not arise from the advertising and promotion of cigarettes and thus fell outside the scope of the preemption provision in the 1969 cigarette labeling act.

Recent years have seen a rise in personal injury litigation against the tobacco industry brought by nonsmokers alleging illnesses associated with environmental tobacco smoke (ETS). An early example was a class action brought by flight attendants in Florida state court for a host of injuries claimed to have been caused by workplace exposure to environmental tobacco smoke. *See* Broin v. Philip Morris Companies, Inc., 641 So.2d 888 (Fla.Ct.App.1994) (settled during trial). Such lawsuits remain unaffected by the *Cipollone* decision. Because the preempted claims announced in *Cipollone* were limited to the scope of the cigarette labeling acts— labeling and advertising of cigarettes—the preemption provisions contained in those statutes have no application to ETS claims. In contrast, ETS plaintiffs allege involuntary exposure to tobacco smoke, so presumably neither the labeling of cigarette packages nor the advertising of cigarettes would play a role in their claims.

In 2008, the U.S. Supreme Court again addressed the scope of preemption under the 1969 cigarette labeling act. The issue in Altria Group, Inc. v. Good, 129 S.Ct. 538 (2008), was whether the plaintiffs' claims that the defendant cigarette manufacturer had deceived them about the health hazards of their so-called "light" cigarettes in violation of a state deceptive practices statute were preempted. Holding that the claims were not preempted by the express preemption provision in the cigarette labeling act, the Court reaffirmed the importance of *Cipollone* in the larger scope of the Court's product preemption doctrine. In particular, the Court emphasized the importance of Congressional intent and restated the presumption against preemption in areas of the law—such as tort law—that are traditionally within the police powers of the state.

b. *Medical Devices: Lohr and Riegel*

Two important Supreme Court cases on express preemption involved the Medical Device Amendments (MDA) to the Food, Drug, and Cosmetic Act. The MDA established three classes of medical devices, classed according to the degree of invasiveness of the device and regulated with increasing rigor. Most preemption decisions have involved Class III medical devices, which include such items as cardiac pacemakers, intraocular lenses, and collagen injections. Thus, the ways these devices may cause injury range from the mechanical to the chemical and often meet the definition of a toxic tort. A Class III device is subject to a premarket approval (PMA) process regarding safety of the device. The PMA regulations are not device-specific, but rather require all manufacturers of Class III devices to provide to the FDA certain detailed information regarding the product's design, manufacture, uses, and labeling. An exemption to the PMA process exists for section 510(k) "substantially equivalent" devices. These devices received marketing approval simply on the basis of a showing that they were the "substantial equivalent" to devices that were on the market at the time of the enactment of the MDA in 1976 and were grandfathered in under the MDA at that time.

The MDA contains a preemption provision that states that "no State ... may establish ... with respect to a device intended for human use any requirement—(1) Which is different from, or in addition to, any requirement applicable under [the MDA], and (2) which relates to the safety or effectiveness of the device...." 21 U.S.C.A. § 360k (West 2010). The scope of the MDA preemption provision is somewhat broader than the analogous provisions in either of the cigarette labeling acts because the FDA has the authority to regulate not just the labeling, but also the design of the product, as reflected in the language of the preemption provision.

In addition, the FDA has promulgated regulations interpreting the preemption provision. *See* 21 C.F.R. §§ 808.1–808.5 (2010). Rules of statutory interpretation dictate that where the plain language of the statute is clear and on point, courts should disregard the agency's interpretation. Chevron v. Natural Resources Defense Council, Inc., 467 U.S. 837 (1984). Otherwise, the agency's interpretation will control, provided that it is reasonable and does not conflict with the intent of Congress. The relevant FDA regulation provides, in pertinent part:

> State or local requirements are preempted only when the Food and Drug Administration has established specific counterpart regulations or there are other specific requirements applicable to a particular device under the act, thereby making any existing divergent State or local requirements applicable to the device different from, or in addition to, the specific Food and Drug Administration requirements.

21 C.F.R. § 808.1(d) (2010). Moreover, the regulations provide that the preemption provision encompasses any state requirement, including statutes, ordinances, regulations, and common-law causes of action. *Id.* § 808.1(b).

i.   Medtronic, Inc. v. Lohr

Medtronic, Inc. v. Lohr, 518 U.S. 470 (1996) involved an action brought by a woman and her husband for claims associated with personal injuries related to a pacemaker manufactured by the defendant. The pacemaker was classified as a Class III device under the MDA and had been marketed as a 510(k) "substantially equivalent" device. The plaintiffs' claims encompassed negligent design and testing, strict liability for defective design, negligent manufacture, and failure to warn. The Supreme Court held that none of the claims at issue in the case was preempted by the MDA. The Court focused closely on the nature of the marketing process for medical devices, emphasizing that the pacemaker in question in *Medtronic* was a 510(k) "substantially equivalent" device. This meant that the marketing approval process for the device consisted almost solely of a determination of *equivalency*, rather than safety. In contrast, the Court noted, a device that has undergone the full PMA process has had a "more rigorous" review.

Conducting an express preemption analysis, the Court held that while the preemption provision could include state common-law tort claims, Congress had not intended to preempt any of the plaintiffs' claims. First, the Court held that the plaintiffs' design defect claims were not preempted by the MDA because the device in question had been marketed as a 510(k) "substantially equivalent" device. The Court reasoned that no specific determination of safety or effectiveness of the device had been made in the 510(k) review process. Thus, the FDA had not established any specific design requirements to which the manufacturer was held.

Second, the Court interpreted the Lohrs' complaint to possibly contain claims for noncompliance with FDA regulations. Any such claims, the Court held, were not preempted by the MDA because they were not "different from, or in addition to" the federal requirements of the MDA.

Third, the manufacturing and labeling claims were not preempted for a different reason. Although the FDA had promulgated regulations with regard to both the manufacture and labeling of medical devices, the regulations contained general language applicable to all devices, not to any particular device. At this point, the Court looked to the FDA's interpretation of the preemption provision, concluding that in the absence of specific regulations by the FDA applicable to a particular device, the claims related to the manufacture and labeling of the devices would not be preempted. The manufacturing and labeling regulations applicable to Lohr's pacemaker were generic in nature, not device-specific.

ii. Riegel v. Medtronic, Inc.

An important question not raised in *Lohr* was whether the MDA preemption provision would preempt product liability claims involving a device that had undergone the full PMA process. In Riegel v. Medtronic, Inc., 552 U.S. 312 (2008), the Court decided this issue in the context of an action for personal injuries related to a Class III cardiac catheter. The claims were similar to those presented in *Lohr*, but the Court found a sufficient distinction between 510(k) "substantial equivalency" and approval under the PMA process to hold that the claims in *Riegel* were preempted. Following closely the analysis in *Lohr*, the Court examined the provisions of the FDA regulation explaining the preemption provision as applicable "only when the Food and Drug Administration has established specific counterpart regulations or there are other specific requirements applicable to a particular device...." 21 C.F.R. § 808.1(d) (2010). The *Riegel* Court held that the PMA process imposes exactly those kinds of "specific requirements applicable to a particular device." This was so, the Court reasoned, because the FDA requires a device that has received pre-market approval to be made with almost no deviations from the specifications in its approval application, on the theory that the FDA has determined that the approved form provides a reasonable assurance of safety and effectiveness. In contrast, the FDA conducts no analogous safety review for "substantially equivalent" devices.

In addition, the Court eroded the part of the express preemption doctrine, relevant in both *Cipollone* and *Lohr*, that had said where state common law applies generally, and not only to the product at issue in the case, tort claims based upon that law would not be barred. Instead, the Court held that "the preempted state requirement [need not] apply only to the relevant device, or only to medical devices and not to all products and all actions in general."

Furthermore, the Court made a broad pronouncement relevant to all cases involving a federal statute with an express preemption provision. Focusing on the fact that the term "requirements" appears in the preemption provisions of any number of federal statutes, the Court stated: "Congress is entitled to know what meaning this Court will assign to terms regularly used in its enactments. Absent other indication, reference to a State's 'requirements' includes its common-law duties." This standardized definition of "requirements," while offering uniformity, restricts the ability of plaintiffs to argue that Congress did not intend state common-law actions to fall within the preemptive scope of some statutes.

c. *Bates and Pesticide Cases*

The labeling and packaging of pesticides are regulated by the Federal Insecticide, Fungicide, and Rodenticide Act (FIFRA), 7 U.S.C.A. § 136 (West 2010). FIFRA is essentially a labeling statute. EPA's regulations promulgated pursuant to FIFRA contain only general labeling requirements and do not prescribe specific label language. Section 136v(b) of FIFRA contains an express preemption provision that provides that a "State shall not impose or continue in effect any requirements for labeling or packaging in addition to or different from those required under this subchapter."

After many years of conflicting decisions in the courts, the United States Supreme Court answered many of the FIFRA preemption questions in Bates v. Dow Agrosciences LLC, 544 U.S. 431 (2005). The case involved peanut farmers who claimed damages to their crops associated with a weedkiller manufactured by the defendant. The Court reversed the Fifth Circuit Court of Appeals and rejected the position of a majority of the federal appellate courts. The Court stated that "[t]he long history of tort litigation against manufacturers of poisonous substances adds force to the basic presumption against pre-emption." The Court observed that FIFRA "authorizes a relatively decentralized scheme that preserves a broad role for state regulation." Turning to the language of § 136v(b), the Court stated that a jury verdict is not necessarily a "requirement" within the meaning of the provision, but that the term may include common-law duties where appropriate. Note that this interpretation of "requirement" is not the absolute definition that the Court espoused three years later in *Riegel*. Under the FIFRA preemption provision, preemption applies only where the state rule is a requirement "for labeling or packaging" and must impose a requirement that is "in addition to or different from" those required under FIFRA. Thus, the Court held that claims for manufacturing defect, design defect, negligent testing, and breach of express warranties are not requirements for labeling and packaging and thus are not preempted. The appearance of the express warranty on the label was irrelevant, as the Court looked at the underlying voluntary contractual commitment to warrant the product.

In contrast, the Court held that the fraud and failure-to-warn claims could be preempted under the provision because those claims essentially alleged that the product's label violated state standards by containing false statements and inadequate warnings. The Court emphasized that for these claims to be preempted, they must contain requirements that are "in addition to or different from"—and not identical to—the requirements under FIFRA. The court remanded these claims for that determination.

3. Product Liability: Implied Preemption

The United States Supreme Court has been less clear about implied preemption, and the cases raise many questions. The decisions sometimes seem contradictory, and the role of implied preemption in toxic torts, particularly drug cases, has yet to be fully understood.

a.   *Wyeth v. Levine*

In 2009, the U.S. Supreme Court analyzed the applicability of implied preemption in a drug product liability action. Wyeth v. Levine, 129 S.Ct. 1187 (2009), involved the provisions of the FDCA applicable to new drugs, but it has far-reaching implications for all other product cases raising implied preemption arguments. The plaintiff claimed that a clinic had administered the defendant's drug Phenergan to her via the IV-push method and accidentally injected the drug into an artery, leading to amputation of the plaintiff's forearm. Although the label stated that care should be taken to avoid intra-arterial injection of the drug, it did not contain any specific warning about the IV-push method of administration. The defendant made both conflict preemption arguments—that it was impossible to comply with both a state tort judgment and the new drug labeling requirements, and that state law presented an obstacle to the accomplishment of the goals and policies of the FDCA.

The portions of the FDCA applicable to drugs do not contain an express preemption provision. The Court found this significant in its analysis of Congressional intent. Indeed, the Court noted that at the time of the enactment of the FDCA's predecessor statute, Congress gave every indication that the Act was intended to supplement state law, not replace it. This purpose continued for the long history of the FDCA, until the FDA abruptly reversed its position in 2006. Accordingly, the long history of acknowledging the role of state law in matters related to prescription drugs persuaded the Court that state tort actions are an important adjunct to the federal statute and its regulations.

Wyeth's first argument was that it could not comply with both state tort-law standards and the federal new drug labeling requirements. Wyeth argued that once the FDA had approved its label, Wyeth could not change it without FDA approval. The Court disagreed, citing a provision that allowed Wyeth to unilaterally strengthen the label while awaiting FDA approval of the change. The second implied preemption argument was that state tort judgments created an obstacle to the effective administration of the federal drug labeling requirements. Wyeth argued that Congress had made a decision that only the FDA was to balance the risks and benefits of drugs and that state tort judgments would inappropriately supplant the expertise of the FDA with the judgment of lay juries. The Court also rejected this second argument. The Court found persuasive the absence of a preemption provision and Congress's certain awareness of the ongoing role of state tort actions in matters related to drug safety. Thus, the Court concluded that "Congress did not intend FDA oversight to be the exclusive means of ensuring drug safety and effectiveness."

Levine was a significant decision, particularly as to the Court's assessment of the role of state tort litigation. But numerous issues remain unresolved.

One such issue making its way through the courts is the role of preemption in generic drug cases. For example, the Fifth Circuit has held that the 1984 Hatch–Waxman Amendments to the FDCA governing generic drugs, and the related FDA regulations, do not preempt failure-to-warn claims against manufacturers of generic drugs, citing *Levine. See* Demahy v. Actavis, Inc., 593 F.3d 428 (5th Cir. 2010).

b.   *Fraud-on-the-FDA Claims*

The United States Supreme Court has stated that neither the express preemption provision nor a saving clause mandates a presumption against *implied* preemption. Geier v. American Honda Motor Co., 529 U.S. 861 (2000). This led the Court to identify an area of implied preemption involving the MDA in Buckman Co. v. Plaintiffs' Legal Committee, 531 U.S. 341 (2001). *Buckman* involved orthopedic bone screws manufactured by AcroMed Corporation that had been inserted into the plaintiffs' spines. The screws were Class III medical devices that underwent the section 510(k) "substantially equivalent" process set forth in the MDA, as described *supra*. The FDA twice denied the application to market the screws for use in the spine, citing lack of equivalency and safety concerns. In its third application, the manufacturer filed two separate section 510(k) applications for two distinct components of the device, seeking substantial equivalency approval separately for each. In addition, AcroMed no longer sought approval of the devices for spinal surgery; rather, it requested approval for insertion in the long bones of the arms and legs. The FDA approved the two applications in 1986. The plaintiffs claimed that AcroMed and its consultant, Buckman Company, had made fraudulent representations to the FDA during the PMA process, particularly with regard to the intended use of the device, thus fraudulently obtaining market approval.

The Supreme Court held that the plaintiffs' fraud-on-the-FDA claims were impliedly preempted by the MDA and, more generally, the FDCA due to a conflict between the state-law claims alleged and the approval and enforcement schemes set forth in the FDCA. Significantly, the Court held that the presumption against preemption did not apply in this case because the federal regulatory scheme empowered the agency to investigate and resolve any alleged fraud complaints before it. The Court emphasized that medical device applicants should be governed by the standards set forth in the MDA and FDCA and not a myriad of state rules in this uniquely federal area of regulation. Important to the Court's analysis was the provision in the FDCA that retains the prerogative of physicians to prescribe drugs or medical devices for reasonable "off-label" uses. In other words, if a physician reasonably believes that it will be safe and effective to do so, the physician could prescribe the bone screws for use in the spine, even though they were approved for use in the long bones of the arms and legs. This, apparently, was what AcroMed was expecting would happen. But whether AcroMed's dealings with the FDA constituted fraud was a separate question that the Court determined was solely within the FDA's jurisdiction to police. This case is examined in a broader context in Jean Macchiaroli Eggen, *Shedding Light on the Preemption Doctrine in Product Liability Actions: Defining the Scope of Buckman and Sprietsma*, 6 Del. L. Rev. 143 (2003).

B. STATUTES OF LIMITATIONS

It is axiomatic that a statute of limitations will bar a cause of action that is commenced after a designated period of time. The rationale for this is to protect defendants from stale claims and to impose some finality on the litigation. The period of time within which the plaintiff may bring the claim runs from the time of accrual of the claim. In many toxic tort actions, the traditional concept of a statute of limitations has proved to be inadequate. When does the action accrue for the purpose of triggering the running of the statutory period? In cases of latent illness, when does the injury actually occur? At the time of exposure, or at the time when the illness manifests itself? Legislatures and courts have struggled with this issue and have taken a variety of approaches.

1. Traditional Exposure Rule

The typical statutory period for the commencement of an unintentional tort claim is between two and four years from the time of injury. For latent illness claims, the traditional approach was that the action accrued at the time of last exposure. Thus, if a person's illness was not manifested until many years following the last exposure—as was the case in many asbestos-related disease cases—the plaintiff's claim would be time-barred. *See* Bassham v. Owens–Corning Fiber Glass Corp., 327 F.Supp. 1007 (D.N.M.1971) (decided on other grounds). As a result of the inequity of such a result, and considering that under traditional concepts of injury the plaintiffs would not have the basis for a claim until manifestation of the illness, courts and legislatures acted to modify the rules governing statutory periods to accommodate toxic injuries.

2. Judicial Discovery Rule

By now, virtually every jurisdiction has remedied the problems inherent in the exposure rule, whether by statutory mandate or by judicial ruling, for most latent illness claims arising from exposure to drugs, chemicals, and asbestos. An early United States Supreme Court case, Urie v. Thompson, 337 U.S. 163 (1949), articulated the equitable reasons for applying a discovery rule to latent illness claims. In that case, which derived from a compensation claim for work-related silicosis under the Federal Employers' Liability Act, the Court emphasized the unfairness of interpreting accrual to preclude a claim before the plaintiff has reason to know of the illness.

This rationale has been accepted by the states. In Louisville Trust Company v. Johns–Manville Products Corp., 580 S.W.2d 497 (Ky.1979), an asbestos case not unlike *Bassham*, the court ruled that the date of accrual of the cause of action was not the time of last exposure, but rather was when the plaintiff knew or should have known of the injury. The court observed that "[a]n action accrues only at the time the plaintiff suffers an actionable wrong," and an actionable wrong is evidenced by some loss or damage. The court applied the discovery rule to actions based on either negligence or product liability theories. Such discovery rules are adaptations of discovery rules that had been employed in many jurisdictions for other kinds of troublesome claims, such as fraud and foreign-object medical malpractice claims.

The Alabama Supreme Court, after a long period of refusal, finally adopted a discovery rule in 2008. Prior to Griffin v. Unocal Corp., 990 So.2d 291 (Ala. 2008), the highest court of the state had maintained that the last exposure rule would apply until and unless the state legislature said otherwise. Following a shift in the composition of the court, the court overruled its prior case law and held 5 to 4 in *Griffin* that the last exposure rule would no longer apply in the state, stating that "a cause of action accrues only when there has occurred a *manifest, present injury*." The Alabama stand-off between the judiciary and the legislature demonstrates that disagreement over the merits of the discovery rule, and the appropriate designation of authority to make the rule, continue in some states.

3. Statutory Discovery Rule

Some state legislatures have enacted statutory discovery rules that have attempted to address the major issues that arise in toxic tort litigation. A statutory discovery rule does not eliminate the need for judicial input, however. The New York statutory discovery rule governs claims for personal injury or property damage "caused by the latent effects of exposure to any substance or combination of substances, in any form, upon or within the body or upon or within property." N.Y. Civ. Prac. L. & R. 214–c(2) (McKinney 2010). The statute provides that the three-year tort limitations period begins to run at the time of discovery of the injury or when the injury should have been discovered through "the exercise of reasonable diligence." This language seems to require some investigative action by the plaintiff after becoming suspicious of a connection between the illness and an earlier exposure. The New York statute places a limit on the time that the plaintiff has for learning the cause of the illness. The statute builds in a tiered system that allows a reasonable time for discovery of the cause, but requires that as a certain amount of time passes, the plaintiff must show that scientific knowledge of causation was not available at a more timely date. Ultimately, however, if the plaintiff has not discovered the cause of the illness within five years from discovering the illness, the claim will be barred.

The language of the New York statute is vague concerning which substances fall within its discovery rule. It refers merely to "substance" and defines "exposure" as "direct or indirect exposure by absorption, contact, ingestion, inhalation, implantation or injection." *See* N.Y. Civ. Prac. L. & R. 214–c(1) (McKinney 2010). In Prego v. City of New York, 541 N.Y.S.2d 995 (N.Y.App.Div.1989), the court held that Section 214–c applied to an action brought by a plaintiff claiming that she contracted HIV from a puncture by a negligently discarded contaminated needle in a hospital setting. The defendant argued that the action should be time-barred because HIV was not within the contemplation of the statute. The court disagreed, holding that "biological transmitters of latent diseases" met the statutory definition. Moreover, the court believed that because the legislature was aware of the various means of transmission of HIV at the time the statute was enacted, it would have expressly excluded it or other biological organisms if it had so intended.

Another question seeking an answer is whether the provisions of Section 214–c(4) extending the statutory time period to allow plaintiffs to discover the cause of a known condition apply only to latent illness. In In re Ephedra Prods. Liab. Litig., 2006 WL 944705 (S.D.N.Y. 2006), the court held plaintiff Giordano's claim time-barred, concluding that the stroke he suffered was not a "latent effect" within the meaning of the New York statute. Giordano claimed that he did not learn of the possible connection between his use of ephedra and his strokes until four years after he suffered the strokes. As of this writing, the Second Circuit, in Giordano v. Market America Inc., 599 F.3d 87 (2d Cir. 2010), has certified this question to the New York Court of

Appeals, along with the related question whether an adverse health effect that occurred twenty-four to forty-eight hours following exposure could be deemed "latent" for the purpose of the statute.

4. Time of Discovery

Regardless of whether the discovery rule is imposed judicially or legislatively, numerous issues have arisen in determining the point at which the plaintiff is deemed to have discovered—or reasonably should have discovered—the injury claimed. Because latent disease can appear slowly, with multiple, progressive symptoms, the cases often focus on the point in the disease process when the plaintiff has sufficient information to proceed with legal action. Similarly, issues arise when the illness is manifest, but the plaintiff does not know the precise cause of the illness. How much suspicion must the plaintiff have of the cause of the injury to trigger the running of the statute of limitations?

In general, the date of accrual will be when the plaintiff was aware of the injury *and* of the potential cause. But what of the situation in which the plaintiff becomes ill, but is unaware of the precise cause of the illness? To what extent is the plaintiff required to investigate the possible causes of the illness by seeking opinions of physicians or other experts so as to preserve the cause of action? In Evenson v. Osmose Wood Preserving Company of America, Inc., 899 F.2d 701 (7th Cir.1990), the plaintiff was treated for nasal polyps and allergic rhinitis for more than three years before being advised by a physician that the condition was related to a workplace chemical. He then filed suit. During the early years of treatment, other physicians had suspected the workplace connection, but upon performing clinical tests, had concluded that the chemical was not the cause. If the initial symptoms and suspicions triggered the running of the applicable two-year statute, the plaintiff's claim would have been time-barred.

The *Evenson* court, refusing to apply a bright line test, held that the running of the statute was triggered by the knowledge of the plaintiff of a "reasonable possibility" that the particular exposure was the cause of the symptoms. Under the facts of *Evenson*, the court stated that "[a] reasonable possibility, while less than a probability, requires more than the mere suspicion possessed by [the plaintiff], a layperson without technical or medical knowledge." Thus, the plaintiff was not aware of a "reasonable" possibility of the workplace cause until after the last physician expressed that opinion, and the action was not time-barred.

A Pennsylvania appellate court expressed a similar view in a non-workplace product liability case in Simon v. Wyeth Pharmaceuticals, Inc., 989 A.2d 356 (Pa. Super. 2009). In 1992, the plaintiff began taking hormone replacement therapy (HRT) for menopausal symptoms and was subsequently diagnosed with breast cancer in May, 2002. Neither the medication package inserts nor the prescribing physicians had warned of any risk of breast cancer from HRT. On July 9, 2002, the NIH published a major study documenting the connection, and the plaintiff learned of the study shortly thereafter from a newspaper article. She commenced her action on July 1, 2004, just shy of two years from the date the study had been released. Pennsylvania has a two-year judicial discovery rule. The court stated: "It is entirely unreasonable that a lay person, completely lacking in medical training, would make the logical connection between HRT and breast cancer prior to the release of the ... study." Likewise, in Pettit v. SmithKline Beecham Corp., 2010 WL 1463479 (S.D.Ohio 2010) (slip op.), the court held that the plaintiff's claim that her use of the drug Paxil while pregnant caused her daughter's congenital heart defect and death ten years later could proceed. The court stated: "Plaintiffs should not be required to have researched the medical literature for drugs prescribed to them eight years earlier." On the other hand, "plaintiffs are not required to receive definitive confirmation of the cause of their harms to be on reasonable notice." Cannon v. Minnesota Mining & Mfg. Co., 2009 WL 350561 (D. Utah 2009) (slip op.).

Often, the determination of the accrual trigger is a close call, and courts have reached different results on similar sets of facts. In Kullman v. Owens–Corning Fiberglas Corp., 943 F.2d 613 (6th Cir. 1991), the court held that the plaintiff should have known that he had an actionable claim when he suspected that the dust he breathed in the workplace might have caused the breathing problems from which he suffered, even though he was not diagnosed with asbestosis until several years later.

His action was time-barred. In contrast, in Joseph v. Hess Oil, 867 F.2d 179 (3d Cir.1989), the court held that the plaintiff's illness, coupled with his knowledge of his exposure to asbestos and an awareness of the hazards of asbestos, was insufficient to satisfy the "knew or should have known" test.

Sometimes knowledge of the broader implications of a diagnosis is imputed to a plaintiff. The plaintiff in Wetherill v. Eli Lilly & Company, 678 N.E.2d 474 (N.Y.1997) had been exposed to DES while in utero. In 1978 and 1979, she was treated for a pre-cancerous condition in her cervix. It was not until 1989—after several miscarriages, discovery of a misshapen uterus, surgery for uterine adhesions, and diagnosis of an incompetent cervix—that she learned she had "classic symptoms" of DES exposure. She sued in 1992. The New York Court of Appeals held that her cause of action accrued more than three years prior to commencement of her action and was time-barred. Interpreting N.Y. Civ. Prac. L. & R. § 214–c, discussed in Section 3 *supra*, the court stated that the language "discovery of injury" means precisely that—discovery of the condition or disease or the symptoms thereof, and not the probable cause. The court determined that by 1988, the plaintiff had enough information to clearly understand her injury. The court rejected the plaintiff's attempt to use the grace period built into the New York statute to extend the time period because she should have known of the connections between her symptoms and DES no later than 1988. The highly publicized nature of the health implications of DES exposure led the court to impute what it believed to be public knowledge to the plaintiff. *Accord* Whitney v. Agway Inc., 656 N.Y.S.2d 455 (N.Y.Sup.Ct.App.Div. 1997) (holding, in a pesticide exposure case, that the claim accrued no later than the time when plaintiff determined there was a "likely connection" between her symptoms and the pesticide and stating that full awareness of the connection is not the trigger).

The Third Circuit has noted that these kinds of discovery questions are usually intensely fact-based, and has disapproved of their disposition on summary judgment. In Debiec v. Cabot Corp., 352 F.3d 117 (3d Cir.2003), the court considered several consolidated cases under the Pennsylvania statute of limitations. In one of the cases, the court stated that even though plaintiffs are expected to use reasonable diligence to investigate their symptoms and possible causes, under some circumstances they may reasonably rely upon medical diagnosis that turns out to be wrong. In *Debiec*, the plaintiff died of chronic beryllium disease after being told by her doctors that it was not likely that she was suffering from the condition. The court held that summary judgment for the defendant was erroneously granted because of material fact questions. *Accord* Keller v. Armstrong World Industries, Inc., 107 P.3d 29 (Or.Ct.App.2005) (imputing to the plaintiff only the "knowledge of all facts that he had a reasonable opportunity to discover" and reversing summary judgment for defendant).

Occasionally, a defendant is found to have obstructed the reasonable opportunity for the plaintiff to discover the cause of his or her illness. Jones v. United States, 2010 WL 668262 (E.D.N.C. 2010), involved a claim of illness caused by a contaminated water supply at the U.S. Marines' Camp Lejeune. The court emphasized the "reasonable diligence" requirement for plaintiffs in discovering the cause of their illness, and held that the plaintiff's claim could proceed. The plaintiff's illness was diagnosed some twenty years after residing at Camp Lejeune. The court found relevant the "Department of the Navy's unwillingness to release information regarding contamination at Camp Lejeune or to provide notice to former residents." As a result, the plaintiff's access to the necessary information was restricted.

A related issue that arises in determining date of discovery involves plaintiffs who develop more than one discrete disease or condition from a single toxic exposure. For example, in Kemp v. G.D. Searle & Company, 103 F.3d 405 (5th Cir.1997), the Fifth Circuit, applying Mississippi's six-year statute of limitations, held that the plaintiff's claim for infertility against the manufacturer of the Copper–7 intrauterine device was time-barred. The court construed the Mississippi latent disease statute, which provided that an action must be brought within six years of the time that the plaintiff discovered, or by reasonable diligence should have discovered, the injury. The plaintiff had suffered from pelvic inflammatory disease (PID) approximately eight years prior to receiving a diagnosis of scarred fallopian tubes, which was the immediate cause of her infertility. She stated that the treating physician for the PID had informed her that PID could lead to tubal scarring, but that he had recommended against diagnostic testing until such later date when the plaintiff had not been successful in becoming pregnant after attempting conception for twelve months—if, in fact, that occurred. The court rejected the plaintiff's argument that infertility was a separate condition from the PID, warranting a separate accrual date for statute of limitations purposes. Calling the infertility part of the "same chain of causality" as the PID, the court held that the limitations period for an IUD plaintiff begins to run upon discovery of the PID, even when infertility is not diagnosed until years later.

Kemp points to the real problem in this kind of latent disease case. The plaintiff will be forced to bring an action for infertility at an early date, when perhaps the true development of the scarring is not known. The result invites speculation about the extent of the plaintiff's injuries. Allowing the action at the time of discovery of the infertility would present a much more precise picture of the injuries sought to be compensated. Moreover, the availability of medical treatments to correct or improve her situation would be accurate at the time of discovery of the infertility.

The *Kemp* court contrasted cases involving what it referred to as two separate and distinct diseases. In this situation, the plaintiff would be able to rely upon a later accrual date for a condition or disease diagnosed later. For example, in Abrams v. Pneumo Abex Corp., 981 A.2d 198 (Pa. 2009), the Pennsylvania Supreme Court, noting that Pennsylvania has recognized the "two-disease rule" for nearly two decades, held that two plaintiffs who had previously brought suit for their non-malignant asbestos-related disease could later bring suit for cancer related to the same exposures without being time-barred. *Accord* Wilson v. Johns–Manville Sales Corp., 684 F.2d 111 (D.C.Cir.1982). Similarly, in Schiro v. American Tobacco Company, 611 So.2d 962 (Miss. 1992), the court allowed a later accrual date for lung cancer, even though the plaintiff, a smoker, had been suffering from emphysema for some years. The distinction is whether the plaintiff is suffering from different symptoms related to the same disease process (e.g. PID and infertility) or different diseases (e.g. asbestosis and mesothelioma). On a related issue, the California Supreme Court, on certified questions from the Ninth Circuit Court of Appeals, held in Grisham v. Philip Morris U.S.A., Inc., 151 P.3d 1151 (Cal. 2007), that earlier awareness of the addictive qualities of smoking did not begin the statute of limitations running for the plaintiff's claims of smoking-related illness that developed later.

5. Property Damage Claims

In some states, the discovery limitations period applies to both actions for personal injuries and actions for property damages. *See, e.g.*, N.Y. Civ.

Prac. L. & R. 214–c (McKinney 2010). Thus, in
Harry Stephens Farms, Inc. v. Wormald Americas,
Inc., 571 F.3d 820 (8th Cir. 2009), the court, applying the discovery rule, determined that genuine
issues of fact existed as to when the plaintiff knew
of the contamination of his property by substances
that had migrated from the defendants' neighboring
chemical plant. Among other things, the court said
that the plaintiff's "undisputed 'worry' and 'concern' about possible environmental contamination
dating back to the mid-1990s was not proper evidence on which to rest the summary judgment
decision." The claims in *Harry Stephens Farms*
were based upon negligence, nuisance, and trespass.

In the context of nuisance claims, courts sometimes apply a rather technical distinction between a
permanent nuisance and a continuing nuisance. A
permanent nuisance is one that cannot be discon-
tinued and will persist indefinitely; presumably, all
damages associated with the permanent nuisance
occur at one time and could be assessed in a single
determination. Therefore, a permanent nuisance
would be subject to a fixed statute of limitations
running from the time of the creation of the nuisance. *See* Phillips v. City of Pasadena, 162 P.2d
625 (Cal.1945). For example, in Dombrowski v.
Gould Electronics Inc., 954 F.Supp. 1006 (M.D.Pa.
1996), the court held that lead contamination of the
air, soil, and groundwater constituted a permanent
trespass or nuisance for statute of limitations purposes. The court stated that the statutory period
began to run from the time the plaintiffs first

should have discovered that the lead contamination was devaluing their property. *See also* Gomez v. Montana, 975 P.2d 1258 (Mont. 1999) (worker's claims arising from toxic exposure to paint products in the workplace do not constitute a continuing tort, and the statutory period began to run when plaintiff first knew, or should have known, of facts constituting the cause of action). In contrast, a continuing nuisance is of a more sporadic or discontinuous nature. Plaintiffs claiming a continuing nuisance may bring successive actions.

Some cases indicate that asbestos abatement claims may not have the benefit of a discovery statute of limitations. In MRI Broadway Rental, Inc. v. United States Mineral Products Co., 704 N.E.2d 550 (N.Y.1998), the New York Court of Appeals held that the statute of limitations started to run in an asbestos abatement case when the asbestos was installed, not when the contamination level exceeded government standards more than a decade later. Similarly, the court in Corporation of Mercer University v. National Gypsum Co., 877 F.2d 35 (11th Cir.1989), after certifying the question to the Georgia Supreme Court, held that property damage claims against asbestos manufacturers for abatement of asbestos in buildings were not subject to the discovery statute of limitations that applied to personal injury claims.

C. STATUTES OF REPOSE

Statutes of repose operate in a manner different from statutes of limitations. They operate in conjunction with statutes of limitations to give defendants maximum protection from stale claims. The plaintiff's claim must be timely under both the statute of repose and the relevant statute of limitations. A statute of repose bars claims brought beyond a certain period of time after a designated action. This is most clearly seen in product liability claims.

In Braswell v. Flintkote Mines, Ltd., 723 F.2d 527 (7th Cir.1983), an asbestos case, the court applied the Indiana Product Liability Act, which established a two-year statute of limitations with an outside limit of ten years from the date of delivery of the product. *See* Ind. Code Ann. § 34–20–3–1(b)(2) (West 2010). Thus, if the ten-year repose statute had run, the claim was barred notwithstanding the possibility that the statute of limitations may not have expired. The court found that the statute was consistent with the goals of repose statutes to give plaintiffs "a reasonable time to present their claims [while protecting] defendants and the courts from having to deal with cases in which the search for truth may be seriously impaired by the loss of evidence."

Baughn v. Eli Lilly & Co., 356 F.Supp.2d 1166 (D.Kan.2005), involved a statute of repose that expired at the end of the product's "useful safe life." Kan. Stat. Ann. § 60–3303 (2009). The statute provides: " 'Useful safe life' begins at the time of delivery of the product and extends for the time during which the product would normally be likely to perform or be stored in a safe manner." Claims alleging harm that occurred more than ten years from delivery raise a presumption that the useful safe life has expired. In *Baughn*, a DES case, the court held that questions of fact existed as to whether the plaintiff fell within exceptions to the ten-year presumption. The plaintiff argued that she fell within either the "prolonged exposure" exception or the exception for injuries occurring within the ten-year period that were not discoverable until after that period expired. *See id.* § 60–3303(b)(2)(D).

A harsher result befell the plaintiff in Montgomery v. Wyeth, 580 F.3d 455 (6th Cir. 2009), a diet drug product liability case. The court applied the Tennessee statute of repose, which provided that claims must be brought within one year of the expiration of the "anticipated life" of the product. Tenn. Code Ann. § 29–28–102 (West 2010) (defining "anticipated life" as determined by the expiration date on the product). The plaintiff argued that the statute of repose should not bar her claim because there were no expiration dates on the product dispensed to her. The court rejected this argument, stating that the statute of repose "does not require that the purchaser have knowledge of the expiration date, but conditions the anticipated life of the product on the expiration date imposed by the manufacturer." The court reasoned that the legislature had intended the statute of repose to bar claims whether or not injured parties were aware of the product's expiration date. *Cf. also* Spence v. Miles Laboratories, Inc., 37 F.3d 1185 (6th Cir. 1994) (holding that claims for HIV contamination of a blood-clotting factor concentrate could be barred by the statute of repose and deciding the case on those grounds, rather than the blood shield statute).

Statutes of repose have not been enacted solely for product liability claims. Often, such statutes appear in reference to conditions of real property, limiting claims to a certain period of time after an improvement on the property. *See, e.g.*, Md. Code Ann., Cts. & Jud. Proc. § 5–108 (2010). In Risch v. Paul J. Krez Company, 678 N.E.2d 44 (Ill.App.Ct. 1st Dist.1997), the court interpreted a statute of repose keyed into construction on or improvement to real property. The statute required a tort action to be brought within ten years after the alleged wrongful act or omission. The plaintiffs' decedents had been exposed to asbestos pipe covering during the 1960s and 1970s; they learned in 1992 that they had mesothelioma. The plaintiffs argued that the defendant's installation activities were only a minor part of its main business, which was the sale of asbestos products, and that sales did not fall within the scope of the repose statute. Using an "activity analysis," the court ruled that the defendant was protected by the ten-year statute of repose because it had substantially participated in the installation of the asbestos products at the job site.

As the cases demonstrate, latent disease claims present some new challenges for the application of statutes of repose. The construction repose statute in *Risch* was obviously intended for property damage claims and accidents, rather than disease claims. Similarly, product repose statutes contemplated accidents, rather than disease. Absent a specific exception in the statute, courts have tended to interpret the repose statute strictly. Thus, in Klein v. DePuy Inc., 506 F.3d 553 (7th Cir. 2007), the Seventh Circuit refused to read a disease exception into the North Carolina statute of repose, stating that a major purpose of the statute was to shield manufacturers from open-ended liability. A new development in Alabama may herald a more lenient approach to statutes of repose in toxic torts personal injury actions. The Alabama statute of repose bars actions brought more than twenty years after the time "they could have been asserted." In Owens–Illinois v. Wells, 2010 WL 1640962 (Ala. 2010) (not yet released for publication), the Alabama Supreme Court held, in an asbestos personal injury action, that the twenty–year statute of repose does not begin to run "until all the essential elements of that claim, including an injury, coexist so that the plaintiff could validly file an action. The rule of repose does not depend solely on the actions of the defendant." In this case, the plaintiff had not manifested symptoms of his illness during the twenty-year period.

D. RES JUDICATA

Res judicata, or claim preclusion, often presents a dilemma for plaintiffs and courts in toxic tort actions. This is because toxic injury does not present itself in the manner of traditional injuries. Take the example of asbestos-related disease. An asbestos

worker, knowing he has been exposed to the substance and learning of the hazards associated with
it, may first believe that he has a claim for fear of
contracting asbestos-related disease or a claim for
increased risk of contracting the disease, two types
of claims discussed in Chapter Nine. The worker
then may manifest asymptomatic pleural plaques in
the lungs, a condition associated with exposure to
asbestos. Subsequently, the worker suffers from
asbestosis, and ultimately, perhaps, suffers from
mesothelioma, a form of lung cancer that is found
in high rates in asbestos workers. If the worker
chooses to bring an action when he suffers from
asbestosis, but not yet from mesothelioma, will a
subsequent claim for mesothelioma be barred by the
doctrine of claim preclusion?

Res judicata generally allows a claimant only one
bite of the litigation apple. When a valid and final
judgment has been taken on a particular claim, res
judicata prevents a subsequent action on the same
claim, with the exception of an action on the judgment if the plaintiff was successful in the first
action. This is the general rule against claim-splitting. To determine what constitutes a claim, the
modern approach is a transactional one. Most
courts follow the rule in Section 24 of the Restatement (Second) of Judgments:

[T]he claim extinguished includes all rights of the
plaintiff to remedies against the defendant with
respect to all or any part of the transaction, or
series of connected transactions, out of which the
action arose.... [A claim is] to be determined

pragmatically, giving weight to such considerations as whether the facts are related in time,
space, origin, or motivation, whether they form a
convenient trial unit, and whether their treatment as a unit conforms to the parties' expectations or business understanding or usage.

Thus, the transactional analysis test encompasses
different evidence, theories, injuries, or remedies.

Although some exceptions to claim preclusion exist, the main issue with respect to toxic tort actions
such as the asbestos situation is identification of
the scope of the transaction, i.e. the scope of the
claim that is extinguished. To what degree should
claim-splitting be allowed? This issue is intimately
connected to the accrual question in statutes of limitations. Assuming the relevant jurisdiction has a
discovery statute, and forbids claim-splitting, a
plaintiff's entire claim (including illnesses related to
the exposure that develop at a later date) would
accrue at the time of discovery of the first injury.
Effectively, a plaintiff could be barred from bringing a claim before the plaintiff even knew of it. This
is similar to the dilemma faced by courts addressing
challenges to statutes of repose. Because of the
close connection between the claim preclusion issues and statutes of limitations, most of the case
law on this question has arisen within the context
of the statutes of limitations. While it is not directly
controlling on the claim preclusion issue, it is safe
to assume that courts prefer to read the accrual
rules and the claim preclusion rules compatibly.

The traditional res judicata approach—and a strict application of claim preclusion rules—would bar any accrued action arising out of the same circumstances as a claim previously adjudicated. *See* Gideon v. Johns–Manville Sales Corp., 761 F.2d 1129 (5th Cir.1985). An emerging trend, however, allows a plaintiff to split the claim under some circumstances.

In Wilson v. Johns–Manville Sales Corp., 684 F.2d 111 (D.C.Cir.1982), the court examined the rationales behind accrual rules, particularly the concern for disappearance of witnesses and evidence over the passage of time. The court said that latent disease cases demand "narrower delineation of the dimensions of a claim," resulting in a more limited bar. The court was closely attuned to the special concerns of toxic tort litigation: "Key issues to be litigated in a latent disease case are the existence of the disease, its proximate cause, and the resultant damage. Evidence relating to these issues tends to develop, rather than disappear, as time passes."

The *Wilson* court looked at another dimension of claim-splitting as well. Traditional rules of tort law allow a plaintiff to recover for all damages, past, present, and future, flowing from the actionable conduct of the defendant. The court noted that traditionally, future damages must be reasonably certain, however, to be recoverable. The difficulty toxic tort plaintiffs would have proving the reasonable certainty of a future illness influenced the court in preferring a rule allowing claim-splitting.

As the *Wilson* case demonstrated, these res judicata issues are also closely tied to the question of
whether courts should recognize present claims for
increased risk of contracting illness in the future.
There has been vigorous reaction to plaintiffs' attempts to bring such claims, with considerable concern for their speculative nature. The allowance of
such claims, if the court is amenable to them at all,
will be closely dependent upon the claim-splitting
rule and the accrual rules in the relevant jurisdiction. A discussion of increased risk claims appears
in Chapter Nine, Sec. B.

A different res judicata problem arose from the
Agent Orange litigation. The Agent Orange class
action was settled in 1984. The settlement established a fund to which class members could apply
for compensation for injuries for a period of ten
years. In Stephenson v. Dow Chemical Co., 273 F.3d
249 (2d Cir.2001), class members who became sick
years after the settlement fund expired brought suit
against the manufacturers of Agent Orange who
were parties to the class action. The defendants
asserted res judicata against the plaintiffs, arguing
that, as class members in the class action, they were
bound to the settlement and could not later bring
suit for their injuries. The Second Circuit held that
res judicata did not bind the plaintiffs. The court
noted that "[r]es judicata generally applies to bind
absent class members except where to do so would
violate due process." Adequate representation of all
class members is crucial to due process, and must

be measured throughout the litigation. The court held:

Because the prior litigation purported to settle all future claims, but only provided for recovery for those whose death or disability was discovered prior to 1994, the conflict between [the plaintiffs] and the class representatives becomes apparent. No provision was made for post-1994 claimants, and the settlement fund was permitted to terminate in 1994. [Thus, the plaintiffs] were not adequately represented in the prior Agent Orange litigation.

In 2003, the United States Supreme Court affirmed by an equally divided Court. Dow Chemical Co. v. Stephenson, 539 U.S. 111 (2003). Thus, the Second Circuit's decision stands, without clear guidance from the Supreme Court.

The Second Circuit's decision was consistent with both long-standing class action case law and the more recent *Amchem* and *Ortiz* decisions of the Supreme Court. In those cases, discussed in Chapter Ten, the Court repeatedly emphasized the likelihood of intra-class conflicts where the class comprised both injured persons and exposed persons who had not yet manifested injury.

Another high profile settlement has also had res judicata implications. In 1998, most states entered into an agreement with the major tobacco companies to resolve any pending or future claims for reimbursement of public expenditures for tobacco-related illness in the state population. Among other provisions, the agreement, known as the Master

Settlement Agreement (MSA), required the tobacco companies to pay $206 billion over a period of twenty-five years to reimburse the states. In return, the states agreed to waive claims for punitive damages. In Brown & Williamson Tobacco Corp. v. Gault, 627 S.E.2d 549 (Ga. 2006), the estate of a smoker who was a citizen of Georgia, one of the signatory states, brought an action against the tobacco company—also a signatory—for both compensatory and punitive damages. The Georgia Supreme Court held that the MSA's release of the defendant for punitive damages was binding on the individual smokers in the state and that the claim for punitive damages could not proceed. The court asserted that the state represented the interests of all citizens of the state in the MSA and that, accordingly, the individual citzens were bound to its provisions.

E.   PLAINTIFF'S CULPABLE CONDUCT

With the tort reform movement that brought comparative negligence, contributory negligence has become far less of a concern for plaintiffs, as generally a finding of contributory negligence will not absolutely bar a plaintiff's claim, but will reduce the plaintiff's overall recovery by the percentage of fault attributable to the plaintiff's conduct. Some states, however, retain some form of bar, but only if the plaintiff's culpable conduct reaches a certain level. *See, e.g.*, Minn. Stat. Ann. § 604.01 (West 2010) (providing that a plaintiff who is more at fault than the person against whom recovery is sought may not recover any damages).

Plaintiff's culpable conduct as a defense to product liability claims has been discussed in Chapter Two, Section E.5, *supra*. Some different issues arise with respect to nuisance claims when the plaintiff's culpable conduct is raised. To determine whether contributory negligence will be available as a defense in a nuisance action, it is necessary to look to the underlying conduct alleged—negligent, intentional, reckless, or abnormally dangerous. According to the Second Restatement, contributory negligence is not available as a defense in nuisance actions based upon intentional or reckless conduct. Restatement (Second) of Torts, § 840B(2) (1977). It may be a defense when negligent conduct is alleged, to the extent that it is available in any other negligence action within the jurisdiction. *Id*. § 840B(1). With respect to nuisance claims based upon strict liability, "contributory negligence is a defense only if the plaintiff has voluntarily and unreasonably subjected himself to the risk of harm." *Id*. § 840B(3). Assumption of the risk is a defense to nuisance claims where the defendant can show that the plaintiff had knowledge of the hazard, appreciated the magnitude of the hazard, and voluntarily encountered it. *Id*. § 840C.

The Restatement of Torts (Third): Apportionment of Liability (2000) has attempted to avoid such fragmented rules. Accordingly, the Restatement of Apportionment refers to "responsibility" of the parties, rather than fault, and in Section 8 sets out factors for determining apportionment in most types of cases.

CHAPTER EIGHT

CAUSATION

A. THE TOXIC CAUSATION PROBLEM

1. Introduction

Legal causation traditionally has included two components—cause-in-fact and proximate cause. Typically, the cause-in-fact requirement is viewed as the easier of the two to satisfy because it requires merely the identification of the series of factual events leading up to an injury. Proximate cause, in contrast, is based in policy, rather than fact. The policy basis of causation directs the court to identify which factual events will be recognized as legal causes of the injury. Toxic torts challenge traditional causation analysis on all fronts.

The most troublesome reality in toxic tort actions is that the plaintiff usually cannot draw a direct factual connection between the defendant's activity or product and the injury alleged. Latent disease, which characterizes toxic injury, is vastly different from traumatic or acute injury that is typical of the traditional tort claim, such as a motor vehicle accident. Consider the example presented by Allen v. United States, 588 F.Supp. 247 (D.Utah 1984), in which the court was confronted with claims of leukemia and other illnesses alleged to have been caused by exposure to radiation during the atomic testing program conducted by the United States Government. The court distinguished the toxic causation presented in the action from standard tort causation:

> In most cases, the factual connection between defendant's conduct and plaintiff's injury is not genuinely in dispute. Often, the cause-and-effect relationship is obvious: A's vehicle strikes B, injuring him; a bottle of A's product explodes, injuring B; water impounded on A's property flows onto B's land, causing immediate damage.

> In this case, the factual connection singling out the defendant as the source of the plaintiffs' injuries and deaths is very much in genuine dispute. Determination of the cause-in-fact, or factual connection, issue is complicated by the nature of the injuries suffered ..., the nature of the causation mechanism ..., the extraordinary time factors and other variables....

One complicating factor in *Allen* was the latency period between the time of the exposures and the manifestation of the illnesses. Because the connection between the exposure and the illness was not immediately apparent, questions arose as to the possibility of intervening events—instead of the initial exposure alleged—that may have caused or contributed to the injury.

A second complicating factor in *Allen* was that the cancers alleged were of a "non-specific nature," appearing not just in the population of persons exposed to radiation during the testing program, but also in the general population in what is referred to as background levels. No clinical distinction could be drawn between the cancers in the plaintiffs and the cancers in the general population. Moreover, although exposure to radiation was known to be associated with the illnesses alleged by the plaintiffs, other exposures and sources were also known to be associated with those illnesses. Therefore, there was no certainty as to which exposure actually did cause the injury.

A related problem is the inability of the scientific community to determine the precise cause of many illnesses. Scientific research has not reached conclusive and comprehensive results on carcinogenesis, mutagenesis, or teratogenesis in humans. Additionally, hard clinical evidence of the causal connection, from the plaintiff's treating physician or other medical specialists, often is lacking. This reality impedes the plaintiff in proving the necessary causal elements of the claim. The relationship between the scientific study of the causes of illness and the legal proof of causation has generated close analysis of the standard for admissibility of scientific evidence, discussed in Section B, *infra*.

2. General Causation and Specific Causation

Every causation analysis, implicitly if not explicitly, makes a determination of both general causation and specific causation. General causation (sometimes referred to in the case law as "generic causation") refers to the determination that the particular exposure was *capable* of causing the kind of injury that the plaintiff has alleged under the circumstances alleged. The next step is specific causation, which demonstrates that the exposure *actually* (or factually) caused the injury in the plaintiff. *See generally* Sterling v. Velsicol Chemical Corp., 855 F.2d 1188 (6th Cir.1988) (bifurcating the trial of causation issues between general causation, to be decided for the entire group of plaintiffs, and specific causation, to be decided later on an individual basis). This dual analysis is usually compressed in the traditional tort action. Thus, for example, a blow on the head such as the one suffered by a plaintiff who struck the windshield during a motor vehicle accident, was *capable* of causing a concussion such as the one suffered by the plaintiff. That the motor vehicle accident *actually* caused the plaintiff's concussion is substantiated by the logical progression of events and supporting evidence, showing that the plaintiff's head hit the windshield with a certain physical force and that symptoms consistent with a concussion were manifested immediately thereafter.

The analysis is attenuated and bifurcated in the toxic tort action. Still, some kinds of cases are easier than others. Asbestos exposure provides an example of this easier kind of toxic causation analysis. Scientific studies have shown that exposure to asbestos fibers is capable of causing a degenerative disease of the lungs called asbestosis. Following a latency period of years or decades, the disease eventually manifests itself in objective symptoms. How can the injured person show that the exposure so many years earlier actually caused this particular occurrence of the disease? Asbestosis is considered a "signature disease" of exposure to asbestos fibers because clinical tests can show with some measure of certainty that asbestos exposure was the causal trigger for the illness. Thus, the precise diagnosis of asbestosis in the plaintiff provides the necessary proof of specific causation. The asbestos plaintiff has an easier task than plaintiffs with other kinds of illnesses because of the existence of the diagnosable "signature disease."

Most illnesses alleged to be caused by toxic exposures cannot be shown to be so closely related to a particular level of exposure as in the "signature disease" situation, however. Returning to the claims in *Allen*, cancers that are indistinguishable from background cancers in the general population make a showing of specific causation virtually impossible. At best, the plaintiff would be able to show that the exposure was capable of producing the illness—in other words, general causation. Many courts have applied the causation requirements strictly, dismissing claims for which the plaintiffs have presented evidence of general causation, but no evidence of specific causation. *See, e.g.,* Cagle v. Cooper Cos., 318 F.Supp.2d 879 (C.D.Cal.2004) (dismissing claims based upon polyurethane foam-coated breast implants).

As a general rule, the standard for proving causation in civil actions is a preponderance of the evidence. The inability to show specific causation may be an insurmountable obstacle for toxic tort plaintiffs in proving their claims. The viability of the claims may be dependent upon the degree to which the court is willing to entertain evidence based upon the probability, rather than the legal certainty, that the defendant's activities or product caused the plaintiff's injury.

3. Frequency, Regularity, and Proximity

Further complicating the causation picture is the difficulty that many plaintiffs have in identifying a particular defendant as the source of their individual injuries. *See, e.g.*, Adams v. I–Flow Corp., 2010 WL 1339948 (C.D. Cal. 2010) (dismissing the plaintiffs' drug and medical device claims for failure to identify a defendant whose product caused the plaintiffs' injuries). Earlier in this book, in Chapter Six, Section E, the indeterminate defendant situation was discussed. That problem typically arises when the plaintiff cannot identify the specific defendant that caused the injuries alleged, but would like to hold collectively liable a group of similarly situated commercial defendants for reasons of public policy. In another common scenario, plaintiffs claim injuries arising from sequential and cumulative exposures, but cannot identify which defendant's product or activities actually triggered the injury. Courts were faced with this issue as early as the *Borel* case, and it is especially common in asbestos litigation.

In Borel v. Fibreboard Paper Products Corp., 493 F.2d 1076 (5th Cir.1973), a major causation issue was whether the plaintiff could prove that each defendant asbestos insulation manufacturer was the cause-in-fact of the plaintiff's injuries. On its way to answering this question, the court drew the significant conclusion that "the disease of asbestosis is cumulative." Although the court acknowledged that it was technically impossible for the plaintiff "to determine with absolute certainty which particular exposure to asbestos dust resulted in injury" to him, the cumulative effect of asbestos allowed the jury to find that "each defendant was the cause in fact of some injury to Borel." Of course, this ruling presupposes that the plaintiff had sufficient evidence to prove that he was exposed to the products of each of the defendants at some point in time.

This exposure theory was developed into a test that has come to be known as the "frequency, regularity, and proximity" test. Many jurisdictions have accepted this test in the context of asbestos litigation. The court in Lohrmann v. Pittsburgh Corning Corp., 782 F.2d 1156 (4th Cir.1986) stated the test as follows: "To support a reasonable inference of substantial causation from circumstantial evidence, there must be evidence of exposure to a specific product on a regular basis over some extended period of time in proximity to where the plaintiff actually worked." This test consistently fits the circumstances of asbestos-exposure litigation in the workplace. *But see* Horton v. Harwick Chemical, 653 N.E.2d 1196 (Ohio 1995) (rejecting frequency-proximity test for causation in asbestos litigation and requiring the plaintiff to prove that the defendant's product was a substantial factor in producing injury). Many jurisdictions have applied this test, especially in asbestos litigation. *See, e.g.*, Gregg v. V–J Auto Parts Co., 943 A.2d 216 (Pa. 2007) (applying the test to claims brought by a plaintiff who had been exposed to asbestos-containing brake parts purchased for his personal automotive use); Gorman–Rupp Co. v. Hall, 908 So.2d 749 (Miss. 2005) (applying the test, but holding that the plaintiffs' evidence was insufficient).

In some jurisdictions, even sufficient proof of frequency, regularity, and proximity may not be enough. In Borg–Warner Corp. v. Flores, 232 S.W.3d 765 (Tex. 2007), the plaintiff had been an auto mechanic who was exposed to "some asbestos" fibers in the course of working on motor vehicle brakes. The Texas Supreme Court stated that the Texas rules of causation had a quantitative component that was missing in the plaintiff's evidence. Although the evidence demonstrated frequency, regularity, and proximity of exposure to the defendant's product, the plaintiff was still required to present "[d]efendant-specific evidence relating to the approximate dose to which the plaintiff was exposed, coupled with evidence that the dose was a substantial factor in causing" the plaintiff's illness. *See also* Adams v. Cooper Indus. Inc., 2007 WL 2219212 (E.D. Ky. 2007) (discussing the importance of presenting evidence of the amount of the toxic substance to which the plaintiff was exposed, but stating that the plaintiff need not determine the exact dose).

Some question has arisen, however, with respect to the application of the "frequency, regularity, and proximity test" to litigation outside the asbestos context. The New Jersey Supreme Court, in James v. Bessemer Processing Company, 714 A.2d 898 (N.J.1998), held that the test applied in a workplace chemical-exposure case. The plaintiff's decedent had worked for the company for twenty-six years during which time he was involved in every aspect of the reconditioning process by which drums used in the petroleum and chemical industries were cleaned and prepared for reuse. James's widow sued the various companies that sent barrels to Bessemer for refurbishing on theories of product liability. The case was made difficult by the fact that Bessemer had destroyed its records that would have shown which defendants had delivered which products to Bessemer and in what quantities. This fact made it impossible for the plaintiff to identify the specific products to which James had been exposed. But lay witnesses were available to provide testimony regarding the types of exposures to which James had been subjected and the frequency, regularity, and proximity of the exposures.

The *James* court announced a sweeping test for causation in occupational toxic tort cases. The court stated: "A plaintiff in an occupational-exposure, toxic-tort case may demonstrate medical causation by establishing: (1) factual proof of the plaintiff's frequent, regular and proximate exposure to a defendant's products; and (2) medical and/or scientific proof of a nexus between the exposure and the plaintiff's condition." Furthermore, in the absence of Bessemer's records, the court held that the jury could rely upon the lay and expert testimony to establish the plaintiff's exposures.

In Green v. Alpharma, Inc., 284 S.W.3d 29 (Ark. 2008), the Arkansas Supreme Court held that the frequency, regularity, and proximity test applied to exposure to any toxic product. The case involved a child's alleged exposure to arsenic-containing chicken excrement, which had been spread as fertilizer over fields in the child's neighborhood. In extending the test beyond asbestos, the court cited *James*.

4. Probabilistic Evidence

The goal of most toxic tort plaintiffs, therefore, is to prove that the *probability* that the exposure caused the injury was sufficiently high to compensate for the lack of cause-in-fact. Probabilistic evidence such as statistical studies and published medical data is the most common form of evidence that toxic tort plaintiffs seek to introduce in support of their causation cases. This contrasts with the heavy reliance in traditional tort actions on direct medical evidence of the plaintiff's condition. Although courts have been amenable to circumstantial evidence of all sorts in traditional tort actions, probabilistic evidence has been viewed with disfavor and even disdain. *See* Troyen Brennan, *Causal Chains and Statistical Links: The Role of Scientific Uncertainty in Hazardous–Substance Litigation*, 73 Cornell L. Rev. 469 (1988).

An example of this judicial attitude may be seen in the Agent Orange litigation. *See* In re "Agent Orange" Prod. Liab. Litig., 597 F.Supp. 740 (E.D.N.Y.1984) (fairness opinion approving settlement of class action). Judge Weinstein noted that traditional notions of causation hold that "statistical correlations alone indicating that the probability of causation exceeds fifty percent are insufficient; some 'particularistic' or anecdotal evidence ... is required." The Agent Orange plaintiffs' inability to provide the particularistic evidence led the court to conclude that "[t]he probability of specific cause would necessarily be less than 50% based upon the evidence submitted." The court's assessment of the plaintiffs' poor likelihood of success in proving causation was one factor in the court's conclusion that the settlement was fair.

Another example of judicial resistance to probabilistic evidence is reflected in the generally negative reaction to the concept of market share liability. *See, e.g.*, Sindell v. Abbott Laboratories, 607 P.2d 924 (Cal.1980) (allowing the plaintiff to join a substantial share of the relevant market and, where a valid claim is proved, to recover from each defendant a proportionate share of the judgment reflecting the particular defendant's share of the market). Even when limited exclusively to the unique circumstances of DES, courts generally have refused to apply some form of collective liability where the plaintiff is unable to identify the specific defendant or defendants who manufactured the product that caused the injury. *See generally* Chapter Six, Section E, *supra*. Market share liability is grounded on statistical percentage shares in the DES market; at least theoretically, the share reflects the probability that the defendant actually manufactured the DES ingested by the plaintiff's mother. What critics dislike so much about market share liability, and about all uses of probabilistic evidence, is the possibility that the defendant who is held to be liable for the plaintiff's injury may not, in fact, have caused the injury or even conducted itself negligently.

5. Legal Certainty Versus Scientific Certainty

Courts and juries are accustomed to applying the preponderance of the evidence standard to causation in civil actions. Scientific evidence complicates this endeavor because scientific certainty and legal certainty are not identical. To the contrary, they are two entirely distinct concepts. Scientists will refrain from pronouncing a causal connection between an exposure and a disease unless the probability of causation is upwards of ninety-five percent. The legal standard of proof is set at fifty-one percent. The real problem is not in the difference between these two numbers, however. Rather, the problem is in translating the scientific standard into a legal standard. There is not a direct correlation between scientific certainty and legal certainty. Thus, a single study concluding that an association exists between a chemical and an illness may not satisfy the legal standard, notwithstanding the significance of the results. Consequently, the legal system has been reluctant to allow a finding of causation in the absence of scientific consensus. The relationship between scientific and legal certainty has provoked much debate over the appropriate evidentiary standard for scientific evidence.

6. "Lone Pine" Orders

Recognizing the importance of causation to plaintiffs' cases, and also recognizing the difficulty plaintiffs will have in supplying the necessary proof, defendants' counsel have sought to require plaintiffs to provide their proof in the pretrial phase of the litigation. Defendants then can use the information supplied as the basis for a summary judgment motion seeking dismissal of the action. The orders requiring production of such proof are called "Lone Pine" orders, taking their name from Lore v. Lone Pine Corp., 1986 WL 637507 (N.J.Law Div.1986), in which the court ordered the plaintiffs to produce documentation of causation, including the facts of each of their exposures and reports of treating physicians and any other experts on the issue of causation. In the federal courts, authority for these orders has been read into Fed. R. Civ. P. 16, which grants courts broad authority to manage litigation at the pretrial stage. "Lone Pine" orders need not appear exactly as the one in the namesake case so long as they require some proof of causal connection. A dismissal sanction may be the result of failure to comply with the requirements of a "Lone Pine" order. *See* Adjemian v. American Smelting & Refining Co., 2002 WL 358829 (Tex.Ct.App.2002).

For an overview of the use of "Lone Pine" orders in toxic tort litigation, see Scott P. DeVries, Alexis MacDowall, & Yelitza V. Dunham, *Use of* Lone Pine *Orders in Cost Effective Management of Mass Tort and Class Actions*, 23 Tox. L. Rptr. 1003 (Nov. 6, 2008).

"Lone Pine" orders appeal to courts so that judicial resources will not be wasted on frivolous lawsuits. Plaintiffs complain that these orders serve the defendants' purposes of keeping the issues from the jury, thus divesting the plaintiffs of their right to a jury trial, and placing excessive emphasis on causation over culpability. *See generally* Allan Kanner, Environmental and Toxic Tort Trials § 8.03 (2004).

B. SCIENTIFIC EVIDENCE

One explanation for judicial resistance to probabilistic evidence may be the unconventional nature of the evidence itself. The scientific and statistical studies that typically accompany a toxic tort plaintiff's claims require specialized knowledge and expertise to interpret. The scientific questions raised by the litigation are often subject to several interpretations, and it is not uncommon to have experts reaching contradictory or inconsistent conclusions. Moreover, the validity of the scientific studies presents a significant evidentiary challenge for the courts. Nearly every toxic torts case involves a dispute over the admissibility of the scientific evidence, not only due to challenges to the type of evidence proffered, but also due to questions about the relationship of the evidence to the specific plaintiff. As judges become more aware of and conversant in the issues of scientific evidence, close scrutiny of the evidence will remain a staple of toxic tort litigation.

Sometimes the claims of toxic tort plaintiffs rest on novel scientific theories. Thus, scientific inquiry on the issues may be in its initial stages. The scientific community may not have reached a consensus on the degree of probability that the exposure may have caused the injury suffered by the plaintiff. Indeed, the emergence of early litigation on a particular subject often encourages—and parties sometimes initiate—study of the relationship between exposure to a substance and a particular disease. This inevitably means that early plaintiffs of this sort may be undercompensated. As the body of scientific evidence develops, a more direct causal connection may emerge, with eventual consensus among experts. Under this scenario, later plaintiffs would be adequately compensated. Of course, the possibility exists that no clear causal connection will ever be found. Most notably, this has turned out to be the case in mass litigation involving the relationship of the morning-sickness drug Bendectin to limb deformities in offspring, silicone gel breast implants to a variety of illnesses, and thimerosol in childhood vaccines to autism. This dilemma has sparked debate over the proper treatment of novel scientific theories in toxic tort actions. Such theories often rely heavily on probabilistic evidence.

Some critics have labeled some, if not all, novel scientific theories as "junk science" and have advocated a ban on all novel scientific evidence in the courtroom. *See generally* Peter W. Huber, Galileo's Revenge: Junk Science in the Courtroom (1991). The "junk science" commentators have argued for strict scrutiny of all scientific evidence with an emphasis on scientific consensus. The high visibility of the advocates of this view has generated strong responses from both supporters and critics. *Compare* Lee Loevinger, *Science and Legal Rules of Evidence: A Review of Galileo's Revenge: Junk Science in the Courtroom*, 32 Jurimetrics J. 487 (1992) (supporting the views of the "junk science" commentators) *with* Jeff L. Lewin, *Calabresi's Revenge? Junk Science in the Work of Peter Huber*, 21 Hofstra L. Rev. 183 (1992) (critiquing the level of scrutiny advocated by "junk science" commentators). The concern over "junk science" has had long legs. In a recent case in which the plaintiffs claimed that a vaccine containing thimerosol caused their child's autism, the Maryland Court of Appeals, affirming summary judgment for the defendant, stated that the state's "jurisprudence engages trial judges in a serious gate-keeping function, to differentiate serious science from 'junk science.'" Blackwell v. Wyeth, 971 A.2d 235 (Md. 2009). It is important to remember, however, that, in the words of one court, "[i]nconclusive science is not the same as junk science." In re Ephedra Prods. Liab. Litig., 393 F.Supp.2d 181 (S.D.N.Y 2005). Most courts would concur that any evidence that meets the reliability and relevance standards should be admissible, regardless of how novel it may be.

1. Procedural Approach

Courts may scrutinize scientific evidence at two distinct procedural stages of the litigation. The first stage is the admissibility stage. While the most common form of challenge to the admissibility of evidence is at trial, by objections made by counsel opposing the introduction of the evidence in question, in toxic tort actions a wholesale challenge to the admissibility of the plaintiff's causation evidence typically occurs in a motion in limine at the outset of the action.

The court's decision on the admissibility of the scientific evidence is not necessarily dispositive of the ultimate issues to which the evidence relates, however. Typically, the defendant brings a summary judgment motion seeking to have the action dismissed on the ground that no genuine issue of fact exists. This is the sufficiency stage. If the plaintiff's scientific evidence—which is usually the most probative evidence of causation—is ruled inadmissible, usually the case will be dismissed. Conceivably, evidence could survive the admissibility inquiry, but the action could be dismissed nonetheless because the plaintiff's causation evidence, although admissible, is insufficient as a matter of law. *See, e.g.,* Brock v. Merrell Dow Pharmaceuticals, Inc., 874 F.2d 307 (5th Cir.1989) (dismissing Bendectin action for insufficiency of evidence of causation); Cagle v. Cooper Cos., 318 F.Supp.2d 879

(C.D.Cal.2004) (holding general causation evidence admissible, but dismissing polyurethane foam-coated breast implant claims for insufficiency of specific causation evidence).

2. Epidemiological Studies

Because direct human experimentation is uncommon, except in the limited area of clinical drug trials, and is generally unacceptable for ethical reasons, plaintiffs have had to seek support for their causation claims in epidemiological studies. Epidemiology is a methodology that employs surveys and statistics to determine the probability of an association between a specified exposure and the occurrence of disease. It examines the frequency and distribution of diseases and studies the factors that may influence their occurrence. Epidemiology does not determine the occurrence of a disease in a specific person. Rather, it looks at groups of persons and draws inferences regarding the causes of illness in each of the groups. Thus, epidemiological studies are probabilistic evidence because they cannot, nor do they purport to, identify actual causes in individual cases. They determine the level of risk of developing a disease that affects the identified group. *See generally* Bert Black & David E. Lilienfeld, *Epidemiologic Proof in Toxic Tort Litigation*, 52 Fordham L. Rev. 732 (1984).

Epidemiological studies often begin with demographic surveys of segments of the population, looking for the rates of occurrence of certain diseases. Such basic studies may result in a figure that repre-

sents the "baseline" level, or essentially background level, of an illness in the general population.
Sometimes, an illness clusters within a certain geo-
graphic area (e.g. residents in the vicinity of a
hazardous waste site), occupation (e.g. mesothelioma among asbestos workers), or other activity (e.g.
smokers and lung cancer). This basic information
can provide the basis of further surveys and statistical studies. The mere demonstration of a cluster of
diseases, however, does not prove causation, absent
other reliable evidence.

Researchers undertake several different kinds of
epidemiological studies when seeking to discover
disease/exposure associations. The epidemiological
studies most commonly discussed in toxic tort litigation are the cohort study and the case-control study.

a. Cohort Studies

Cohort studies are prospective studies that follow
a group of individuals exposed to a particular substance over a period of time to determine whether
they contract a particular illness. The information
is then compared with information collected from a
non-exposed group. Statistical studies may then cal-
culate whether the exposed group has demonstrated
an increased risk of developing the illness over
members of the non-exposed group. If the relative
risk of developing the illness is greater in the exposed group than in the non-exposed group, the
information is examined to determine whether a
causal connection may exist. Epidemiologists do this
by calculating the "attributable risk" and then un-

dertaking a more subjective analysis of the biological plausibility of the proposed causal connection. These criteria are designed to verify the assumptions made in translating a statistical association into a biological inference of causation.

One example of a high-profile prospective epidemiological study was a study begun in 1951 to determine the effects of smoking on health. The study involved tens of thousands of British physicians, with the researchers using questionnaires to ascertain their smoking habits. The researchers then followed the participants for a period of years, examining causes of death to determine any differences in death rates between the group of smokers and the group of non-smokers. The death rates demonstrated "a significant and steadily rising mortality from deaths due to cancer of the lung as the amount of tobacco smoked increases." Richard Doll & A. Bradford Hill, *The Mortality of Doctors in Relation to Their Smoking Habits: A Preliminary Report*, 2 Brit. Med. J. 1451 (1954).

b.   Case–Control Studies

The case-control study is retrospective in nature, as it begins by identifying a group of persons who have contracted a certain illness ("case" group) and a group who has not contracted the illness ("control" group), then surveys the two groups to determine whether the members of the case group have any characteristics in common that may be associated with the disease. An example of such a study might look at persons with mesothelioma compared to persons without the illness. The study might reflect that a certain percentage of persons with mesothelioma worked in the asbestos industry for a period of time, while the control group contained a much smaller percentage of asbestos workers. Statistical analyses then make a determination of whether an association exists between the illness in the case group and any factors identified in the study.

Critics of case-control studies point out that they are susceptible to bias in the design, where a researcher begins with a certain predisposition toward finding a particular causal connection and designs the study around that. A further problem could be the recall bias of the participants in the study, as the study may seek information over a period of decades. Early retrospective studies examining the relationship between lung cancer and smoking were criticized for the choice of subjects, which were usually hospital patients, many of whom had underlying, non-smoking related medical conditions that may have caused or contributed to their deaths. Allan M. Brandt, The Cigarette Century 142 (2007).

Case-control studies are preferable to cohort studies when time is of the essence, however, as cohort studies could take years before any meaningful data are collected. On the other hand, the relative speed of case-control studies makes them likely to be commissioned specifically for litigation. Studies produced for litigation are often criticized for bias in the design because their goal is to achieve a certain result in the litigation.

c.   Other Drawbacks of Epidemiological Studies

In addition to problems of bias in the design of a study, epidemiological studies may yield questionable results for several reasons. First, the researcher must study a sufficiently large sample size to obtain significant statistically valid results. For results to be distinguishable from background levels, an appropriately sized sample must be used for subtle distinctions to be accurately assessed. Second, due to the long latency period associated with some diseases, a study may not follow the subjects for a sufficiently long time to accurately reveal the rate of disease in the group studied. Third, some diseases may be caused by a combination of factors or by alternative factors. Fourth, a correct analysis of the data may be masked by confounding factors. For example, cigarette smoking, in addition to the exposure under study, may be a confounding factor in studies of certain lung conditions. For a discussion of these and other issues presented by the use of epidemiological studies, see Jeffrey Dintzer & Jonathan Mosher, *Epidemiologic Evidence in Toxic Tort Cases*, 17 Natural Resources & Env't 222 (2003).

3.   Toxicological Studies

Toxicological studies are laboratory studies that may be conducted either in vivo (on animal tissue) or in vitro (on cultures in a laboratory container).

They have some clear advantages over epidemiological studies. The carefully controlled manner in which these tests are properly conducted allows researchers to obtain reasonably accurate information in all respects, including exposure (dose). Toxicological studies are more problematic than epidemiological studies, however, as any conclusions require extrapolation from the laboratory data to humans.

a. *Animal Studies*

Animal laboratory studies, which compare a dose group with a control group, have been widely criticized for the assumptions that researchers make in extrapolating to humans from the animal data. This task is referred to as species-to-species extrapolation. One such criticism is that human systems are sufficiently different from animal systems—metabolically and in other ways—to render any extrapolated data misleading. Another major criticism is that dose-response data—i.e. the manner in which the animals' system responds to exposure at different doses—does not accurately predict human responses at human doses. Further, the large doses of chemicals that researchers often use in animal studies to achieve results in a relatively speedy time frame, when translated into human doses may result in amounts far in excess of any exposure that humans could realistically anticipate. Researchers commonly extrapolate down from large doses to estimate the effect at lower doses. Critics find this kind of extrapolation very problematic, and there is much disagreement over the method of extrapolation for estimating carcinogenicity at low doses.

One illustration demonstrates several of these shortcomings. In General Electric Co. v. Joiner, 522 U.S. 136 (1997), the district court had ruled inadmissible certain animal studies introduced by the plaintiff to demonstrate that he had developed cancer from exposure to PCBs in the workplace. The Supreme Court held that the district court had not abused its discretion in excluding the evidence. The Court reasoned:

> The studies involved infant mice that had developed cancer after being exposed to PCBs. The infant mice in the studies had had massive doses of PCBs injected directly into their peritoneums or stomachs. Joiner was an adult human being whose alleged exposure to PCBs was far less than the exposure in the animal studies. The PCBs were injected into the mice in a highly concentrated form. The fluid with which Joiner had come into contact generally had a much smaller PCB concentration.... The cancer that these mice developed was alveologenic adenomas; Joiner had developed small-cell carcinomas. No study demonstrated that adult mice developed cancer after being exposed to PCBs. One of the experts admitted that no study had demonstrated that PCBs lead to cancer in any other species.

Judging by these standards, plaintiffs seeking admissibility of animal study data to prove that exposure to a substance caused their illness are not likely to achieve success unless the study data has a much closer connection to the plaintiff.

Notwithstanding these problems, animal studies have proven useful in suggesting a relationship between an exposure and illness in humans. Regulatory agencies often use animal studies in deciding whether a substance presents a health hazard to humans that should be regulated. Courts, on the other hand, have approached animal studies with reservation and prefer to see some corroborating epidemiological or clinical evidence in conjunction with the animal studies when offered for proof of causation in personal injury actions. *See* Longmore v. Merrell Dow Pharmaceuticals, Inc., 737 F.Supp. 1117 (D.Idaho 1990). *See generally* Jack L. Landau & W. Hugh O'Riordan, *Of Mice and Men: The Admissibility of Animal Studies to Prove Causation in Toxic Tort Litigation*, 25 Idaho L. Rev. 521 (1988–89).

b. Short–Term Tests

These tests are highly problematic, and their use in toxic tort litigation to prove causation has been so vehemently questioned as to effectively marginalize their utility in that context. Nevertheless, such studies may accompany and corroborate other types of scientific evidence introduced on the issue of causation. The best known short-term test, referred to as the Ames test, generally studies the mutagenic effect of a suspected toxic substance on bacteria cultured in a laboratory container. Because the bacteria reproduce rapidly, many generations may be examined during the course of the study. Although the test directly tests mutagenicity, scientists believe that a meaningful correlation exists between mutagenicity and carcinogenicity, so the test is also used to suggest a carcinogenic effect.

The short-term tests are subject to some of the same criticisms as animal studies, but to an even greater degree. The Ames test has been sharply criticized by its founder for certain conclusions regarding the relationship between chemicals and cancer that have been drawn from the test data. Moreover, the test has been known to yield a high percentage of false positives, perhaps skewing results. All of these problems combine to render the short-term test of negligible value in proving causation in toxic tort actions. These tests are better used to formulate an approach to other kinds of studies that will be more useful in toxic tort litigation and regulation.

c. *Biomonitoring Studies*

Biomonitoring studies have been around for a long time, but the public's interest in a systematic approach to biomonitoring and in determining its broader utility is relatively new. Biomonitoring studies measure levels of chemicals in the human body. Interpreting the studies, researchers attempt to estimate concentrations of chemicals that the human body could tolerate without harm. The Centers for Disease Control (CDC) have been conducting ongoing studies of this sort for approximately thirty years through the National Biomonitoring

Program (NBP). The NBP is retrospective in the sense that it measures levels of chemicals from exposures that have already occurred. But the information obtained from the studies is intended to form the basis of future policy and regulatory decisions. The program has several interrelated goals, among which are: (1) enabling public health groups and government regulators to prioritize risks for action through identifying high-risk populations and providing accurate exposure data and (2) evaluating existing prevention measures. *See* Dep't of Health & Human Services, Centers for Disease Control and Prevention, Fourth National Report on Human Exposure to Environmental Chemicals viii (2009); Ken Sexton, Larry L. Needham, & James L. Pirkle, *Human Biomonitoring of Environmental Chemicals*, 92 Amer. Scientist 38, 42 (2004).

States are also seeing the value of biomonitoring studies in developing data on environmental exposures and in setting priorities for their own public health programs. *See* Cal. Health & Safety Code § 105441 (2009) (establishing California Environmental Contaminant Biomonitoring Program, effective in 2007).

Biomonitoring studies may be particularly useful in setting parameters for regulation and in the development of public health measures. In the courtroom, however, they are open to the same criticisms as most other scientific studies, including the need to extrapolate from the studies of populations to individuals. On a more individual level, even if a chemical has been detected in a plaintiff's body, demonstrating that it caused the illness from which the plaintiff suffers is still difficult without indication of the ways in which the chemical acted and reacted in the plaintiff's body. These studies may have greater utility in forming a basis for medical monitoring claims, however. *See generally* Chapter Nine, *infra*.

d.   Genetic Studies

A rapidly evolving type of novel scientific methodology with great relevance to toxic causation is toxicogenomics. Scientists in this field work to identify physical changes in the human body at a much earlier time than previously available, thus shedding light on the biological changes in a person during the latency period before manifestation of symptoms. Scientists are also optimistic that these studies will provide information on the interaction between environmental exposures and genetic predisposition to illness. Accordingly, scientists may be able to discern the characteristics of illness that arise from exposures and differentiate them from the characteristics of the same illness caused by hereditary factors. Genetic evidence of this sort is still far from meeting evidentiary standards. But eventually these studies will challenge the judicial system in unprecedented ways. *See generally* G. Marc Whitehead, *The Use and Abuse of Genetic Testing: Toxicogenomics in the Courtroom*, 17 Toxics L. Rptr. 963 (Oct. 10, 2002) (discussing admissibility issues raised by the coming wave of genetic information).

C. ADMISSIBILITY OF SCIENTIFIC EVIDENCE IN THE COURTS

Evidentiary challenges to plaintiffs' causation evidence are standard in toxic tort actions. This can be the most significant aspect of the lawsuit because exclusion of even some of the plaintiff's expert testimony on causation can be fatal to the case. The admissibility issues relate to the evidence of both plaintiffs and defendants. As a practical matter, because plaintiffs bear the burden of proof, admissibility is a more dispositive issue for plaintiffs than for defendants.

1. Traditional Admissibility Standard

Prior to the United States Supreme Court's decision in Daubert v. Merrell Dow Pharmaceuticals, Inc., 509 U.S. 579 (1993), the standard for admissibility of scientific evidence in the federal courts was established in Frye v. United States, 293 F. 1013 (App.D.C.1923). *Frye* served as the standard for state rulings on the admissibility of scientific evidence as well. *Frye* pre-dated the Federal Rules of Evidence by half a century. But even after the promulgation of the Federal Rules, the influence of the *Frye* doctrine continued to dominate the federal cases. Today, many states still adhere to the *Frye* doctrine and have not changed their admissibility rules to reflect the impact of *Daubert*.

a. The Frye Doctrine

Frye v. United States, 293 F. 1013 (App.D.C. 1923) was a criminal case involving the admissibility of blood pressure deception measurements to prove the defendant's guilt. The court stated: "[W]hile courts will go a long way in admitting expert testimony deduced from a well-recognized scientific principle or discovery, the thing from which the deduction is made must be sufficiently established to have gained general acceptance in the particular field in which it belongs." This test apparently was intended to exclude all novel or developing scientific theories. Following the promulgation of the Federal Rules of Evidence in 1975, courts reached different conclusions as to whether the *Frye* requirement of "general acceptance" survived or whether it was supplanted by the relevant Federal Rules. Because the Federal Rules were silent on the *Frye* issue, courts were left to speculate on the impact of the Rules on the *Frye* doctrine. Currently, a significant minority of states—including New York, California and Illinois—continues to adhere to a version of the *Frye* doctrine. *See, e.g.,* Goeb v. Tharaldson, 615 N.W.2d 800 (Minn.2000) (stating that *Frye* "ensures that the persons most qualified to assess scientific validity of a technique have the determinative voice").

Thus, in Blackwell v. Wyeth, 971 A.2d 235 (Md. 2009), the Maryland Court of Appeals employed the *Frye* rule to exclude novel evidence sought to be introduced by the plaintiffs to prove that thimerosol in a vaccine had caused their child's autism. The court noted that under *Frye*, "seminal scientific technologies may be rejected, because the 'Frye standard retards somewhat the admission of proof based on new methods of scientific investigation by requiring that they attain sufficient currency and status to gain the general acceptance of the relevant scientific community . . . .' " (quoting Reed v. State, 391 A.2d 364, 370 (Md. 1978)).

b. *Federal Rules of Evidence*

Several provisions in the Federal Rules of Evidence are applicable to a federal court's decision whether to admit scientific evidence as proof of causation. State evidentiary rules have analogous, if not always identical, provisions.

Rule 402 of the Federal Rules makes all relevant evidence admissible. It is limited by Rule 403, which provides that relevant evidence "may be excluded if its probative value is substantially outweighed by the danger of unfair prejudice, confusion of the issues, or misleading the jury, or by considerations of undue delay, waste of time, or needless presentation of cumulative evidence." Defendants argue that some kinds of scientific evidence are too speculative and have the effect of confusing the jury, who might grant such evidence the same weight as more definitive evidence, either because the expert makes a highly credible and persuasive presentation or because the distinctions between various pieces of evidence are too complex and technical to be fully understood by laypersons.

Two federal rules directly address expert testimony. Rule 702, as amended in 2000, provides:

If scientific, technical, or other specialized knowledge will assist the trier of fact to understand the evidence or to determine a fact in issue, a witness qualified as an expert by knowledge, skill, experience, training, or education, may testify thereto in the form of an opinion or otherwise, if (1) the testimony is based upon sufficient facts or data, (2) the testimony is the product of reliable principles and methods, and (3) the witness has applied the principles and methods reliably to the facts of the case.

Rule 703 addresses the basis of the expert's opinion:

The facts or data in the particular case upon which an expert bases an opinion or inference may be those perceived by or made known to the expert at or before the hearing. If of a type reasonably relied upon by experts in the particular field in forming opinions or inferences upon the subject, the facts or data need not be admissible in evidence in order for the opinion or inference to be admitted.

Of course, the party offering the expert testimony must qualify the person as an expert qualified to give the opinion. Rule 703 makes clear that a testifying medical expert need not actually have examined the plaintiff, as experts may base their opinions on information (e.g. clinical test results, reports of examinations, studies conducted by others) reviewed by them. Moreover, it is irrelevant that the underlying information may be inadmissible hearsay, provided that it is "of a type reasonably relied upon by experts in the particular field.''

2. The Rule of *Daubert v. Merrell Dow Pharmaceuticals, Inc.*

Until the 2000 amendments, the Federal Rules of Evidence remained silent on whether the general acceptance rule of *Frye* was intended to be incorporated into them. Courts reached widely diverging opinions on the role of general acceptance under the Federal Rules. *Compare* Christophersen v. Allied–Signal Corp., 939 F.2d 1106 (5th Cir.1991) (incorporating *Frye* into broad Federal Rule analysis); United States v. Smith, 869 F.2d 348 (7th Cir.1989) (adopting *Frye* doctrine virtually unchanged) *with* United States v. Downing, 753 F.2d 1224 (3d Cir. 1985) (rejecting a pure *Frye* standard and developing its own reliability inquiry that included general acceptance as one element); Ferebee v. Chevron Chemical Co., 736 F.2d 1529 (D.C.Cir.1984) (rejecting *Frye* in a case involving a novel scientific theory). In the toxic tort case of Daubert v. Merrell Dow Pharmaceuticals, Inc., 509 U.S. 579 (1993), the United States Supreme Court clarified the role of *Frye* and established a new standard for expert evidence under the Federal Rules, thus prompting the amendments of 2000.

a. *The Bendectin Litigation*

Daubert involved product liability claims related to the drug Bendectin, which was prescribed to alleviate the symptoms of ''morning sickness'' during pregnancy. Plaintiffs brought actions against the manufacturer of the drug for damages for limb deformities in children allegedly caused by first trimester, in utero exposure to Bendectin. More than thirty epidemiological studies had been conducted on the effects of Bendectin, but no study had found the drug to be teratogenic in humans. In most cases, the defendant's experts convincingly showed that maternal use of Bendectin during the first trimester of pregnancy had not been shown to be a risk factor for the deformities alleged. Consequently, Bendectin plaintiffs began to employ less traditional scientific evidence to support their cases.

The Bendectin plaintiffs relied upon a variety of studies. First, they proffered both in vivo and in vitro laboratory studies that showed a connection between Bendectin and certain defects. They also employed pharmacological studies that analyzed the chemical structure of Bendectin and identified similarities between it and other substances known to cause birth defects. The most controversial evidence proffered by the plaintiffs was a reanalysis of the published epidemiological studies on Bendectin. The reanalysis recalculated data from the earlier studies that had found no connection between Bendectin and birth defects. Upon reanalysis, the plaintiffs' experts were of the opinion that a causal connection did in fact exist. The reanalysis had not been published or otherwise offered for peer review. Among the cases in which plaintiffs had relied upon this same evidence were Brock v. Merrell Dow Pharmaceuticals, Inc., 874 F.2d 307 (5th Cir.1989) (holding that the evidence was insufficient as a matter of law) and Richardson v. Richardson–Merrell, Inc., 857 F.2d 823 (D.C.Cir.1988). Historically, defendants have been overwhelmingly successful in the Bendectin cases, often on summary judgment motions. *See generally* Joseph Sanders, *The Bendectin Litigation: A Study in the Life Cycle of Mass Torts*, 43 Hastings L.J. 301 (1992). Yet, in many cases that actually went to trial, the juries found for the plaintiffs. *See generally* Joseph Sanders, *From Science to Evidence: The Testimony on Causation in the Bendectin Cases*, 46 Stan. L. Rev. 1 (1993).

b. *Daubert v. Merrell Dow Pharmaceuticals, Inc.*

The Supreme Court's decision in Daubert v. Merrell Dow Pharmaceuticals, Inc., 509 U.S. 579 (1993) settled the dispute among the federal courts over the applicability of *Frye* to the Federal Rules. In a unanimous opinion on this point, Justice Blackmun wrote that the general acceptance test of *Frye* was replaced by the Federal Rules of Evidence. The Court stated that "under the Rules, the trial judge must ensure that any and all scientific testimony or evidence admitted is not only relevant, but reliable." The reliability analysis derives from Rule 702 in conjunction with several other Rules, including Rules 403, 703, and 706.

The Court interpreted Rule 702 to require "a valid scientific connection to the pertinent inquiry as a precondition to admissibility." The Court was especially concerned about the relationship between science and the law:

The adjective "scientific" implies a grounding in the methods and procedures of science. Similarly,

the word "knowledge" connotes more than subjective belief or unsupported speculation.... Proposed testimony must be supported by appropriate validation.... In short, the requirement that
an expert's testimony pertain to "scientific
knowledge" establishes a standard of evidentiary
reliability.

The Court acknowledged that "arguably, there are
no certainties in science," because scientific knowledge is constantly evolving. But certainty is required in the law—at least, a measure of certainty
at the time a decision is rendered in a particular
lawsuit. Thus, the Court acknowledged the difficulty presented by novel scientific evidence: the scientific knowledge is in an initial or developing stage,
but the law requires a decision.

The *Daubert* Court vacated the decision of the
appellate court and remanded the case for further
proceedings. Initially, the Court stated that pursuant to Federal Rule 104(a), trial courts are expected
to undertake a preliminary inquiry on admissibility,
most commonly by a hearing on a motion in limine,
to determine whether the proposed expert testimony constitutes *scientific knowledge* and whether
that knowledge will assist the factfinder in determining a fact in issue. Thus, the "fit" between the
expert's opinion and the precise issue to be decided
in the case is crucial.

The Court then offered several "general observations," which essentially amount to a multi-factored

test. These observations ask trial courts to consider: (1) whether the scientific technique or theory has been tested; (2) whether the study has been published or has undergone some other form of peer review; (3) the rate of error associated with the scientific technique used; and (4) whether the theory is generally accepted in the relevant scientific community. The Court was careful to note that no single factor is necessarily determinative of admissibility. Thus, if the theory does not have general acceptance in the relevant community, testimony based on the theory may still be admissible if other indicia of reliability are present. The Court also emphasized that the trial court's inquiry must focus only on the "principles and methodology" of the scientific evidence. The trial court may not subject the conclusion of the expert to the analysis.

The *Daubert* Court also expressed confidence in the ability of the traditional mechanisms of the jury system, such as cross-examination, to assure that appropriate evaluations of scientific evidence are made. This faith in the jury system was consistent with an apparent rejection by the Court of the position of the "junk science" commentators. *See generally* Jean Macchiaroli Eggen, *Toxic Torts, Causation, and Scientific Evidence After Daubert*, 55 Pitt.L.Rev. 889 (1994) (discussing in detail the *Daubert* opinion in the context of toxic torts).

c. *Refinement of the Daubert Doctrine*

The United States Supreme Court has revisited the *Daubert* test in two major cases. The first of these cases was General Electric Co. v. Joiner, 522 U.S. 136 (1997), which resolved the question of the appropriate standard that federal appellate courts should use in reviewing the evidentiary determinations of trial judges. *Joiner* was another toxic tort case, involving a personal injury claim for lung cancer resulting from workplace exposures to PCBs. The district court granted summary judgment for the defendants partially on the ground that the expert testimony submitted by the plaintiff did not show a nexus between his exposure to PCBs and the particular kind of cancer from which he suffered. The Eleventh Circuit reversed, and the case, on certiorari to the Supreme Court, raised the issue whether *Daubert* had intended to change the traditional use of the abuse of discretion standard to review such evidentiary rulings. The Supreme Court unanimously held that the abuse of discretion standard continued to be the proper standard of review.

The nonunanimous portion of the *Joiner* opinion added fuel to the admissibility fire. Applying the abuse of discretion standard in this case, the Court upheld the exclusion of the testimony. In reaching this conclusion, the Court disagreed with the Eleventh Circuit's view that the district court should have limited its examination to the reliability of the methodology. The Supreme Court stated that "conclusions and methodology are not entirely separate from one another." This statement appears to contradict an important aspect of *Daubert*—that the trial court should scrutinize the *methodology* to determine scientific validity and evidentiary reliability. Thus, *Joiner* may signal a turn away from the strict language of *Daubert* and a return to the questionable practice of judicial scrutiny of experts' conclusions. Finally, the Court said that scientific evidence should not be admitted solely on the basis of the ipse dixit—essentially, the say-so—of the expert. Sometimes, the Court stated, the "analytical gap" between the underlying data and the expert's conclusion is simply too great.

The second significant Supreme Court decision construing *Daubert* was Kumho Tire Co. v. Carmichael, 526 U.S. 137 (1999). The evidentiary issue raised in the case was whether the *Daubert* test of reliability must be applied to expert testimony that is not considered "scientific." The evidence involved in *Kumho Tire* was testimony by the plaintiffs' engineering expert as to whether an automobile tire had been defective, thereby causing the accident that gave rise to the lawsuit. The Court unanimously held that the trial court's gatekeeping role, pursuant to *Daubert*, applies not just to scientific testimony, but to all expert testimony. The Court observed that Rule 702 does not distinguish between "scientific" knowledge and "technical" or "other specialized" knowledge. Characterizing the plaintiffs' engineer's testimony as "technical," rather the "scientific," the Court held that a *Daubert* analysis should be applied to the evidence, as it should also be applied to any evidence that falls within the scope of Rule 702.

The *Kumho Tire* decision has raised questions about the applicability of the factors listed in *Daubert*, which were uniquely suited to scientific studies. In *Kumho Tire*, the Court stated that the factors listed in *Daubert* were not intended to constitute a definitive checklist for determining reliability. Rather, the *Daubert* analysis was intended to be flexible and keyed into the facts of the particular case in question. With respect to the engineering testimony in *Kumho Tire*, the Court held that the trial court had not abused its discretion in excluding it. Although the trial court had not objected to the expert's methodology generally, the court had excluded the testimony because the methodology could not establish tire failure in this particular case. With the flexibility noted by the Court comes a heavy burden on trial courts to step into the shoes of scientists to determine not just whether the evidence is reliable, but also which factors should be used in making that reliability determination. That task may render trial judges not just gatekeepers, but creators of the password as well.

d. Impact of Daubert

Daubert could be interpreted to represent a more liberal approach to the admissibility of scientific evidence than the *Frye* doctrine. While this appears true from the language of the opinion, *Daubert* has not had the effect of opening the courtroom doors wide to dubious scientific evidence, as some had feared. With respect to Bendectin cases, *Daubert* made no difference at all. See, e.g., DeLuca v. Merrell Dow Pharmaceuticals, Inc., 6 F.3d 778 (3d Cir.1993) (affirming, in light of *Daubert* decision, district court's holding that plaintiff's scientific evidence was inadmissible). Arguably, the decision has made little, if any, difference in the determination of the admissibility of scientific evidence in other kinds of cases as well. In fact, a study by the RAND Institute for Civil Justice, released in 2002, concluded that post-*Daubert*, courts applying the rule of *Daubert* have found more evidence to be unreliable and have excluded more evidence. Lloyd Dixon & Brian Gill, Changes in the Standards for Admitting Expert Evidence in Federal Civil Cases Since the Daubert Decision (RAND Institute 2002).

Perhaps the most visible change effected by the *Daubert* decision was the 2000 amendment to Rule 702 of the Federal Rules of Evidence. Rule 702 now contains language reflecting *Daubert*'s emphasis on reliability and relevance of the facts, data, and methods. While Rule 702 stops short of codifying the *Daubert* factors, the Committee Note states that "[t]he standards set forth in the amendment are broad enough to require consideration of any or all of the specific Daubert factors where appropriate." The Committee Note also listed five additional factors to be considered.

While *Daubert* applies explicitly to the federal courts, many states have adopted the *Daubert* doctrine as well. In 2010, the Iowa Supreme Court reaffirmed its commitment to the rule of *Daubert* in the context of a toxic tort case. In Ranes v. Adams

Labs., Inc., 778 N.W.2d 677 (Iowa 2010), the plaintiff claimed brain injury following ingestion of a prescription cough and cold remedy containing phenylpropanolamine (PPA). Applying the *Daubert* test, the court excluded as unreliable critical portions of the plaintiff's evidence. *See also, e.g.*, McDaniel v. CSX Transportation Inc., 955 S.W.2d 257 (Tenn.1997) (developing a doctrine similar to *Daubert* for state trials where the state had previously adopted Federal Rules of Evidence for state courts); E.I. duPont de Nemours & Co. v. Robinson, 923 S.W.2d 549 (Tex.1995) (applying *Daubert* in state court where the Federal Rules of Evidence have been adopted for state trials). Other states have rejected *Daubert* and cling to the general acceptance test of *Frye*. *See, e.g.,* Slay v. Keller Industries, Inc., 823 So.2d 623 (Ala.2001); Ramirez v. Florida, 651 So.2d 1164 (Fla.1995); Goeb v. Tharaldson, 615 N.W.2d 800 (Minn.2000).

Another result of *Daubert* has been the creation of resources for trial judges to assist in the evaluation of the admissibility of scientific evidence. Chief among these resources is the Federal Judicial Center's Reference Manual on Scientific Evidence (2d ed. 2000), which provides both procedural and substantive information about analyzing scientific methodologies. Reviewing courts have also relied on the Manual in determining whether a lower-court decision on admitting scientific evidence should be upheld. For example, in Wintz v. Northrop Corp., 110 F.3d 508 (7th Cir.1997), the court, in determining whether the district court had properly excluded the expert testimony of a toxicologist, explicitly relied on the Manual's recommendations. In particular, the Manual stated that a toxicologist should be able to present specific testimony of the relationship of the plaintiff's exposure to the development of the disease alleged—in this case, in utero exposure to bromide used by the infant's mother in her workplace, alleged to have caused a genetic disorder. Because the toxicologist had not offered specific evidence of the mother's exposure, the Seventh Circuit held that the trial court had properly excluded the evidence. Resources like the Manual create a much more scientifically sophisticated judiciary than in the early years of toxic tort litigation, and raise the bar for plaintiffs to present scientifically sound evidence.

e. *Novel Scientific Evidence*

In *Daubert*, the Court treated novel theories in the same manner as more established theories, applying the same factors. Novel scientific methodologies are likely not to have been peer reviewed or to have earned general acceptance. Thus, they are likely to face exclusion under *Daubert*. One message that *Daubert* sends to litigants is that theories that are too speculative or unfounded in scientific methodology will not be tolerated, including those relying on novel methodologies. *See, e.g.*, O'Conner v. Commonwealth Edison Co., 13 F.3d 1090 (7th Cir. 1994) (excluding evidence of radiation as the cause of the plaintiff's cataracts because it was merely subjective opinion); Chikovsky v. Ortho Pharmaceutical Corp., 832 F.Supp. 341 (S.D.Fla.1993) (excluding causation testimony relying on a study of a substance similar, but not identical, to the medication to which the plaintiff was exposed).

Some courts have looked for ways to give the benefit of the doubt to the novel nature of some scientific evidence and the fact that such evidence is not generally accepted in the relevant scientific community. In Smith v. General Electric Co., 2004 WL 870832 (D.Mass.2004), the plaintiff claimed that the decedent's rare form of leukemia was caused by chronic, low-dose exposure to ingested or inhaled plutonium and americium alpha emitters. The plaintiff's scientific theories were "novel and controversial" because little scientific information existed connecting low-level radiation exposures of the kind experienced by the decedent with the particular type of leukemia from which he had suffered. As a threshold issue, the court determined that the plaintiff's experts were "serious scientists with controversial views that are in many respects on the periphery of the mainstream, but views that are not so divorced from a scientific method of investigation that they can be dismissed as quackery or armchair conjecture." Accordingly, the court held the plaintiff's expert evidence admissible, even though the court thought the defendant's evidence was stronger. The court stated: "Daubert neither requires nor empowers trial courts to determine which of several competing scientific theories has the best provenance."

f. Clinical Medical Evidence of Causation

One key issue raised by *Kumho Tire* is how broadly the terms "scientific," "technical," and "other specialized" knowledge will be treated by the courts. For example, will the testimony of clinicians who examined the plaintiff be subject to the same scrutiny as the testimony of other kinds of experts? Clinical medical testimony typically differs from other kinds of expert testimony in toxic tort cases because it derives from first-hand examination of the plaintiff, either by a treating physician or by another medical specialist. *Kumho Tire*'s focus on experience-based expert evidence is broad enough to encompass clinical medical testimony. The next question that arises is whether clinical medical testimony should be treated like "hard science" in the *Daubert* analysis, or be judged on its own terms. If so, by what criteria should it be judged?

Courts have taken different approaches to the admissibility of clinical medical testimony under *Daubert*. In Moore v. Ashland Chemical Inc., 151 F.3d 269 (5th Cir.1998) (en banc), the Fifth Circuit excluded the conclusion of the plaintiff's medical specialist that the cause of his reactive airways distress syndrome (RADS) was his workplace exposure to toluene. This doctor, a pulmonary and environmental medicine specialist, based his opinion on the following: (1) examination of the plaintiff and medical test results; (2) the fact that the manufacturer's MSDS for toluene warned that exposure to the fumes could cause lung injury; (3) the fact that the plaintiff's RADS symptoms appeared shortly after his exposure to the toluene solution; (4) an existing scientific study on the relation between toluene and respiratory illness; and (5) his training and experience. Nevertheless, the court held that the district court reasonably concluded that this basis was not enough to pass muster under *Daubert*. The court discounted the study as containing some self-doubts and qualifiers. The MSDS was of limited value, the court said, because the types of tests underlying it were unknown, and no information was given on the exposure level necessary to sustain the injuries warned. The court also discounted the proximity of onset of the injuries to exposure as inadequate without other studies to demonstrate a scientific connection. Finally, the Fifth Circuit pointed to certain facts about the plaintiff's lifestyle and personal medical history that weighed against the specialist's opinion, i.e. that the plaintiff was a smoker, had recovered from pneumonia shortly before his exposure to the toluene, and had suffered from asthma as a child. Three judges dissented, objecting that the majority had improperly interpreted the *Daubert* factors to require all expert testimony to meet a standard within the "hard science" community. Generally accepted clinical medical methodology, the dissent noted, could not meet this standard.

In contrast, in Westberry v. Gislaved Gummi AB, 178 F.3d 257 (4th Cir.1999), the Fourth Circuit was more accepting of clinical medical methodologies. The plaintiff suffered from severe sinus infections allegedly caused by his industrial exposure to talc.

The defendant challenged the admissibility of the expert testimony of the plaintiff's physician, who concluded that the plaintiff's condition was caused by his inhalation of the talc. The defendant argued that because the physician had no epidemiological studies, peer-reviewed published studies, animal studies, or laboratory data to support his conclusion, his opinion would not survive *Daubert* scrutiny. Moreover, the defendant noted, the physician had no tissue samples showing that talc was found in the plaintiff's sinuses. Rather, the doctor merely relied on a differential diagnosis and the temporal proximity of the exposure to the onset of symptoms.

The technique of differential diagnosis typically includes physical examinations, review of the patient's medical history, and review of various clinical tests, including laboratory tests, following which the physician determines the most probable cause of the illness or condition. Part of the process is the generating of possible causes for the symptoms and eliminating those that can be ruled out. In *Westberry*, the court found it irrelevant that the physician did not know the precise amount of talc to which the plaintiff was exposed and had no means of assessing the level of exposure that was sufficient to produce sinus irritation in the plaintiff. The court found the MSDS relevant, which indicated that inhalation of talc dust "in high concentrations irritates mucous membranes." Sufficient evidence existed to provide anecdotal proof of "high concentrations" in the plaintiff's work environment. Furthermore, the court stated that evidence of temporal proximity of the exposure to the onset of the plaintiff's symptoms "can provide compelling evidence of causation." In this case, temporal proximity was demonstrated. *Westberry* is significant in its recognition of clinical medical differential diagnosis as a discrete methodology which, when properly followed, may satisfy the standards of *Daubert* independently. For a detailed discussion of the admissibility issues relating to clinical evidence of causation and differential diagnosis, see Jean Macchiaroli Eggen, *Clinical Medical Evidence of Causation in Toxic Tort Cases: Into the Crucible of* Daubert, 38 Houston L. Rev. 369 (2001).

Courts that follow the rule of *Daubert* are becoming more amenable to admitting clinical medical evidence of causation, provided that the technique of differential diagnosis was rigorously followed in the clinical setting. In In re Paoli Railroad Yard PCB Litig., 35 F.3d 717 (3d Cir. 1994), the court stated that "differential diagnosis generally is a technique that has widespread acceptance in the medical community, has been subject to peer review, and does not frequently lead to incorrect results." The Third Circuit then proceeded to squeeze the differential diagnosis analysis into the factors of the *Daubert* case. In Best v. Lowe's Home Centers, Inc., 563 F.3d 171 (6th Cir. 2009), the Sixth Circuit endorsed the *Paoli* court's recognition of differential diagnosis as medically sound and adopted that court's test, but did not feel the need to make the methodology fit the *Daubert* factors so closely. Thus, a causation opinion based upon differential diagnosis would need to demonstrate that the procedure followed was one in which the physician

> (1) objectively ascertains, to the extent possible, the nature of the patient's injury ..., (2) "rules in" one or more causes of the injury using a valid methodology, and (3) engages in "standard diagnostic techniques by which doctors normally rule out alternative causes" to reach a conclusion as to which cause is most likely.

(quoting *Paoli*). *Accord* Ruggiero v. Warner–Lambert Co., 424 F.3d 249 (2d Cir. 2005); Glastetter v. Novartis Pharm. Corp., 252 F.3d 986 (8th Cir. 2001).

D. THE PROBLEM OF INDETERMINATE PLAINTIFFS

The problems involving indeterminate *defendants* have been discussed elsewhere. See Chapter Six, Sec. E, *supra*. That situation focused upon the problems inherent in the DES litigation rendering plaintiffs unable to identify the precise defendant whose product caused the injuries alleged. While the unique circumstances of the DES litigation created significant causation problems for the plaintiffs, some courts have managed those problems by allowing the "indeterminate defendants" to be treated under special rules of collective liability, such as market share liability. *See, e.g.,* Sindell v. Abbott Laboratories, 607 P.2d 924 (Cal.1980).

The problem of indeterminacy also occurs with respect to plaintiffs. The indeterminate plaintiff situation arises in toxic torts in two ways. First, some persons who have been exposed to a particular substance and have become ill may actually have contracted the illness from another cause. Assuming the absence of a "signature disease," and due to the inability of toxic tort plaintiffs to show cause-in-fact, the precise cause of their illness may never be known. A second kind of indeterminate plaintiff is the future claimant. This situation arises because latency periods for the development of disease are unequal from individual to individual. Not everyone who has been exposed to a particular substance over the same period of time gets sick at the same time. Thus, all liability of a defendant for the injuries resulting from a single course of conduct cannot be resolved simultaneously, nor even sometimes within the same decade. The future claimant issue is addressed in Chapters Nine and Ten, *infra*.

The first kind of plaintiff indeterminacy has generated judicial and scholarly interest because of the issue of causal indeterminacy. Some courts and commentators have struggled to find a means to resolve all claims arising out of exposure to the defendants' product or to hazardous substances for which the defendants are responsible in a single proceeding. The notion of collective recovery mechanisms has met with some resistance, however. In contrast to the indeterminate *defendant* situation, in which collective liability was imposed upon the defendants so as to advance the policy goals of deterrence, loss shifting, and loss spreading, collective recovery in the indeterminate *plaintiff* situation would likely result in overcompensation of some persons, most notably those whose illness was not actually caused by the alleged exposure.

This was one of the issues discussed by the court in Allen v. United States, 588 F.Supp. 247 (D.Utah 1984). The court proposed a relaxation of the cause-in-fact requirement in the situation presented. The court noted that the leukemias and other conditions alleged by the plaintiffs to have been caused by exposure to ionizing radiation released during the United States Government's atomic testing program were identical to the same illnesses existing in the general population without such an exposure. Nevertheless, the court held that sufficient statistical evidence existed to demonstrate a close association between low-level exposure to radiation and the cancers alleged by the plaintiffs. The court stated that where the defendant has acted negligently in putting the plaintiffs at risk and the statistical evidence consistently shows "substantial, appropriate, persuasive, and connecting factors" associating the exposure with the injuries alleged, the factfinder could reasonably make a finding of causation. The court also required an analysis of a variety of factors applicable to individual plaintiffs—including exposures to other substances and personal variables such as the type of cancer alleged—for a determination of consistency with the known scientific data. At that point, the burden would shift to the defendants to disprove the causal connection.

Another proposal has been a collective, or class, solution to the indeterminate plaintiff problem. *See* Richard Delgado, *Beyond Sindell: Relaxation of Cause–In–Fact Rules for Indeterminate Plaintiffs*, 70 Calif. L. Rev. 881, 899–902 (1982). This proposal imagines collective recovery based upon factors similar to those recommended by the *Allen* court, but with payment on a pro rata basis, rather than individualized recovery. Along these lines, Judge Weinstein endorsed a class-wide approach in the Agent Orange litigation. There, Judge Weinstein was responsible for examining the fairness of a proposed settlement of over two million personal injury claims arising from the United States Government's use of the defoliant known as Agent Orange during the Vietnam War. For a discussion of the various aspects of managing the Agent Orange class action, see Chapter Ten, Sec. B & passim, *infra*. In approving the $180 million settlement, Judge Weinstein rejected an individualized assessment of causation in favor of a collective approach. He advocated a class-wide assessment of overall harm to the plaintiffs and holding the defendants liable to each plaintiff for a pro rata share of damages. *See* In re "Agent Orange" Prod. Liab. Litig., 597 F.Supp. 740 (E.D.N.Y.1984).

Most judicial efforts to settle mass toxic tort litigation have logged a considerable amount of time contemplating the appropriate treatment of indeterminate plaintiffs. Further, the use of aggregative procedures to resolve mass toxic tort litigation reflects the tension between the desire for individualized resolution of causation and the efficiency of collective resolution. These procedures are discussed in Chapter Ten, Sections B & C, *infra*.

CHAPTER NINE

INJURIES AND DAMAGES

A. EMOTIONAL DISTRESS

As a general rule, a plaintiff who recovers on a claim for personal injury is entitled to compensation for all damages for injury past, present, and future arising out of the circumstances giving rise to the action. Dan B. Dobbs, The Law of Torts § 302, at 822 (West 2000). Thus, a plaintiff who proves a claim for physical injury resulting from exposure to chemicals from a hazardous waste site may recover for both the physical illness and any emotional distress associated with it.

Many potential toxic tort plaintiffs claim emotional distress without any accompanying illness or other physical injury, however. These claims are sometimes referred to as "fear of cancer" claims or as the misnomer "cancerphobia." The law has had considerable difficulty recognizing such claims without some objective proof of their validity. Concern for imagined claims or fraudulent and frivolous lawsuits has prevented most jurisdictions from recognizing emotional distress claims without some additional corroboration. Moreover, courts have expressed concern that emotional distress may be so fleeting and short-lived that it should not be compensated.

1. Outrageous Conduct

If the conduct of which the plaintiff complains is extreme and outrageous, courts may allow a claim for intentional or reckless infliction of emotional distress absent a physical injury. Because of the outrageous nature of the conduct, juries may reasonably infer that the plaintiff suffered emotional distress. A draft of the Restatement (Third) of Torts: Liability for Physical and Emotional Harm (Tent. Draft No. 5 2007) states: "An actor who by extreme and outrageous conduct intentionally or recklessly causes severe emotional disturbance to another is subject to liability for that emotional disturbance and, if the emotional disturbance causes bodily harm, also for the bodily harm." This provision accurately reflects the state of the law on the tort of intentional infliction of emotional distress, sometimes called the tort of outrage.

For example, in Capital Holding Corp. v. Bailey, 873 S.W.2d 187 (Ky.1994), the plaintiff alleged, among other claims, a claim of outrageous conduct causing severe emotional distress. He had contracted with the defendant building owner to remove pipes and ducts from the basement of a building, but allegedly had not been told that those items were contaminated with asbestos. He stated further that the owner knew of the asbestos contamination before hiring him, but did not inform him of the hazard. Upon learning of the contamination approximately two years later, the plaintiff underwent medical diagnostic tests that revealed no present illness. He was told, however, that he had an increased risk of developing asbestosis and mesothelioma. The court allowed the outrageous conduct claim to stand, finding that the record showed that for several months the plaintiff had been "knowingly and recklessly exposed" to the asbestos.

In Franklin Corp. v. Tedford, 18 So.3d 215 (Miss. 2009), the Mississippi Supreme Court focused on the need for the plaintiff to demonstrate that the defendant directed its intentional (or reckless) and outrageous conduct specifically at the plaintiff. The plaintiffs in this case were employees of the defendant furniture maker who claimed exposure to the neurotoxin propyl bromide in the workplace. They alleged that the workplace was not ventilated, nor was the air adequately tested, and that no protective gear had been provided. These failures, they claimed, continued after the defendant had ample knowledge of the hazards of the chemical, including direct warnings from the manufacturer. The state workers' compensation statute permitted workers to sue their employers for intentional torts. The court held that the plaintiffs had stated claims for intentional torts because the plaintiffs had sufficient evidence of intent, directed specifically at the plaintiffs, to maintain their action.

Other courts have not allowed claims for intentional infliction of emotional distress, even on facts indistinguishable from the cases allowing such claims. Thus, in Contreras v. Thor Norfolk Hotel,

292 F.Supp.2d 798 (E.D.Va.2003), the court held, on facts similar to *Capital Holding*, that a worker had no claim for emotional distress because he had no diagnosed disease and the defendant's conduct had not been directed at him personally. In Whitlock v. Pepsi Americas, 681 F.Supp.2d 1116 (N.D.Cal. 2010), the plaintiffs claimed emotional distress as a result of exposure to hazardous waste contamination of proerty in the vicinity of the defendant's site. The court held that the plaintiffs could not maintain claims for intentional infliction of emotional distress because (1) they were not present at the time of contamination and (2) the defendants were completely unaware of their existence. Therefore, under California law, the defendants' conduct was not directed at the plaintiffs. The court stated that "it is not enough to show that the defendant knew or should have known that there may be people in the area who might be affected by defendants' conduct."

2. Negligent Infliction of Emotional Distress

a. *Physical Injury Requirement*

The allegation of negligent conduct is more problematic. Traditionally, courts have required that for such a claim to be viable the plaintiff must allege physical harm. Section 436A of the Restatement (Second) of Torts sets forth the general rule under these circumstances: "If the actor's conduct is negligent as creating an unreasonable risk of causing either bodily harm or emotional disturbance to another, and it results in such emotional disturbance alone, without bodily harm or other compensable damage, the actor is not liable for such emotional disturbance." The physical harm may be—but is not required to be—caused directly by the defendant's conduct; physical harm that results from the emotional distress may be sufficient to satisfy the requirement. While courts have moved away from an absolute physical injury requirement, situations involving toxic exposures and fear of future disease have caused most courts to cling to some version of that requirement in toxic tort actions.

In Payton v. Abbott Labs, 437 N.E.2d 171 (Mass. 1982), the court, answering certified questions, held that the physical injury rule applied in a class-action brought by persons who were exposed to DES, but who had no present manifestation of illness. The court discussed the concept of reasonable foreseeability of injury that has traditionally been a requirement in the law of negligence. In the court's opinion, this requirement could be satisfied in appropriate cases either where emotional distress is caused by or causes physical injury. The court applied the following test:

> [The plaintiff] must allege and prove she suffered physical harm as a result of the conduct which caused the emotional distress.... [F]urther, ... a plaintiff's physical harm must either cause or be caused by the emotional distress alleged, and ... the physical harm must be manifested by objective symptomatology and substantiated by expert testimony. Finally, the emotional distress

for which compensation is sought must be reasonably foreseeable....

Under this test, the plaintiff's compensation will be
for an amount of emotional distress that a reasonable person would have suffered under the circumstances.

Variations of this test have been applied by many
courts. The Texas Supreme Court, in a unanimous
opinion in Temple–Inland Products Corp. v. Carter,
993 S.W.2d 88 (Tex.1999), reaffirmed the physical
injury rule. The case arose out of the exposure of
two electrical workers to asbestos in a laboratory in
which they were installing electrical outlets. When
the work was almost complete, the laboratory manager warned the workers of the danger of asbestos
exposure. The physician who examined the workers
eighteen months later concluded that they had no
asbestos-related disease at that time, but asserted
that they had an increased risk of developing a
disease from the exposure. The physician characterized the risk as a "high possibility," but not a
probability. The Texas Supreme Court rejected the
plaintiffs' claims for fear of developing asbestos-
related disease, holding that such claims, in the
absence of manifest disease, were too speculative
and would lead to a flood of "prophylactic" lawsuits. Furthermore, the court held that the inhalation of asbestos fibers was not a physical injury that
would trigger a claim for negligent infliction of
emotional distress.

The Pennsylvania Supreme Court reached a similar result in a case brought by a plaintiff with asymptomatic pleural thickening, a benign condition related to asbestos exposure that may be a precursor to more serious impairment and asbestos disease. In Simmons v. Pacor, Inc., 674 A.2d 232 (Pa.1996), the court held that "non-impairing, asymptomatic pleural thickening" did not constitute a sufficient physical injury to be compensable as a matter of law. Accordingly, applying the physical injury rule to the negligent infliction of emotional distress claim, the court held that the condition did not satisfy the physical injury requirement to provide the basis for emotional distress damages. The court noted, however, that if the plaintiff should develop asbestosis or mesothelioma in the future, he could sue at that time for physical and emotional damages.

The United States Supreme Court also has expressed support for the physical injury requirement in toxic tort cases. In Metro–North Commuter Railroad v. Buckley, 521 U.S. 424 (1997), an asbestos-exposure case involving a claim for emotional distress damages under the Federal Employers Liability Act (FELA), the Court held that plaintiffs without physical disease or symptoms may not recover under FELA for emotional distress damages. In so ruling, the Court distinguished an earlier Supreme Court case, Consolidated Rail Corp. v. Gottshall, 512 U.S. 532 (1994), in which the Court had ruled that a plaintiff suffering a "physical impact" may bring a claim for emotional distress absent a physical injury. The Court in *Metro–North* stated that "physical impact," as conceived in *Gottshall*, did not encompass exposure to a substance that might cause a latent illness. The Court stated in *Metro–North* that such physical impact "does not include a simple physical contact that might cause a disease at a substantially later time—where that substance, or related circumstance, threatens no harm other than that disease-related risk." The difficulty with defining and applying "impact" has caused most states to move away from a rule based on impact only.

b. *Bodily Presence of a Toxin as Physical Injury*

An appellate court in New York has extended the meaning of "physical injury" to include evidence of the presence of a toxin in the plaintiff's body, whether or not traditional injury has manifested. In DiStefano v. Nabisco Inc., 767 N.Y.S.2d 891 (N.Y. App. 2003), the court held that the plaintiff guardian had not established sufficient physical injury for the infant to recover for negligent infliction of emotional distress. The plaintiff alleged the infant's exposure to volatile organic compounds (VOC), but had no evidence of illness. The court stated:

> To maintain a cause of action to recover damages for emotional distress following exposure to a toxic substance, a plaintiff must establish both that he or she was in fact exposed to a disease-causing agent and that there is a "rational basis" for his or her fear of contracting a disease.... This Court has construed "rational basis" to

mean "the clinically-demonstrable presence of a toxin in the plaintiff's body, or some other indication of a toxin-induced disease". . . .

The same court reaffirmed this principle in Cleary v. Wallace Oil Co., 865 N.Y.S.2d 663 (N.Y. App. 2008) (slip op.), which involved contamination of the plaintiffs' home with more than 900 gallons of heating oil that the defendant allegedly improperly pumped. The court followed *DiStefano* and held that the plaintiffs' emotional distress claims must be dismissed because they failed to present the requisite clinical evidence.

This line of cases in New York is intriguing because it suggests that clinical evidence demonstrating the mere presence of the chemical in the plaintiff's body, along with proof of exposure, would satisfy the physical injury rule. As the technology to detect small amounts of a chemical in a person's body tissues or bodily fluids progresses, jurisdictions adopting this type of rule would be faced with an increase in claims for negligent infliction of emotional distress.

c. *Relinquishment of Physical Injury Requirement*

The California Supreme Court, for well articulated policy reasons, has taken the bold step of allowing claims for negligent infliction of emotional distress in the absence of physical harm. In Potter v. Firestone Tire and Rubber Company, 863 P.2d 795 (Cal.1993), the court addressed the claims of several landowners who alleged exposure to toxic substances due to the proximity of an adjacent landfill containing toxic waste. None of the plaintiffs was suffering from any disease or other physical condition. They did allege, however, that they were subject to an increased, but unquantified, risk of developing cancer in the future. In rejecting the physical injury requirement in this case, the court stated:

[T]he physical injury requirement is a hopelessly imprecise screening device—it would allow recovery for fear of cancer whenever such distress accompanies or results in any physical injury, no matter how trivial, yet would disallow recovery in all cases where the fear is both serious and genuine but no physical injury has yet manifested itself.

Nevertheless, the *Potter* court did place some significant limitations on a plaintiff's ability to recover for emotional distress. The court stated that the plaintiff can only recover for emotional distress that is reasonable and serious. Reasonableness is not established merely by the fact of exposure, however. The court required that the plaintiff show that the emotional distress was based upon a knowledge that the likelihood of developing cancer is more likely than not.

To meet this test, the plaintiff has the daunting task of presenting reliable medical or scientific testimony quantifying the risk of developing cancer as greater than fifty percent. The court acknowledged that in some cases it may be difficult for the risk to be quantified, but noted that in other types of cases involving the risk of developing a disease, plaintiffs have been able to acquire the requisite expert evidence. The court believed that the quantification of risk requirement best served the policy considerations of keeping litigation within manageable limits and assuring that persons who recover for emotional distress are those with legitimate claims.

In abandoning the physical injury requirement, the *Potter* court implicitly recognized that risk alone may be as concrete an injury as physical injury. It is important to remember that in emotional distress claims the compensation is for *fear* of developing a disease for which there is an increased risk. Claims based on fear have some tradition in the law that allows courts to have a certain comfort level with the developing doctrines in the latent disease context. In contrast, claims that seek compensation for the increased risk itself, for which there is very little legal context, have caused courts considerable discomfort. *See* Section B, *infra*.

d.   *Fear of HIV/AIDS*

Courts have had particular difficulty applying the rules for negligent infliction of emotional distress to fear of AIDS cases. Many of the cases have been resolved under a version of the rule of parasitic recovery, i.e. if the plaintiff can prove a physical injury, he or she will be entitled to damages for emotional distress that flow from it. In the fear of AIDS cases, a substantial number of courts have translated the concept of physical injury into a requirement of proof of actual exposure to HIV.

Thus, in Majca v. Beekil, 701 N.E.2d 1084 (Ill. 1998), the Illinois Supreme Court, in the first of two consolidated cases, required that a clerical worker claiming emotional distress damages for fear of contracting HIV from a scalpel cut she received demonstrate that she was actually exposed to the virus. A podiatrist who later died of AIDS had used the scalpel the day before. The plaintiff was unaware of the podiatrist's medical condition at the time of the cut and discarded the scalpel after receiving medical attention. As a result, the plaintiff was unable to prove whether she was actually exposed to HIV. The court stated: "Without actual exposure to HIV, a claim for fear of contracting AIDS is too speculative to be legally cognizable." Other jurisdictions employ the same actual exposure rule as a means of distinguishing between speculative claims and those based upon a genuine fear of AIDS. *See, e.g.,* Brzoska v. Olson, 668 A.2d 1355 (Del.1995); Carroll v. Sisters of Saint Francis Health Services, Inc., 868 S.W.2d 585 (Tenn.1993).

Some courts have shown special concern for plaintiffs who are unable to determine whether they were actually exposed to HIV. In Hartwig v. Oregon Trail Eye Clinic, 580 N.W.2d 86 (Neb.1998), the Supreme Court of Nebraska noted that the purpose of the actual exposure rule is generally a means of "objectively quantifying the reasonableness of a plaintiff's fear of contracting AIDS." But the actual exposure rule need not apply, the court held, where (1) the plaintiff has been exposed by a "medically sufficient channel of transmission to the tissue, blood, or body fluid of another" and (2) it is "impossible or impracticable to ascertain" whether the tissue or fluid is HIV positive. In this circumstance, a plaintiff will be allowed to recover for the reasonable fear of AIDS. The court also applied a "window of anxiety" to limit the amount of time for which the plaintiff could recover emotional distress damages. The "window" would run from the time of exposure to the time when the plaintiff knew or should have known that he or she was not infected with HIV. The court suggested that the outside time would be following a series of tests reasonably recommended by the plaintiff's physician. The court observed that the medical community treats potentially HIV-infected persons as though they were actually infected by advising them to conduct their lives as though they were infected until a certain period of time has passed with negative HIV tests. The court stated that for the law to ignore a person's reasonable fear of contracting HIV during that period of time would be unfair. *Accord* Madrid v. Lincoln County Medical Center, 923 P.2d 1154 (N.M.1996) (holding that the "window of anxiety" would be six months from date of exposure). In Williamson v. Waldman, 696 A.2d 14 (N.J.1997), the New Jersey Supreme Court followed this approach, but also held that the determination of the reasonableness of the plaintiff's emotional distress would be measured against "a reasonable person of ordinary experience who has a level of knowledge that coincides with then-current, accurate, and generally available public information about the causes and transmission of AIDS." This approach is clearly intended to minimize claims based upon unwarranted hysteria, while allowing claims rooted in genuine, justifiable fear.

B. INCREASED RISK OF DISEASE

Claims for increased risk of disease—sometimes called enhanced risk—seek compensation for the risk of developing the disease, whether or not the person ever becomes ill. This is a separate claim from fear of developing the disease; rather, if allowed, it compensates purely for the risk. The typical plaintiff asserting an increased risk claim has been exposed to a toxic substance known to be associated with latent disease, but either has no physical symptoms of illness or has a condition that is known to be a precursor to a more serious illness. Thus, a person exposed to toxic chemicals in the drinking water supply, but who has not manifested symptoms of illness, may seek to bring an increased risk claim. Similarly, an asbestos worker with pleural thickening, a benign and often asymptomatic conditions that has been associated with exposure to asbestos, may seek compensation for the increased risk of developing lung cancer.

Increased risk claims are the most problematic claims that courts confront in the toxic tort context, and courts have displayed a good deal of hostility toward them. One reason is that these claims do not comport with traditional notions of what constitutes an injury. Under traditional concepts of standing, courts are accustomed to seeing civil cases that seek redress for an injury that has occurred. A claim that has not accrued usually will not be entertained. Claims for increased risk do not dispute that the ultimate claim for the disease has not yet accrued. The question that these claims beg is whether they should be recognized as independent claims: Because the risk is present and continuing, is not the claim for risk legally cognizable? This conceptual question is not the entire problem, however. If courts do entertain such claims, what are the parameters?

In the 1980s and 1990s, when plaintiffs were first struggling to find cognizable claims based upon risk of disease, these claims for compensatory damages based upon risk seemed appealing. But most jurisdictions have rejected them, at least where the plaintiff has no present manifestation of illness. Instead, plaintiffs increasingly have turned their attention to medical monitoring claims, which are also based upon the risk of future illness created by the defendant. These claims are discussed in more detail in Section C, *infra*. In the current legal climate, increased risk claims seeking compensatory damages are generally more trouble than they are worth.

1. The Challenge to Traditional Doctrines

Increased risk claims implicate several traditional doctrines and ask the court to apply them in a novel manner. A fundamental concept of tort law is that the plaintiff may recover all damages arising from the defendant's conduct, past, present, and future. This traditional rule, however, assumes some present injury to person or property, which is absent in the increased risk claims. The second doctrine is res judicata. The prohibition against claim-splitting requires that once a cause of action accrues and a plaintiff brings an action, the plaintiff must include all claims arising from the same transaction or series of transactions. *See* Restatement (Second) of Judgments, § 24 (1982). Subsequent claims arising from the same transaction will be barred. *See generally* Chapter Seven, Section D, *supra.* If an increased risk claim is allowed, the logical extension of the res judicata doctrine would be to bar any subsequent claim for actual injury based upon the same conduct. If compensation for the increased risk is considered to be full compensation for all injuries that might arise in the future, the result will be overcompensation for some (i.e. those who never develop the disease) and undercompensation for others (i.e. those who do develop the disease and suffer injuries in excess of the predicted amount previously compensated).

If some form of claim-splitting is allowed under these circumstances, different problems arise. On the one hand, if the plaintiff is compensated early for the risk of developing disease, and eventually also recovers on a later claim after becoming ill, concern arises over the extent to which the plaintiff may be obtaining a double recovery. On the other hand, if the plaintiff recovers now for risk and never develops the illness, the present recovery would be a windfall for the plaintiff. And, more troubling, it may make money unavailable for persons similarly situated who had the poor luck of becoming ill after the plaintiff obtained the judgment.

Regardless of the approach taken to claim-splitting, there is a crucial interrelationship between the res judicata rule and the rules of accrual for statutes of limitations. A claim cannot be actionable unless recognized by the applicable rules as having accrued. If a claim has accrued, the statutory period will begin to run—and eventually run out. Thus, some coordination must exist between the applicable accrual rule for statute of limitations purposes and the rule on claim-splitting in the same jurisdiction.

2. Cases Relying on Present Injury

Some courts require, explicitly or implicitly, a present physical injury to provide some objective basis for the increased risk claim. A relatively early case, not arising in the toxic tort context, recognized a claim for decreased chance of survival based upon statistical percentages. In Herskovits v. Group Health Cooperative, 664 P.2d 474 (Wash.1983), the court held that the plaintiff's decedent's decreased chance of survival resulting from a physician's negligence in misdiagnosing lung cancer presented a cognizable claim. The plaintiff alleged that at the time the decedent first saw the physician for lung symptoms, he was not diagnosed with lung cancer.

The complaint alleged that had he been properly diagnosed and treated at that time, he would have had a thirty-nine percent five-year survival possibility. At the time he was actually diagnosed, his chance of survival after five years was reduced to twenty-five percent. This represented a thirty-six percent reduction in his overall chance of survival after five years. He died approximately two years after the diagnosis of cancer.

The court ruled that these allegations were sufficient to take the case to the jury for a determination of proximate cause between the increased risk and the decedent's death. It was not necessary for the plaintiff to show that it was certain that the decedent would have lived had he been properly diagnosed in the first place, or that he would have had more than a fifty percent chance of survival if he had been properly diagnosed at the earlier date.

Herskovits, while relying on risk as the primary element of the claim, nevertheless involved an undisputed physical injury—the course of the decedent's lung cancer and his eventual death. Similarly, in Petriello v. Kalman, 576 A.2d 474 (Conn. 1990), another medical malpractice case, the plaintiff alleged that during a routine D & C, the physician perforated her uterus and suctioned portions of her small intestine, then negligently repaired the intestine. The court allowed a claim for an approximately sixteen percent increased risk of bowel obstruction in the future.

In the toxic tort context, the court in Brafford v. Susquehanna Corp., 586 F.Supp. 14 (D.Colo.1984), allowed an increased risk claim upon a showing of present physical injury. The *Brafford* plaintiffs alleged that they had experienced an increased risk of future disease as a consequence of exposure to radiation from a uranium tailing pile at the defendant's mining facility. The court defined present physical injury as "immediate, present damage to ... cellular and subcellular structures, incurred proportionately to the amount and duration of the radiation exposure." This rather broad definition of physical injury would accommodate many toxic tort plaintiffs' claims of increased risk of illness. Whether most exposed plaintiffs could prove the present injury is another issue.

3. Claims Based Upon Risk Only

The majority of courts that have addressed the issue have refused to recognize claims for increase risk of disease without current manifestation of illness. As the Supreme Court of Rhode Island stated in Kelley v. Cowesett Hills Associates, 768 A.2d 425 (R.I. 2001), "the possibility of contracting cancer resulting from mere exposure to a carcinogen, although potentially increasing one's risk of developing cancer, is too tenuous to be a viable cause of action." The plaintiff had no present physical manifestation of asbestos-related illness. *Accord* Bonnette v. Conoco, Inc., 837 So.2d 1219 (La. 2003) (rejecting the plaintiffs' claims for "slightly increased risk" of developing cancer as a result of a slight exposure to asbestos in the soil on their property).

A few courts have been amenable to increased risk claims, but have set strict requirements for the plaintiffs. In Ayers v. Township of Jackson, 525 A.2d 287 (N.J.1987), the New Jersey Supreme Court addressed a variety of claims brought by persons arising out of the contamination of their drinking water supply. None of the plaintiffs claimed to be suffering from any illness associated with the toxic chemicals. The court held that for a plaintiff to recover on a claim of increased risk, the likelihood of the plaintiff developing the disease must be reasonably certain. This meant that the risk must be quantified. In *Ayers*, the plaintiffs' expert expressly stated that although the plaintiffs had an increased risk of cancer, he was unable to quantify the extent of the increased risk because of a lack of scientific information on the interaction of the various chemicals to which they were exposed. Thus, the court refused to recognize their increased risk claims.

The *Ayers* court also addressed the res judicata impact of increased risk claims. Although this matter was not directly at issue in the case, the court stated that under New Jersey law, plaintiffs who bring increased risk claims—or claims based upon any other early injury—would not be barred by either the statute of limitations or the rules of claim preclusion from bringing a later claim after an illness has manifested. Analyzing this issue within the context of New Jersey's discovery statute of limitations, the court noted that the cause of action for the later disease would not accrue until the symptoms of the disease appeared and the plaintiff was aware of the likely cause. The court also said that the rule against claim-splitting would not apply:

[The rule] cannot sensibly be applied to a toxic-tort claim filed when disease is manifested years after the exposure. . . . In such a case, the rule is literally inapplicable since . . . the second cause of action does not accrue until the disease is manifested; hence, it could not have been joined with the earlier claims.

If a plaintiff who later develops an illness related to a prior exposure is allowed to bring the claim after the illness has manifested, what purpose does an earlier increased risk claim serve? This may help explain why so many courts have refused to recognize these claims. Still, some plaintiffs may continue to bring increased risk claims for fear that the defendant will be judgment-proof when illness manifests, or that proof will be lost or destroyed.

4. What Constitutes "Reasonable Certainty" of Risk?

Ayers is representative of decisions recognizing the validity of some claims for increased risk of future disease, provided that the plaintiff can demonstrate future illness is "reasonably certain." In Hagerty v. L & L Marine Services, Inc., 788 F.2d 315 (5th Cir.1986), the court established a standard that "the toxic exposure more probably than not *will* lead to cancer." *See also* Potter v. Firestone Tire & Rubber Company, 863 P.2d 795 (Cal.1993) (stating that the more-likely-than-not standard is the best measure of the existence of a cognizable risk of future disease). In Sterling v. Velsicol Chemical Corp., 855 F.2d 1188 (6th Cir.1988), the court stated that it was not necessary to use the term "reasonable medical certainty," but indicated that the degree of certainty must be greater than "possibly" or "could have." Proof of group risk, through the introduction of epidemiological evidence, will not suffice alone to prove the quantified risk required. The risk must be personalized to the plaintiff. Thomas v. FAG Bearings Corp., 846 F.Supp. 1400 (W.D.Mo.1994). Presenting expert testimony that the specific plaintiff is more likely than not to develop cancer or another disease from an exposure, when that plaintiff has no present symptoms of illness, is a difficult task indeed. Thus, even when courts may be amenable to increased risk claims, the bar may be too high for plaintiffs.

C. MEDICAL MONITORING

Courts have been more receptive to claims for medical monitoring, or medical surveillance, than claims for increased risk. Generally, the medical monitoring plaintiffs exhibit the same characteristics as those who bring increased risk claims— showing some significant exposure, but often manifesting no physical symptoms of disease. The claim for medical monitoring—which some courts refer to as a claim, but others see as a remedy—is for costs associated with periodic medical examinations and diagnostic tests to detect the onset of disease at the earliest possible stage. It is prospective in nature. But it does not seek to compensate for any damages associated with the likelihood of contracting the disease in the future, nor does it compensate in any way for the plaintiff's fear of becoming ill. In that respect, medical monitoring claims are distinguishable from increased risk claims and emotional distress claims. What medical monitoring has in common with these other claims, however, is that the basis for recovery is risk. Thus, some jurisdictions refuse to recognize a medical monitoring claim absent a present physical injury. *See, e.g.,* La. Civ. Code Ann. art. 2315(B) (West 2010); Hinton *ex rel.* Hinton v. Monsanto Co., 813 So.2d 827 (Ala.2001). Indeed, the United States Supreme Court lent support to this position in Metro–North Commuter Railroad v. Buckley, 521 U.S. 424 (1997), an asbestos-exposure case under FELA discussed *supra* in the context of negligent infliction of emotional distress. The Court expressed concern for a flood of "less important" cases and the threat of unlimited liability.

1. Courts Requiring Present Physical Injury

In the past decade, the number of medical monitoring cases has increased; many of the cases are class actions. Yet the courts remain sharply split as to whether to require some evidence of present physical harm as a basis for ordering medical monitoring damages. In Paz v. Brush Engineered Mate-

rials, Inc., 949 So.2d 1 (Miss. 2007), the Mississippi
Supreme Court, responding to a certified question
from the Fifth Circuit Court of Appeals, considered
this issue in an action brought by workers exposed
to beryllium in the workplace. None of the plaintiffs
complained of any physical symptoms, but they
alleged that exposure to beryllium is known to
cause chronic beryllium disease, a latent disease
that affects the lungs and could lead to death. The
court emphasized that ordinary negligence requires
a physical manifestation of injury and that exposure
to a hazardous substance is not an injury. In the
court's opinion, there was no reason to alter this
basic doctrinal principle when the plaintiffs seek
medical monitoring. The court supported its ruling
by stating its concerns for a flood of "trivial" litigation and for depletion of defendants' assets for
medical monitoring, leaving fewer funds for compensation of persons who become ill.

Similarly, in Wood v. Wyeth–Ayerst Labs, 82
S.W.3d 849 (Ky. 2002), the court refused to allow
a medical monitoring claim in the absence of a
present physical injury. The court quoted the Restatement in defining "physical harm" as "physical impairment of the human body." Restatement
(Second) of Torts, § 7, cmt. e (1965). In the
court's opinion, mere ingestion of the drug alleged
to increase the risk of illness did not qualify as
"physical impairment." *Accord* Houston County
Health Care Auth. v. Williams, 961 So.2d 795 (Ala.
2006); Henry v. Dow Chemical Co., 701 N.W.2d
684 (Mich. 2005).

2. Courts Not Requiring Present Physical Injury

In contrast, other courts see medical monitoring claims as a viable compromise—not as costly in the short run as increased risk or emotional distress damages, and potentially limiting costs in the long run if early diagnosis leads to successful management of an illness. These courts often have a different view of the concept of present injury. Thus, in Gates v. Rohm and Haas Co., 618 F.Supp.2d 362 (E.D. Pa. 2007), the court stated that the costs of medical monitoring constituted a compensable injury under the law of Illinois.

Courts allowing medical monitoring claims without current physical injuries tend to agree on the elements of the claim. While their language may differ, the same basic requirements are present. In addition, the elements of the claim must be proven through expert testimony. In re Paoli Railroad Yard PCB Litigation, 35 F.3d 717 (3d Cir.1994), construing Pennsylvania law in the context of PCB contamination, is representative of the approach taken by these courts. The court set forth the elements that the plaintiff must prove as follows:

1.   Plaintiff was significantly exposed to a proven hazardous substance through the negligent actions of the defendant.

2.   As a proximate result of exposure, plaintiff suffers a significantly increased risk of contracting a serious latent disease.

3. That increased risk makes periodic diagnostic medical examinations reasonably necessary.

4. Monitoring and testing procedures exist which make the early detection and treatment of the disease possible and beneficial.

Accord, e.g., Bower v. Westinghouse Electric Corp., 522 S.E.2d 424 (W.Va.1999). The plaintiff need not show any present symptoms of illness. But in at least one jurisdiction, the plaintiff must have been *directly* exposed to the hazardous substance. *See* Theer v. Philip Carey Co., 628 A.2d 724 (N.J.1993) (holding that the wife of an asbestos worker, who was exposed to asbestos through washing her husband's clothes, was exposed indirectly and did not qualify for medical monitoring damages). Failure to satisfy any one of the above elements may lead to dismissal of the claim. *See* In re Tobacco Litig. (Med. Monitoring Cases), 600 S.E.2d 188 (W.Va. 2004).

A major concern in determining whether a claim for medical monitoring should be allowed is the necessity of the monitoring itself. The level of risk that may form the basis of a medical monitoring award is typically lower than that required for increased risk claims. Courts have used different terminology in articulating the medical monitoring test, but seem to agree that the plaintiff must show that the medical monitoring is reasonably necessary to diagnose the onset of disease. *See, e.g.,* In re Paoli Railroad Yard PCB Litigation, 35 F.3d 717 (3d Cir.1994); Ayers v. Township of Jackson, 525 A.2d 287 (N.J.1987); Askey v. Occidental Chemical Corp.,

477 N.Y.S.2d 242 (N.Y.App.Div.1984) (stating that plaintiffs must establish to a reasonable degree of medical certainty that expenditures for medical monitoring are reasonably anticipated to be incurred as a result of exposure).

There are several reasons behind the receptivity of these courts to medical monitoring claims. First, courts dismissing various claims of toxic tort plaintiffs often express regret that the law provides no remedy for a particular injury. Medical monitoring claims provide some assistance to plaintiffs with significant exposures, but who would not otherwise be able to maintain a present claim. Second, courts view medical monitoring as a much less costly alternative to increased risk claims, and one without the disadvantage of overcompensation to persons who ultimately never become ill. Third, medical monitoring claims may deter defendants from engaging in negligent conduct. The initiation of some financial obligation on the part of the defendant soon after the release or other conduct that caused the exposure will apply more pressure to defendants than allowing them to be free of responsibility until the plaintiffs' illnesses become manifested. Finally, when exposed persons seek early diagnosis and treatment, the illness may be cured or successfully managed, thus advancing public health interests and reducing the overall future costs of claims.

3.   Subcellular Changes as Present Injury

In Donovan v. Philip Morris USA, Inc., 914 N.E.2d 891 (Mass. 2009), the Massachusetts Supreme Judicial Court addressed the notion of present injury on certified questions from the federal district court. In *Donovan*, smokers and former smokers without present illness sought medical monitoring. They alleged that smoking has caused subcellular bodily changes that have predisposed them to developing lung cancer in the future. Thus, the plaintiffs alleged:

> [T]he plaintiffs' experts aver that the particles and gases inhaled as cigarette smoke cause an inflammatory reaction in the bronchi and bronchioles leading to an accumulation of inflammatory cells and secretions, impairments of [lung tissues], . . . causing bronchioconstriction. Further, they state that cigarette smoke shifts the balance of cellular protein synthesis and degradation in the lung, resulting in the over-distention and destruction of functional airspaces. Finally, the inhaled carcinogens allegedly damage the genes of the airway cells and impair the repair mechanisms that protect against genetic damage, resulting in increased carcinogenic genetic mutations and loss of protective repair processes.

The plaintiffs further alleged that a new technology, low-dose computed tomography (LDCT) scans of the chest, is capable of detecting and diagnosing cancer at an early stage, allowing for higher rates of cure and survival than previously possible. The court concluded that "the physiological changes with the attendant substantial increase in risk of cancer, and the medical necessity of monitoring with its attendant cost, may adequately establish the elements of injury and damages." Further, the court stated: "No particular level or quantification of increase in risk of harm is necessary, so long as it is substantial and so long as there has been at least a corresponding subcellular change."

At least some courts disagree with a definition of present injury that includes subcellular changes. In Dumontier v. Schlumberger Tech. Corp., 543 F.3d 567 (9th Cir. 2008), the court considered this issue in the context of the Price–Anderson Act, the federal legislation setting up Government liability for nuclear radiation exposure. The court held that the Act required "bodily injury," and that damage to cells or DNA did not fit that definition. The court stated:

> Plaintiffs presented evidence that radiation always "damage[s] the DNA or other important cellular components." But this damage does not establish that there is or will be pain or interference with bodily functions.... Plaintiffs' expert also explained that these subcellular alterations increase the risk of cancer. The Act, however, permits recovery for disease—not simply a risk of disease. We have previously held that such a risk isn't compensable.

This case shows the tenacity of the traditional definition of bodily injury in tort law.

As new technologies are developed, both to diagnose and treat disease and to detect subcellular changes that predispose exposed persons to disease, more courts may move in the direction of the *Dono-*

van court. At the present time, however, courts are sharply split on whether to allow claims for medical monitoring in the absence of physical harm that falls within the traditional definition of injury.

4. Medical Monitoring Payments

How should the award for medical monitoring be paid? In Ayers v. Township of Jackson, 525 A.2d 287 (N.J.1987), the New Jersey Supreme Court expressed a preference for a court-supervised fund to administer the payments. The fund would limit payment to amounts actually spent. In contrast, a lump-sum payment is problematic because of the inability to predict the amounts that will be needed for the monitoring. The court-supervised fund supports the goal of ensuring the availability of funds for judgments payable to persons who develop illnesses in the future.

In general, payments will be ordered only for those extraordinary monitoring expenses that are associated with the defendant's conduct, and not for those medical tests and examinations that reasonable persons would be expected to undergo as a matter of course. *See* Potter v. Firestone Tire & Rubber Co., 863 P.2d 795 (Cal.1993).

5. CERCLA Issues

Medical monitoring also has become an issue within the context of CERCLA. CERCLA provides that private parties may recover the "necessary costs of response" (i.e. cleanup) of a site. There has been a split among the federal district courts as to whether "necessary costs" include the medical monitoring expenses of private persons who were exposed to hazardous substances from the site. The federal circuits that have considered the issue have agreed that medical monitoring costs—at least as they are defined under the common law—are not included in the necessary costs of response. In Daigle v. Shell Oil Co., 972 F.2d 1527 (10th Cir.1992), the Tenth Circuit held that the medical monitoring costs available under CERCLA were those "necessary to prevent contact with hazardous substances," not prospective monitoring to detect the development of disease in persons exposed at an earlier date. Moreover, the court noted that in enacting CERCLA, Congress had deliberately rejected any personal rights to recovery of medical expenses. *See also* Syms v. Olin Corp., 408 F.3d 95 (2d Cir. 2005); Price v. U.S. Navy, 39 F.3d 1011 (9th Cir. 1994).

In a district court case that reached the opposite conclusion, Brewer v. Ravan, 680 F.Supp. 1176 (M.D.Tenn.1988), the court found medical monitoring expenses necessary to "monitor, assess, and evaluate a release." Thus, the court held that such expenses were within the definition of "removal" pursuant to Section 101(23) of CERCLA and therefore an element of response costs. The court distinguished between those medical costs necessary to "assess the effect of the release or discharge on public health or to identify potential public health problems presented by the release," which were recoverable, and costs of treatment of personal injuries or disease caused by the release, which were not recoverable.

D. INTERGENERATIONAL TORTS

Sometimes a toxic tort action is brought for a tort that was committed on a parent of the injured plaintiff prior to the plaintiff having been conceived. In recent years, the question of the liability of defendants for preconception torts has arisen in the more attenuated context of the "DES grandchildren" litigation. The classic DES case is one brought by a child of the woman who ingested the DES while pregnant with that child. This is essentially a prenatal tort—alleging that the tortious act of the defendant directly injured the plaintiff by an exposure in utero prior to birth. The grandchildren, however, cannot allege that they were exposed directly to the DES, thus causing courts to question their right to recovery.

Courts are divided on public policy grounds as to the treatment of preconception claims. A few courts addressing this type of claim have allowed it. In Jorgensen v. Meade Johnson Laboratories, 483 F.2d 237 (10th Cir.1973), the court allowed a cause of action by the father of twins born with genetic defects. The twins' mother had ingested birth control pills prior to the twins' conception, and the complaint alleged that the birth control pills had caused an alteration in the mother's chromosomal structure that led to the genetic defect in her children. Although *Jorgensen* alleged a preconception tort, it was a "second-generation" claim, not a "third-generation" claim as in the DES grandchild situation. This may have made it more palatable to the court to allow the claim to stand.

A similar situation was presented in Renslow v. Mennonite Hospital, 367 N.E.2d 1250 (Ill.1977), but with a more protracted time frame. This court also recognized the claim for a preconception tort. The facts of *Renslow* involved a woman who allegedly received incompatible Rh-positive blood transfusions almost a decade before her child was born. The plaintiff claimed that the transfusions caused the injuries with which the child was born. The court found the existence of "a contingent prospective duty to a child not yet conceived but foreseeably harmed by a breach of duty to the child's mother." Thus, the court used an analysis of duty to justify allowing this preconception tort claim in the medical malpractice context.

These two cases, even though they involve preconception torts like the DES grandchildren cases, are actually more akin to the standard DES child case in the generational proximity to the tortious conduct. In fact, the court in *Renslow*, in dicta, drew the line at claims that may be brought by subsequent generations for genetic damage. Because the *Renslow* plaintiff was not claiming a genetic injury, liability was allowed, and the issues raised by intergenerational claims were not directly addressed.

The DES cases have presented the clearest example of the problems of allowing intergenerational liability. In Enright v. Eli Lilly & Co., 570 N.E.2d 198 (N.Y.1991), the grandmother had ingested the prescription drug DES while pregnant with her daughter. In the complaint, the daughter and her daughter ("the granddaughter") alleged that the daughter's exposure to DES in utero had resulted in a condition that prevented her from carrying a baby to term. Such physical problems were known to be associated with in utero exposure to DES. Years later, the granddaughter was born prematurely as a result of this condition. The granddaughter suffered from injuries related to her premature birth. The court disallowed the granddaughter's claim "to confine liability within manageable limits." The court recognized the far-reaching implications if such a claim were allowed: "[T]he cause of action plaintiffs ask us to recognize here could not be confined without the drawing of artificial and arbitrary boundaries. For all we know, the rippling effects of DES exposure may extend for generations."

Similarly, in Grover v. Eli Lilly & Co., 591 N.E.2d 696 (Ohio 1992), the court rejected a DES grandchild's claims on a set of facts similar to those in *Enright*. The court in *Grover*, however, used language of foreseeability and duty to justify its decision. The court stated: "An actor does not have a duty to a particular plaintiff unless the risk to that plaintiff is within the actor's 'range of apprehension'." Citing the Restatement, the court found that the recognizable risk that the DES manufacturers created was to the class of persons actually exposed to the drug and that the manufacturers could not reasonably have anticipated injury beyond that generation of persons. *See* Restatement (Second) of Torts, § 281m, cmt. c (1965). The court stated:

It is one thing to say that knowledge of a propensity to harm the reproductive organs is sufficient to impose liability for a variety of different injuries to the reproductive organs. It is yet another thing to say that this generalized knowledge is sufficient to impose liability for injuries to a third party that occur twenty-eight years later.

. . . [[T]he grandchild's] injuries are not the result of his own exposure to the drug, but are allegedly caused by his mother's injuries from her *in utero* exposure to the drug. Because of the remoteness in time and causation, we hold that [the grandchild] does not have an independent cause of action.

Thus, the court kept the litigation within manageable limits. *See also* Sorrells v. Eli Lilly & Co., 737 F.Supp. 678 (D.D.C.1990) (applying Maryland law) (rejecting a claim brought by a DES grandchild). *But see* McMahon v. Eli Lilly & Co., 774 F.2d 830 (7th Cir.1985) (applying Illinois law) (holding that the DES manufacturer's knowledge of the hazards of the drug was sufficient to subject it to liability for injuries to grandchildren of women who ingested the drug).

Undoubtedly, the courts in *Enright, Grover*, and like cases foresaw the more troublesome class of intergenerational torts referenced in *Renslow*. At least one incident of alleged genetic injury, causing the DES "signature" cancer in a granddaughter of a woman who ingested the drug, has been reported. *See* Marisa L. Mascaro, *Preconception Tort Liability: Recognizing a Strict Liability Cause of Action for DES Grandchildren*, 17 Am. J.L. & Med. 435, 449–50 (1991). Genetic injury claims are especially problematic because a genetic mutation may not be expressed for several generations, extending the potential period for claims indefinitely. Thus, it is likely that courts will place strict limits on such claims in the same manner that the physical injury claims of *Enright* and *Grover* were prohibited.

E.　"TOXIC TRESPASS" CLAIMS

Some commentators have noted a trend toward claims for "toxic trespass," which have more in common with the tort of battery than with the tort of trespass. The underlying concept views the presence of a chemical substance in the plaintiff's body as proof of an actionable harmful contact, even though the plaintiff may not be aware of the presence of the substance in his or her body and has no signs or symptoms of illness or any indication of an asymptomatic disease process. This type of claim shares with battery the elements of intent, harmful or offensive contact (the substance in the plaintiff's body), and lack of consent. Presumably, intent would be defined to include knowing with substantial certainty that the necessary contact would occur. What toxic trespass shares with the traditional tort of trespass is that recovery is based upon the interference, without the need to demonstrate harm. In this case, the interference would be in the plaintiff's interest to bodily integrity free from invasion by foreign substances. The necessary proof to demonstrate contact would likely be biomonitoring evidence indicating the presence of a chemical in the plaintiff's body that is traceable to the defendant. Biomonitoring is discussed in Chapter Eight, Section B.3.c., *supra*.

A major deterrent to bringing an action for toxic trespass in which the plaintiff claims that the presence of the substance is a "harmful" contact is proof of causation. The plaintiff would be required to show that the contact created the harm. But, as some have argued, a plaintiff relying instead on a "offensive" contact has a looser causation requirement. *See* Jim Langlais & Doug Arnold, *Toxic Trespass Claims: The Elephant in the Room*, 23 Toxics L. Rptr. (BNA) 499 (June 12, 2008) (arguing that a handful of cases and local ordinances recognize the concept of toxic trespass and predicting more claims of this type in the courts); *see also* Steven N. Geise & Hollis R. Peterson, *Toxic Trespass Claims: Beyond the Lab Results*, 24 Toxics L. Rptr. (BNA) 49 (Jan. 8, 2009) (discussing defense strategies to toxic trespass claims).

Those relying on such claims may be splitting hairs, and their claims may or may not go far in the courts. But theories such as the "toxic trespass" theory demonstrate, at the very least, that a certain amount of legal creativity may be necessary for plaintiffs to bend traditional doctrines to fit newly evolving evidence and theories of injury.

F. QUALITY OF LIFE

The Restatement (Second) of Torts § 929 (1979) states that one of the types of damages recoverable for invasions of an interest in property is damage for "discomfort and annoyance." Courts have held that diminution in the quality of life is recoverable as part of the damages for nuisance. In Ayers v. Township of Jackson, 525 A.2d 287 (N.J.1987), the plaintiffs complained that as a result of the contamination of their drinking water supply they suffered intolerable conditions from being cut off from their drinking water supplies and left without running water for almost two years. Their complaints included general inconvenience, plus specific problems with obtaining drinking water from barrels supplied to them as a replacement for their usual supply. The court held that the plaintiffs' claims for diminished quality of life were associated with the interference with the use and enjoyment of their property.

The court in Sterling v. Velsicol Chemical Corp., 855 F.2d 1188 (6th Cir.1988), in allowing a claim for reduced quality of life, stated that even though nuisance is a property action, its basis is interference with the lives and well-being of the plaintiffs. The treatment of this type of injury as an aspect of nuisance implies that for damages for diminished quality of life to be recoverable, the plaintiff must demonstrate the elements of a claim for nuisance.

G. STIGMA DAMAGES

Courts have seen an increase in claims for "stigma" damages associated with property on which contamination had been remediated, but where property values continue to be adversely affected. In In re Paoli Railroad Yard Litigation, 35 F.3d 717 (3d Cir.1994), the Third Circuit acknowledged that under some circumstances an award of remediation costs may not fully compensate a plaintiff, as where the value of the property does not return to its previous level on the market. When this happens, the court said, "plaintiffs should be compensated for their remaining loss. Absent such an approach, plaintiffs are permanently deprived of significant value without any compensation." To state a proper claim, the plaintiff must prove that (1) the defendant caused a temporary physical damage to the plaintiff's property; (2) remediation will not cause the property value to return to its prior level; and (3) some ongoing risk to the land exists. Similarly, the Fifth Circuit, in Bradley v. Armstrong Rubber Company, 130 F.3d 168 (5th Cir. 1997), held that stigma damages may be recovered for diminished property values lingering after remediation.

Courts generally will not allow stigma damages in the toxic tort context unless there is proof of actual injury to the property or interference with use of the property. In Smith v. Kansas Gas Service Co.,

169 P.3d 1052 (Kan. 2007), the Kansas Supreme
Court rejected a claim for stigma damages, even
though the plaintiffs provided expert testimony
showing a five percent loss of value of the homes
located within one-quarter mile of a natural gas
storage yard from which gas had been released. The
plaintiffs had not provided evidence that their property had been contaminated or otherwise harmed by
the release. In Adams v. Star Enterprise, 51 F.3d
417 (4th Cir.1995), the district court refused to
allow stigma damages because the plaintiffs' basis
for the damages was merely public fears of future
contamination. The plaintiffs made no allegations
that they had experienced any actual odors, groundwater contamination, or other interference with
their property. Moreover, as the Fourth Circuit
noted, the offending source of the alleged diminished property values was "not visible or otherwise
capable of detection from the plaintiffs' property."
Cf. Carter v. Monsanto, 575 S.E.2d 342 (W.Va.2002)
(rejecting "property monitoring" as a remedy where
the plaintiffs sought inspection and monitoring to
determine future contamination).

More recently, stigma damages may become an
issue in the proliferation of cases claiming property
damage and/or personal injuries due to defective
drywall imported from China. Because home sellers
will likely be required to disclose the presence of the
drywall, stigma may become an issue in this emerging category of toxic torts. For an overview of issues
related to Chinese drywall, see Allan Kanner, *The
Evolving Crisis Over Defective Chinese Drywall: An*

Overview of Legal Claims and Legislative Efforts,
24 Toxics L. Rptr. (BNA) 1337 (Nov. 19, 2009).

H. PUNITIVE DAMAGES

Punitive damages are distinct from compensatory
damages and are viewed as a kind of quasi-criminal
penalty within the civil justice system. The dual
goals of punitive damages are to punish and deter
the defendant, goals that are shared with the criminal justice system. Punitive damages claims generally require a showing of egregious conduct on the
part of the defendant. Typically, this requirement is
satisfied by intentional or reckless conduct, but it
may also be satisfied by malicious or grossly negligent conduct. Moreover, a fair number of states
have enacted laws that establish a standard of clear
and convincing evidence for proof of a punitive
damages claim. *See, e.g.*, Alaska Stat. § 09.17.020(b)
(2009); Cal. Civ. Code § 3294 (West 2010); Ky. Rev.
Stat. Ann. § 411.84(2) (West 2010).

After a determination is made that the standard
for an award of punitive damages has been met, the
jury then sets the amount of the punitive damages
based upon what is necessary to both punish and
deter the defendant. The defendant may introduce
evidence of its financial worth in mitigation of the
damages. The goal of punitive damages is not to
drive the defendant company out of business, although many defendants have complained that punitive damages do have that effect, particularly in
the context of mass tort litigation. The award be-

comes part of the plaintiff's judgment, unless state law provides that a portion of the punitive award goes to the state, as discussed in Section Three, *infra*.

1. Due Process Standards for Punitive Damages Awards

a. Procedural Due Process and Judicial Review

The United States Supreme Court established the due process standard for review of an award of punitive damages in Pacific Mutual Life Insurance Company v. Haslip, 499 U.S. 1 (1991). The case arose from a claim of fraud by an insurance agent in the collecting and processing of insurance premiums. The Court approved the Alabama process for review of punitive damages and upheld the punitive damages award. The Court stated that there is no bright line between an award that is constitutionally acceptable and one that is not. Rather, a general standard of reasonableness should apply.

The Court examined the Alabama post-trial procedures for scrutinizing punitive damages awards. The procedure was two-tiered: first, the trial court reviewed the jury's award for excessiveness, and then the appellate court conducted its own independent review. In *Haslip*, the Court held that this review process satisfactorily assured that the punitive damages award was not excessively disproportionate to the reprehensible character of the defendant's conduct. The Alabama scheme required both the trial court and the Alabama Supreme Court to examine certain factors to determine whether the award of punitive damages was proper. Those factors included such considerations as the culpability of the defendant's conduct, the duration of the conduct, the existence of similar past conduct, the degree to which the defendant profited from its wrongful conduct, the financial position of the defendant, and the amount of criminal sanctions or other civil awards for the same conduct. In a later case, Cooper Industries, Inc. v. Leatherman Tool Group, Inc., 532 U.S. 424 (2001), the Supreme Court held that appellate review of excessiveness of a punitive damages award under due process standards should be conducted de novo.

An issue that arose in the wake of *Haslip* was whether due process mandated a two-tiered, multi-factored review process of the type established by Alabama. In TXO Production Corp. v. Alliance Resources Corp., 509 U.S. 443 (1993), the United States Supreme Court held that the West Virginia procedure for review of punitive damages awards satisfied due process standards, even though it was not identical to the Alabama procedure addressed in *Haslip*. The Court emphasized that the West Virginia review process included the same general factors as the process in Alabama. But in Honda Motor Co. v. Oberg, 512 U.S. 415 (1994), the Court held that the Oregon procedure violated due process because it virtually eliminated post-verdict review of the amount of a punitive damages award.

b. *Substantive Due Process: Amount of Award*

The key factor for judicial consideration in the Alabama scheme in *Haslip* was a determination of whether a reasonable relationship existed between the punitive damages award and the harm that actually occurred, as well as the harm that might have resulted from the defendant's conduct. The Supreme Court viewed this factor as the core of the substantive due process test. An important and persistent question that has arisen is whether due process requires a particular ratio between the harm—characterized by the compensatory damages—and the punitive damages. The punitive damages award in *Haslip* was roughly four times the amount of the compensatory award. The Court commented that this ratio "may be close to the line" of due process, but found that it "did not lack objective criteria."

The Supreme Court has addressed the ratio issue in several subsequent decisions. In TXO Production Corp. v. Alliance Resources Corp., 509 U.S. 443 (1993), the Court considered the question of the relationship between compensatory damages and punitive damages. The case involved an alleged conspiracy over oil and gas rights in West Virginia. The jury awarded the defendant, on the counterclaim, punitive damages in an amount that was 526 times the compensatory award. In holding that the award did not violate due process, the Supreme Court found it "appropriate to consider the magnitude of the potential harm that the defendant's conduct would have caused to its intended victim if the wrongful plan had succeeded, as well as the possible harm to other victims that might have resulted if similar future behavior were not deterred." Thus, the Court again refused to draw a bright line for due process purposes. If no compensatory damages are awarded, however, an award of punitive damages will probably not be appropriate. *See* Oliver v. Raymark Industries, 799 F.2d 95 (3d Cir.1986) (applying New Jersey law). *But cf.* Jacque v. Steenberg Homes Inc., 563 N.W.2d 154 (Wis. 1997) (holding that nominal damages can support a punitive damages award in a claim for intentional trespass to land).

In BMW of North America, Inc. v. Gore, 517 U.S. 559 (1996), the Court established more cohesive guidelines on the due process parameters of a punitive damages award. The plaintiff in *Gore* complained that the defendant had failed to disclose that the new automobile purchased by the plaintiff had been repainted. The plaintiff contended that the failure to disclose constituted fraud. The jury found the defendant liable for $4000 in compensatory damages and $4 million in punitive damages. Subsequently, the Alabama Supreme Court reduced the punitive damages award to $2 million. The U.S. Supreme Court held that the punitive damages award was excessive. The Court first stated that the award should be analyzed in relation to the defendant's conduct that occurred solely within Alabama, and not nationally. Next, the Court observed that none of the aggravating factors typically associated with highly reprehensible conduct was present in this case. The harm was purely economic, no third parties were threatened, the defendant did not display any indifference or recklessness in regard to the health or safety of persons, and the company arguably could have interpreted the relevant disclosure statute to create an exclusion for its conduct.

With regard to the ratio between the compensatory damages and the punitive damages, the Court held fast to its previous rejection of a bright line test. The Court stated that while circumstances may exist to allow a high punitive damages award in relation to a small compensatory damages award, the ratio in some cases will trigger suspicion: "When the ratio is a breathtaking 500 to 1, however, the award must surely 'raise a suspicious judicial eyebrow.' " (quoting *TXO*). Thus, the court concluded that the punitive damages award in this case was more than was necessary to punish and deter the defendant's conduct. *Gore* has cast a long shadow, however, and its three principles of due process analysis have come to be known as the "Gore Guideposts": (1) the reprehensibility of the defendant's conduct; (2) the reasonableness of the ratio between the amount of punitive damages and the amount of compensatory damages; and (3) a comparison of other sanctions available for the same conduct under relevant criminal or civil statutes.

In State Farm Mutual Automobile Insurance Co. v. Campbell, 538 U.S. 408 (2003), the Supreme Court continued to reject a bright line test for ratio, but stated that "in practice, few awards exceeding a single-digit ratio ... will satisfy due process." The Court also stated that when compensatory damages are substantial, a lesser award of punitive damages would probably suffice to effect the necessary punishment and deterrence. Further, in line with *Gore* the Court was concerned about the degree to which the court below had relied on the defendant's practices in other states, particularly considering the fact that the out-of-state conduct alleged was significantly different from the conduct alleged in the plaintiffs' case. Among the many problems with considering out-of-state conduct was the possibility that the conduct may have been legal where it occurred.

State Farm v. Campbell has made an impact in the courts. For example, in Boerner v. Brown & Williamson Tobacco Co., 394 F.3d 594 (8th Cir. 2005), the Eighth Circuit reduced a punitive damages award made to the estate of a smoker from $15 million to $5 million. Using *Gore* and *State Farm*, the court held that in light of the substantial compensatory damages award of more than $4 million, a ratio of slightly more than one to one would satisfy due process.

2. Multiple Punitive Awards for the Same Conduct

For a long time, a problematic and unanswered issue of punitive damages in toxic tort litigation was the due process propriety of multiple punitive damages awards against the same defendant for the same conduct. The classic example is that of the asbestos industry. Repeated punitive damages awards have been assessed against the same asbestos manufacturers in cases brought by different plaintiffs, all arguably arising out of the same general course of conduct in failing to make known the hazards of asbestos at a time when the industry first became aware of the danger and in failing to provide instructions for the safe handling of asbestos-containing materials. The asbestos manufacturers' objection to these multiple awards was not merely a matter of fairness. The manufacturers also faced the prospect of insolvency if forced to pay a continuing series of punitive awards of the magnitude of the awards already made.

In *State Farm*, the United States Supreme Court inched toward these issues, but stopped short of addressing them fully. The Court did state, however, that while the defendant's conduct toward others may have some relevance in setting the punitive damages award, the award should be based primarily on the conduct of the defendant toward the particular plaintiff in the case.

In Philip Morris USA v. Williams, 549 U.S. 346, 353 (2007), the Supreme Court picked up the loose thread left dangling in *Gore* and *State Farm* and moved closer to answering the issue of multiple awards for the same conduct. In *Williams*, the Court expressed concern that the punitive damages award, which was based upon a deceit claim, may have been based in part on harm to persons outside the litigation, i.e. other smokers using the defendant's product. The jury had assessed a punitive award that was almost 100 times the compensatory damages award. The Court stated: "In our view, the Constitution's Due Process Clause forbids a State to use a punitive damages award to punish a defen-

dant for injury that it inflicts upon ... those who
are, essentially, strangers to the litigation.'' The
Court was especially concerned that a defendant
would not be able to present an effective defense
when such other persons are not before the court.
But the prohibition was not absolute. The Court
further stated that sometimes evidence of the defendant's conduct toward others outside the present
litigation would be allowed, specifically for the purpose of demonstrating reprehensibility of the conduct, pursuant to the first *Gore* guidepost.

The *Williams* rule is difficult to apply. Would a
jury be able to separate the reprehensibility analysis
from the process of assessing the amount of punitive damages? Is *Williams* just a rule for appellate
courts? Regardless of these difficulties of application, it is clear that the Supreme Court is saying
that the punitive award in a particular case should,
as accurately as possible, reflect the conduct of the
defendant directed at the plaintiff(s) in that case.

Williams does not directly address the question of
multiple awards for the same conduct, however. In
mass torts, as plaintiffs bring their cases, seriatim,
the same evidence will be offered to demonstrate
reprehensibility. Logically, repeated awards for the
same general course of conduct would overlap, in
small or substantial part. Some courts have considered ways to avoid the problem of multiple awards,
but all have procedural difficulties and raise fairness questions. In Owens–Corning Fiberglas Corp.
v. Malone, 972 S.W.2d 35 (Tex.1998), for example,
the Supreme Court of Texas opined that limiting

punitive damages to the first or first several judgments involving the same course of conduct would arbitrarily reward the first-comers to the litigation.

Proposals to limit punitive damages are problematic. To be effective, many of these proposals would require uniformity among the states, an accomplishment that is widely acknowledged as unlikely to occur. One such proposal is to set an individual cap on the punitive damages allowed for each plaintiff. *See* Fischer v. Johns–Manville Corp., 512 A.2d 466 (N.J.1986) (stating that such a cap would be ineffective unless applied uniformly). An aggregate cap is another suggestion, but this solution would create the same race to the courthouse as the single-award solution. Still, many states have undertaken the task of legislatively imposing limits on punitive damages awards, as discussed next.

3. Legislative Punitive Damages Reform

Substantial legislative activity has occurred at the state level with respect to punitive damages. These reforms have taken several approaches. First, states have enacted various provisions directed at tightening the circumstances under which punitive damages will be available. For example, several states have elevated the standard for proving a punitive damages claim to that of "clear and convincing" evidence. *See, e.g.,* Cal. Civ. Code § 3294 (West 2010); Ky. Rev. Stat. Ann. § 411.184(2) (West 2010). In addition, a few states have codified a type of "government standards" defense, according to which, in certain kinds of cases, the defendant's compliance with government regulatory standards will operate as a defense to punitive damages claims. *See, e.g.,* Ariz. Rev. Stat. Ann. § 12–701(A)(1) (West 2010) (FDA approval of drugs); Utah Code Ann. § 78B–8–203(1)(a) (West 2009) (FDA approval). New Hampshire imposes an outright ban on punitive damages. N.H. Rev. Stat. Ann. § 507:16 (2010).

States have also legislatively limited the amounts of awards. These limits have taken the forms of setting a monetary cap on each award, providing a maximum ratio between punitive damages and compensatory damages, or keying the award into the defendant's annual gross income or net worth. *See, e.g.,* Ala. Code § 6–11–21 (2008) (limiting punitive damages to three times the compensatory damages or $500,000, whichever is larger); Colo. Rev. Stat. Ann. § 13–21–102(1)(a) (West 2010) (limiting punitive damages to the equivalent of the amount of compensatory damages awarded); Kan. Stat. Ann. § 60–3701(e) (2009) (capping punitive damages at annual gross income or $5,000,000, whichever is less); Miss. Code Ann. § 11–1–65(3)(a) (West 2009) (providing a sliding scale of limitations on punitive damages based upon the net worth of the defendant); Tex. Civ. Prac. & Rem. Code § 41.008 (Vernon 2009) (limiting punitive damages to the greater of two times the amount of economic damages plus an amount equal to noneconomic damages found by the jury up to $750,000, or $200,000); Va. Code.

Ann. § 8.01–38.1 (West 2009) (capping punitive damages at $350,000).

Third, some states have enacted "split-recovery" statutes, which legislatively mandate that a portion of each punitive damages award should go directly to the state. Barring some other designation in the statute, those states that have taken a portion of the plaintiff's punitive damages award have placed the money in the general state fund. *See* Alaska Stat. § 09.17.020(j) (2009) (providing that fifty percent of any punitive damages award must go to "the general fund of the state"). The split-recovery statutes containing more specific designations vary considerably. For example, the Iowa statute provides that seventy-five percent of each punitive damages award must be deposited in a civil reparations trust fund, to be "disbursed only for purposes of indigent civil litigation programs or insurance assistance programs." Iowa Code Ann. § 668A.1(2)(b) (West 2010). Missouri has created a public Tort Victims Compensation Fund, into which fifty percent of each punitive damages award must be deposited. The fund provides compensation to tort victims who were unable to collect the full amount of compensatory damages awarded in their actions. Mo. Ann. Stat. § 537.675 (West 2009). In Indiana, seventy-five percent of each punitive damages award must go to the state fund to compensate victims of violent crimes. Ind. Code Ann. § 34–51–3–6(c) (West 2009).

At least one state has used its punitive damages reform statute to address the issue of multiple punitive awards against the same defendant arising out of the same conduct. The Georgia legislature has enacted a provision limiting punitive damages in product liability cases to one award in a Georgia court per defendant, per product, "regardless of the number of causes of action which may arise from such act or omission." Seventy-five percent of that single punitive damages award, after attorney fees and costs, must be deposited in the state treasury. Ga. Code Ann. § 51–12–5.1 (West 2010).

In addition to state legislative reforms, punitive damages have been targeted by those who seek reforms on the federal level for product liability law and tort law generally. Various bills introduced in Congress have contained caps on punitive damages awards as well as other restrictions. While federal action would have the advantage of creating uniformity, many have not been persuaded by the merits of the individual proposals. Recently, the activity on the state level has eclipsed any federal efforts. There is every reason to believe, however, that supporters of national punitive damages reform will continue to propose measures for Congressional consideration.

CHAPTER TEN

MASS TOXIC TORTS

Toxic substance litigation has transformed the legal system. Professors Marcus and Sherman have identified three characteristics of modern complex litigation, all of which are particularly descriptive of mass toxic torts. First, they observe that the courts, and more frequently the federal courts, are being used to resolve disputes involving multi-faceted, problematic substantive issues, such as those of science and technology. This has inevitably led to the creation of new types of actions. Second, the numbers of parties have multiplied, creating new procedural issues and challenging case management. Third, the monetary stakes in litigation are much higher now, particularly with the increase in punitive damages awards. Richard L. Marcus & Edward F. Sherman, Complex Litigation: Cases and Materials on Advanced Civil Procedure 1–2 (4th ed. 2004). Mass toxic torts manifest these characteristics in the extreme.

A. THE PROBLEM OF MASS TOXIC TORTS

The problems of latent disease claims create special challenges in the mass tort context. When many people have been exposed to one or more toxic substances under the same or similar circumstances, discrepancies typically exist in individual routes and amounts of exposure. This is true whether the injured persons are claiming unrelated exposures to the same consumer product or exposure to the same contaminated land, air, or water. Likewise, latency periods vary among individuals. Some persons become ill sooner, others later or not at all. Matters of specific causation in the individual claims must still be addressed in mass tort litigation. When the claimants are geographically diverse, difficult choice-of-law questions arise as well. Attempts to resolve the similar toxic-exposure claims of many persons become complex and problematic when viewed in this light.

In much mass toxic tort litigation, some form of aggregative procedure is essential to achieve the goals of efficiency and consistency. It is crucial to the effective operation of the judicial system, however, that individualized justice not be totally abandoned in an effort to achieve judicial economy. As the court in Malcolm v. National Gypsum Co., 995 F.2d 346 (2d Cir.1993) stated in reversing the district court's consolidation of 600 asbestos cases: "The systemic urge to aggregate litigation must not be allowed to trump our dedication to individual justice, and we must take care that each individual plaintiff's—and defendant's—cause not be lost in the shadow of a towering mass litigation."

While the class action device tends to be the most high profile aggregative procedure, it is by no

means the only one. Multidistrict litigation transfer
and consolidation have been used very effectively in
some mass torts. This chapter begins with a look at
these aggregative procedures in the mass toxic tort
context. Courts not only must decide whether the
use of aggregative procedures generally will best
serve the litigants, but also must choose which
aggregative procedure is most appropriate in a particular type of litigation. Nor does the court's special role in mass litigation end at that point. The
court is constantly involved in determining and
executing case management procedures focused on
the particular problems of the mass toxic tort case.

The vast numbers of parties in actions such as
asbestos litigation make it necessary to fashion
mechanisms for processing these claims while avoiding duplicative efforts and maintaining due process.
The public law/private law nature of toxic torts
often leads to the question whether the resolution
of mass claims may be more properly handled by
the legislature rather than the courts. In Amchem
Products, Inc. v. Windsor, 521 U.S. 591 (1997), the
United States Supreme Court chastised the proponents of the litigation for usurping the role of
Congress and attempting to establish a quasi-legis-
lative claim resolution mechanism in an inappropriate manner. For a discussion of *Amchem*, see Section B *infra*.

Matters of attorney ethics also arise in the context of mass tort litigation. Multiple plaintiffs may
have conflicting interests, even though their claims

are similar. Attorneys may become overly enthusiastic in soliciting clients for mass tort litigation. And attorney fee issues are often hotly debated. The public furor over plaintiff attorney fees generated by several settlements between various states and the tobacco industry will not soon dissipate.

Despite some procedural deterrents, the use—or attempted use—of the class action device has grown in the area of toxic torts. This is particularly true of actions that seek, solely or in conjunction with other forms of relief, medical monitoring damages. Mass toxic torts encompass both environmental pollution and alleged toxic product liability, and have alleged personal injuries, property damages, economic losses, and the risk of future illness. Litigation based upon bisphenol A (BPA) in baby bottles and children's cups, radiation exposure from diagnostic CT scans, prescription and over-the-counter drugs of all sorts, exposure of military service persons and other personnel to toxic releases in Iraq and Afghanistan, and all measure of food products (e.g. alleging that fast-food grilled chicken products should be accompanied by a warning that grilling could increase the risk of cancer) is now common. The 2010 oil spill and continuing leak in the Gulf of Mexico has spawned many suits in just the first few months since the incident, from commercial shrimpers, environmental groups, and governmental entities. This explosion of litigation demands a reassessment of the procedural mechanisms available to manage them in the courts.

B. CLASS ACTIONS

When the Advisory Committee to the 1966 amendments to Rule 23 of the Federal Rules of Civil Procedure stated that the class action device was not appropriate for mass torts, the Committee was contemplating a completely different type of mass tort. The mass accidents of the 1960s, confined in space and time, were very different from the latent disease claims of the past several decades. Now, it is generally agreed that the class action device may be an appropriate method of managing certain kinds of mass tort litigation. Class actions not only serve the goals of efficiency and conservation of resources, but they also provide a means of representation for a class of persons who may not otherwise pursue their legal claims. In a class action, the class may consist of plaintiffs or defendants. Because most toxic tort claims for which class certification is sought involve plaintiff classes, this section will focus exclusively on the plaintiff class. In a class action, one or several persons bring the action on behalf of the class. These persons are called the class representatives, and they and their attorneys determine the course of the litigation, the result of which becomes binding on all class members (sometimes referred to as absent class members) who have not chosen to opt out of the class action (where opting out is available).

Although procedures for certifying class actions exist under both federal and state law, this chapter employs the federal class action device, as set forth in Rule 23 of the Federal Rules of Civil Procedure, as a model for understanding the procedural requirements and issues inherent in the mechanism. The Agent Orange litigation, filed in 1979 and settled in 1984, was the first well-documented example of the use of the class action device in mass toxic tort litigation in federal court. As a result, the Agent Orange litigation gives a cradle-to-grave picture of a mass toxic tort class action, and even a glimpse into its legal afterlife. The action arose from the use of the herbicide 2,4,5–trichlorophenoxyacetic acid, commonly known as "Agent Orange," in United States military operations during the Vietnam War. The course of the litigation demonstrated judicial efforts to manage the numerous complex procedural problems of a mass toxic tort, through the efforts initially of Judge Pratt and later Judge Weinstein. While recent legal developments cast substantial doubt over the continued availability of the class action device in mass tort actions with the characteristics of the Agent Orange litigation, the case nevertheless offers critical lessons in the issues raised by litigation on such a massive scale. Thus, this litigation will be cited frequently throughout this section, as it remains the mostly broadly instructive toxic tort class action.

A variant of the class action, known as the settlement class action, has arisen largely due to toxic tort litigation. Amchem Products, Inc. v. Windsor, 521 U.S. 591 (1997) was an example of a case that was presented to the court as a settlement class action. Essentially, *Amchem* was commenced at its end; that is, a complaint and proposed settlement agreement were filed together, with the settling parties seeking both class certification and judicial approval of the settlement. The purpose of the action was to settle all future claims by persons exposed to asbestos products, including spouses of asbestos workers. The settlement encompassed persons currently ill, but who had not yet filed suit, as well as those exposed to asbestos, but who had not yet manifested illness. The settlement established a massive administrative mechanism containing a schedule of payments for various disease categories. Although the Supreme Court held that the Third Circuit had been correct in decertifying the class action, the Court recognized that settlement class actions, where appropriate, may be maintained, provided that they meet the requirements of Rule 23. *Amchem* and settlement class actions are discussed further in Section F.1, *infra*.

Amendments to Rule 23 in 2003 have provided more detailed guidance to courts in managing class actions within their jurisdiction, including provisions on appointment of class counsel and awards of attorney fees. In addition, Congress enacted the Class Action Fairness Act of 2005, which will have the effect of moving many state class actions into federal court, at the discretion of the defendant.

1. Certification Requirement

A case cannot proceed as a class action in federal court unless expressly certified as one by the court. Rule 23(c)(1)(A) requires that "at an early practicable time" after the commencement of an action brought as a class action (referred to as a "putative class action"), the court shall determine whether it may proceed as a class action. If the court determines that the action meets the requirements of Rule 23(a) and (b), the court issues a certification order. Pursuant to Rule 23(c)(1)(B), the order must define the class and list the class claims or defenses. Once the federal court has issued a class certification decision, the court has a fair amount of latitude to shape the procedural mechanisms to respond to the unique issues of a particular class action. A party may seek an immediate interlocutory appeal of the certification decision from the appropriate Circuit Court of Appeals which, pursuant to Rule 23(f), has the discretion to permit an appeal.

2. Prerequisites to a Class Action

By definition, class actions challenge due process. They bind absent class members to the judgment or settlement without complete individualized resolution of their claims. Accordingly, Rule 23 contains a series of prerequisites designed to ensure that the action is appropriate for class adjudication. In addition, a further, implicit, requirement is that an appropriately defined class be identified.

a. *Identifying the Class*

Rule 23 presupposes that an appropriate class is available. In toxic tort actions, the definition of the class may pose certain problems. This is especially true because tort law tends to be a creature of state law, but mass toxic torts often have a nationwide effect. Despite problems relating to causation, as well as the vast numbers of class members, the Agent Orange litigation was certified as a class action. *See* In re "Agent Orange" Prod. Liab. Litig., 100 F.R.D. 718 (E.D.N.Y.1983). Judge Weinstein defined the class as those members of the United States, New Zealand, and Australia armed forces in or near Vietnam between 1961 and 1972 who were injured by exposure to Agent Orange or other phenoxy herbicides. The class was defined as those who claimed injury, rather than the broader category of those who were exposed.

More recently, the Supreme Court has made clear that attempts to certify classes that include both persons claiming current injury and those who have been exposed to a toxic substance, but who are currently without injury, will be disfavored. Even actions seeking medical monitoring because of the risk of future illness raise these problems because some class members may have present illnesses while others do not. The decision in Amchem Products, Inc. v. Windsor, 521 U.S. 591 (1997) rejected a proposed settlement class in the asbestos personal injury context, partially on the ground that exposed-only plaintiffs had interests that conflicted significantly with the plaintiffs claiming current injuries. The Court stated:

> In significant respects, the interests of those within the single class are not aligned. Most saliently, for the currently injured, the critical goal is generous immediate payments. That goal tugs

against the interest of exposure-only plaintiffs in ensuring an ample, inflation-protected fund for the future. . . .

. . . .

   . . . Many persons in the exposure-only category . . . may not even know of their exposure, or realize the extent of the harm they may incur. Even if they fully appreciate the significance of class notice, those without current afflictions may not have the information or foresight needed to decide, intelligently, whether to stay in or opt out.

These conflicts of interest infected the entire class certification question, in the Court's view. They are directly relevant to the Rule 23(a) prerequisites of typicality and adequacy of representation, as discussed further *infra*. In *Amchem*, the broad definition of the class presented fatal problems for the proponents of the class action. Among other things, the Court noted that for settlement class actions, there may be a need for heightened attention to class definition because of the interaction between the certification provisions of Rule 23 and the settlement.

b. *Numerosity*

The first explicit prerequisite of a federal class action is numerosity of the class. *See* Fed. R. Civ. P. 23(a)(1). There is no bright line identifying when numerosity exists. And it is not necessary for the plaintiffs to identify the class members. Indeed, inability to identify the specific class members makes the class action device preferable because joinder would be impracticable under those circumstances. *See* Doe v. Charleston Area Medical Center, Inc., 529 F.2d 638 (4th Cir.1975).

c. *Commonality*

The second prerequisite to a class action, identified in Rule 23(a)(2), is commonality. Commonality requires that questions of law or fact common to the class are presented by the action. This is just a general screening requirement, and at this stage there is no mandate that the common questions predominate over individual questions. It merely suffices that some common questions of law or fact exist.

In the Agent Orange litigation, the court identified questions of both law and fact that were suitable for a collective decision. These included the Government contractor defense, general causation, and the determination whether Agent Orange was a defective product. *See* In re "Agent Orange" Prod. Liab. Litig., 506 F.Supp. 762 (E.D.N.Y.1980). In general, the court believed that most of the affirmative defenses could be handled on a class-wide basis.

d. *Typicality*

The typicality requirement of Rule 23(a)(3) assures that the representative plaintiffs' claims are typical of the claims held by the class members. Differences among the claims of the class members will not necessarily render class treatment impossible. Rule 23(c)(4) makes clear that a class action may proceed on particular issues or that the class may be divided into subclasses, with each subclass being subject to the provisions of Rule 23 for class actions generally. Typicality can be a fatal problem in class certification of mass toxic tort actions. The larger and more diverse the plaintiff class, the more difficult will be the task of appointing class representatives who are truly typical of the various plaintiffs, in terms of exposure, type of injury, and causation.

e. Adequacy of Representation

This prerequisite is intended to assure that the class representatives "will fairly and adequately protect the interests of the class." Fed.R.Civ.P. 23(a)(4). This prerequisite necessarily generates concern about the attorneys who represent the class. The court will be concerned that the class attorneys have a true interest in representing the interests of all class members, and not just the representatives, and that they have the skill and resources to adequately do so. The court will want to be assured that the class representatives will fully pursue claims and appeals in which the class has an interest and that no conflict of interest exists between the representatives and the class. Adequacy of representation is especially subject to re-evaluation later, when the circumstances of the parties may change due to events occurring during the course of the litigation. *See* Gonzales v. Cassidy, 474 F.2d 67 (5th Cir. 1973). In the Agent Orange litigation, Judge Weinstein noted the causation problem and ordered the plaintiffs' counsel to choose a representative claimant for each type of injury alleged.

In *Amchem*, the Supreme Court was troubled by the representation issues raised by the unique characteristics of the proposed settlement class action. Counsel for the Center for Claims Resolution (CCR), a consortium of twenty former asbestos manufacturers, were instrumental in fashioning the settlement, which proposed to bind all future asbestos personal injury claimants, including those who were currently injured and those who had been exposed to asbestos, but without currently manifested disease. The Supreme Court observed that "the terms of the settlement reflect essential allocation decisions designed to confine compensation and to limit defendants' liability." The Court concluded that the proposed settlement constituted "a global compromise with no structural assurance of fair and adequate representation for the diverse groups and individuals affected." Moreover, there was no assurance "that the named plaintiffs operated under a proper understanding of their representational responsibilities." Notwithstanding the unique circumstances of *Amchem*, the Court's concerns and close scrutiny of the representation issue are important lessons for those who seek class certification in all mass toxic torts.

3. Types of Class Actions

Rule 23(b) sets forth descriptions of several kinds of class actions that may be certified following the court's finding that the 23(a) prerequisites have been met. The action must fit into one of the 23(b) categories to be maintainable as a federal class action. In toxic tort litigation, the 23(b)(1)(B) and 23(b)(3) class actions have received the most attention. This section will describe all four categories, with emphasis on the foregoing two types.

a. General Provisions

Rule 23(b) provides that a class action may be certified where:

(1) the prosecution of separate actions by or against individual members of the class would create a risk of

(A) inconsistent or varying adjudications with respect to individual members of the class which would establish incompatible standards of conduct for the party opposing the class; or

(B) adjudications with respect to individual members of the class which would as a practical matter be dispositive of the interests of the other members not parties to the adjudications or substantially impair or impede their ability to protect their interests; or

(2) the party opposing the class has acted or refused to act on grounds generally applicable to the class, thereby making appropriate final injunctive relief or corresponding declaratory relief with respect to the class as a whole; or

(3) the court finds that the questions of law or fact common to the members of the class predominate over any questions affecting only individual

members, and that a class action is superior to other available methods for the fair and efficient adjudication of the controversy.

The class actions described in sections (b)(1) and (b)(2) are mandatory class actions, i.e. actions in which all class members are bound and, unless the court orders otherwise, none is permitted to be excluded from the judgment. A 23(b)(3) class action permits class members to opt out of the action, within a certain period of time after certification as set by the court, and to proceed with an individual action.

b.   *Rule 23(b)(1)(A) Class Actions*

The types of actions set forth in 23(b)(1) address some of the difficulties that arise if individual actions by members of the class were to go forward. 23(b)(1)(A) is concerned that the party opposing the class action (the defendant, for the present purposes) not be held to conflicting standards of conduct by incompatible results of individual lawsuits. Although this would appear to fit with mass tort actions, the Advisory Committee seems to have had a different type of action in mind. Some examples given in the Advisory Committee notes are "[s]eparate actions by individuals against a municipality to declare a bond issue invalid ... [or] to prevent or limit the making of a particular appropriation or to compel or invalidate an assessment." Fed. R. Civ. P. 23, adv. comm. note. Rule 23(b)(1)(A) actions may not be appropriate in actions for money damages. *See* La Mar v. H & B Novelty & Loan Co., 489 F.2d

461 (9th Cir.1973) (stating that "the defendants in [money damages actions] can continue the conduct of which the plaintiffs complain even if the plaintiffs are successful ... in their individual actions" and the plaintiffs' success "does not fix the rights and duties owed by the defendants to others").

In a mass accident case arising out of the collapse of skywalks in the lobby of the Hyatt Regency Hotel in Kansas City, the district court initially certified a 23(b)(1)(A) class action, finding that a mass tort action fit the requirements of the rule. The decision was later vacated. *See* In re Federal Skywalk Cases, 93 F.R.D. 415 (W.D.Mo.1982). Some have suggested that if 23(b)(1)(A) were intended to apply to actions such as the *Skywalk* litigation, the rule would necessarily encompass all money damages actions that involved multiple plaintiffs—a result undoubtedly not contemplated by the rulemakers. *See* Richard L. Marcus & Edward F. Sherman, Complex Litigation: Cases and Materials on Advanced Civil Procedure 301–02 (4th ed. 2004). The court in the Agent Orange litigation stated that 23(b)(1)(A) was "*not* meant to apply ... where the risk of inconsistent results in individual actions is merely the possibility that the defendants will prevail in some cases and not in others, thereby paying damages to some claimants and not others." In re "Agent Orange" Prod. Liab. Litig., 506 F.Supp. 762 (E.D.N.Y.1980).

c. *Rule 23(b)(1)(B) Class Actions*

The interests sought to be protected in a 23(b)(1)(B) class action differ from the interests in a

23(b)(1)(A) class action. This kind of class action acknowledges that in some instances, if multiple actions proceed on an individual basis, the later claimants may be prejudiced by an inability to collect on their judgments against the defendants. This is called a "limited fund" class action because it is sometimes invoked in situations where, if the individual actions were to go forward without class certification, judgments in favor of early claimants would deplete the defendant's resources, thus leaving later claimants unable to obtain compensation for their injuries. *See* Fed. R. Civ. P. 23, adv. comm. note.

The 23(b)(1)(B) class action has been attractive to some mass tort litigants, particularly in cases in which punitive damages claims have been asserted. Its utility is limited, however, as demonstrated by the example of the Dalkon Shield litigation. In In re Northern District of California "Dalkon Shield" IUD Prods. Liab. Litig., 693 F.2d 847 (9th Cir. 1982), the court found error in the district court's certification of a (b)(1)(B) class for punitive damages. Taking note of the fact that over one thousand lawsuits had already been filed against the defendant manufacturer, the district court had conditionally certified a nationwide punitive damages class under 23(b)(1)(B), as well as a statewide class action on the issue of liability under 23(b)(3).

The Ninth Circuit was especially concerned with the lack of documentation as to whether later claims would in fact be impaired if the actions were allowed to proceed individually. The district court had certified the "limited fund" class action without having before it sufficient information regarding the finances, including insurance coverage, of the manufacturer. Moreover, the record was silent on the number of Dalkon Shield claims that had already been paid. The court stated: "Rule 23(b)(1)(B) certification is proper only when separate punitive damage claims necessarily will affect later claims. The district court erred by ordering certification without sufficient evidence of, or even a preliminary fact-finding inquiry concerning Robins' actual assets, insurance, settlement experience and continuing exposure." Several other federal courts have denied certification of 23(b)(1)(B) class actions for essentially the same reasons. *See, e.g.,* In re Bendectin Prods. Liab. Litig., 749 F.2d 300 (6th Cir.1984).

In Ortiz v. Fibreboard Corp., 527 U.S. 815 (1999), the United States Supreme Court cast serious doubt on the viability of the 23(b)(1)(B) class action in mass toxic tort litigation. The *Ortiz* settlement class action arose from a negotiated settlement between class plaintiffs, who had been exposed to asbestos, and Fibreboard Corp., in the context of an insurance coverage dispute between Fibreboard and its insurance carriers. As with the arrangement in *Amchem*, the purpose of the action was to achieve a global settlement of all future asbestos personal-injury claims against the defendant. The class thus included both persons currently injured and those who had been exposed to Fibreboard's products, but who had no present injury. The district court certified the action as a 23(b)(1)(B) "limited fund." The Supreme Court ultimately held that the class certification was erroneous, objecting both to the broad definition of the class of future claimants and to the use of the "limited fund" class action.

The Court noted that the historical limited fund model involved claimants to trust assets, a bank account, insurance proceeds, or other limited assets, pointing out that "the Advisory Committee did not contemplate that the mandatory class action ... would be used to aggregate unliquidated tort claims on a limited fund rationale." The Court also criticized the lower courts' uncritical acceptance of the parties' characterization of the available fund as limited. Rather, the Court said, the district court should have demanded specific proof of the limit on and insufficiency of the fund available to pay claims. Accordingly, the Court expressed the opinion that 23(b)(1)(B) class actions are perhaps best left to those cases that fit the historical limited fund model. Thus, while not absolutely excluding the use of the 23(b)(1)(B) class action in mass tort litigation, the Court demonstrated patent hostility toward its use in that context.

In In re Simon II Litigation, 407 F.3d 125 (2d Cir.2005), the Second Circuit vacated a 23(b)(1)(B) limited fund class action for punitive damages in a tobacco suit based upon alleged fraudulent conduct. The plaintiffs argued that the fund should be limited by the amount that would be appropriate to punish and deter the defendants, a theory referred to by the court as a "limited punishment" theory. The court rejected the theory because there was

> no evidence by which the district court could ascertain the limits of either the fund or the aggregate value of punitive claims against it, such that the postulated fund could be deemed inadequate to pay all legitimate claims, and thus plaintiffs have failed to satisfy one of the presumptively necessary conditions for limited fund treatment under *Ortiz*.

Thus, the requirement of demonstrating a true limited fund continues to have force.

d.   *Rule 23(b)(2) Class Actions*

The 23(b)(2) class action is designed to reach litigation in which final injunctive relief or declaratory relief is sought affecting the entire class. The Advisory Committee notes make clear, however, that this kind of class action "does not extend to cases in which the appropriate final relief relates exclusively or predominantly to money damages." Fed. R. Civ. P. 23, adv. comm. note. The classic (b)(2) case is a case alleging the violation of civil rights. Most toxic tort actions, even where they seek injunctive relief, will seek money damages as well, thus rendering the 23(b)(2) class action inappropriate.

Some toxic tort actions may seek primarily injunctive relief. A 23(b)(2) class will still probably be inappropriate, however. For example, a public nuisance action often seeks abatement of the nuisance.

See, e.g., Village of Wilsonville v. SCA Services, Inc., 426 N.E.2d 824 (Ill.1981) (disposal of hazardous waste). When brought by a municipality to vindicate a public right, a class action is rendered unnecessary. When brought instead by private individuals who have suffered a special injury, it is likely that money damages would be requested in addition to an injunction, most likely rendering 23(b)(2) inappropriate. *See generally* Chapter Three, Section C.2, *supra*. Thus, the 23(b)(2) class action is of very limited use in toxic tort litigation.

e.   *Rule 23(b)(3) Class Actions*

By far the most common kind of federal class action in the toxic tort context is the 23(b)(3) class action. In many ways, the requirements of the 23(b)(3) action are less narrow than those of the other 23(b) types. Moreover, it is more flexible in that it permits class members to opt out of the class action to pursue their own individual lawsuits. Nevertheless, the 23(b)(3) requirements have been applied strictly, and the provision is not a catch-all.

In certifying a 23(b)(3) class action, the court must determine that the common questions of law or fact that had been found to exist in the 23(a)(2) prerequisite inquiry actually predominate in the litigation over the questions affecting individual class members. Further, the court must find the class action device superior to other means of handling the complex litigation. Rule 23(b)(3) offers the following factors to assist the court in its determination of whether this type of class action should be certified:

(A) the interest of members of the class in individually controlling the prosecution or defense of separate actions; (B) the extent and nature of any litigation concerning the controversy already commenced by or against members of the class; (C) the desirability or undesirability of concentrating the litigation of the claims in the particular forum; (D) the difficulties likely to be encountered in the management of a class action.

The Advisory Committee notes state that a mass tort action "is ordinarily not appropriate for a class action because of the likelihood that significant questions, not only of damages but of liability and defenses to liability, would be present, affecting the individuals in different ways." The Advisory Committee was concerned that class certification in litigation involving numerous individual questions would "degenerate in practice into multiple lawsuits separately tried."

Notwithstanding these concerns, courts have read the Advisory Committee notes as not prohibiting the use of the 23(b)(3) class action device in mass torts, but rather emphasizing the predominance and superiority requirements. In the Agent Orange litigation, the court stated that so long as common questions of law or fact constitute a "significant aspect" of the case and are appropriate for resolution on a class basis, the predominance requirement is met. In that case, significant common questions existed on certain defenses that were applicable to the class as a whole. This, the court held, sufficed to meet the test. As to the individual questions of causation, the court found that no barrier to the certification of a 23(b)(3) class action existed provided that the plaintiffs' counsel chose representatives for each type of injury alleged. The court further held that the superiority requirement was met. The defendants noted the size and geographical breadth of the class and argued that because the separate substantive product liability laws of the individual states would apply to the individual plaintiffs, the class action should not be certified. The court rejected this argument, concluding that sufficient general uniformity existed in state substantive law. Because the Agent Orange litigation settled prior to trial, there was no opportunity to evaluate the success of class treatment in the factfinding process.

In contrast, an effort to certify a 23(b)(3) class action in the Dalkon Shield litigation ultimately failed. The Ninth Circuit concluded that too many issues requiring individual determination were present in the case, including individual case histories of plaintiffs regarding their use of the Dalkon Shield and their alleged injuries. *See* In re Northern Dist. of California "Dalkon Shield" IUD Prods. Liab. Litig., 693 F.2d 847 (9th Cir.1982). The district court judge who had originally certified the class, Judge Spencer Williams, has criticized the Ninth Circuit's decision, insisting that his certification of an "issues-only" class precluded a challenge on the predominance grounds because individual questions were not part of the matters certified. *See* Hon. Spencer Williams, *Mass Tort Class Actions: Going, Going, Gone?*, 98 F.R.D. 323 (1983).

Many courts hesitate to certify 23(b)(3) class actions in toxic tort litigation because of problems related to causation. Thus, the court in Mertens v. Abbott Laboratories, 99 F.R.D. 38 (D.N.H.1983) held that proof of general causation of the adverse effects of in utero exposure to DES did not constitute a predominating common question, because individual proof would be required of each plaintiff on the matter of specific causation. Likewise, in Yandle v. PPG Industries, Inc., 65 F.R.D. 566 (E.D.Tex.1974), an asbestos case, the court denied class certification because "there is not a single act of negligence or proximate cause which would apply to each potential class member and each defendant in this case."

In Amchem Products, Inc. v. Windsor, 521 U.S. 591 (1997), discussed *supra*, the Supreme Court decertified an unusually expansive 23(b)(3) class action. The district court had held that the predominance requirement was met by the fact that all members of the class had been exposed to asbestos and by the existence of the class members' common interest in just and speedy adjudication and their need to minimize the risks and costs of litigation through reaching an early settlement. The Supreme Court stated that the "predominance inquiry tests whether proposed classes are sufficiently cohesive to warrant adjudication by representation," and concluded that the vast class of injured and non-injured persons in this case did not meet that test. The Court held that individual questions far exceeded the common questions among the class members. These individual questions included such matters as time, manner, and extent of exposure, type of injury (or lack thereof), and the existence of intervening causes such as smoking. Furthermore, the Court noted, differences in applicable state law exacerbated these individual differences.

It is difficult to determine how much impact *Amchem* has had on class action certification in mass tort cases, but it has likely had a chilling effect. In Nafar v. Hollywood Tanning Sys., Inc., 2009 WL 2386666 (3d Cir. 2009), an action brought by indoor tanners who claimed the defendant failed to warn of the risks of ultraviolet light, the Third Circuit vacated class certification. Although the court ruled primarily on the deficiencies of the certification order itself, it directed the district court, on remand, to consider closely whether the individual issues of causation predominated. Still, federal district courts have continued to certify class actions where they deemed the requirements of Rule 23 were met. *See, e.g.,* Sher v. Raytheon Co., 261 F.R.D. 651 (M.D. Fla. 2009) (certifying a 23(b)(3) class action in a groundwater contamination case); Klein v. O'Neal, Inc., 222 F.R.D. 564 (N.D.Tex.2004) (certifying a nationwide drug product liability class action and stating that differences in applicable state laws "do not present insurmountable obstacles to class certification"). *Amchem* does, however, serve as a reminder that the requirements of Rule 23 should be applied strictly, and that mass toxic torts present challenges to using the class action device to aggregate large numbers of claims.

f. *Notice in 23(b)(3) Class Actions*

An integral part of the 23(b)(3) class action is the notice requirement, which is mandated by due process to give class members the opportunity to opt out and pursue individual actions. Rule 23(c)(2)(B) provides that in a 23(b)(3) class action, "the best notice practicable under the circumstances" must be given to the class members, "including individual notice to all members who can be identified through reasonable effort." These requirements reflect almost verbatim the general procedural due process requirements set forth in Mullane v. Central Hanover Bank & Trust Co., 339 U.S. 306 (1950). Rule 23(c)(2)(B) also provides that the notice shall state that the class member may affirmatively opt out of the action by a certain date and that if the class member does not opt out, any judgment in the action will become binding on the class member.

The notice ordered in the Agent Orange litigation demonstrates the lengths to which courts may have to go to assure that due process is satisfied in notifying class members in a 23(b)(3) action. The court ordered notice in several forms, in a hierarchy that related to the ability of the plaintiffs' attorneys to identify class members individually. Thus, where class members had already participated to any degree in litigation on Agent Orange or were represented by counsel, or were listed in the V.A.'s "Agent Orange Registry," the court ordered individual mailings. For the remainder of the class, notice was appropriate by radio and television announcements or in newspapers and magazines. Moreover, the court ordered notice to the Governors of the states to identify potential class members who may be known to state organizations established to assist Vietnam veterans. *See* In re "Agent Orange" Prod. Liab. Litig., 100 F.R.D. 718 (E.D.N.Y.1983).

4. Settlement of Class Actions

Rule 23(e)(1) provides that a class action may not be dismissed or settled without court approval and that notice of the dismissal or settlement must be given to all class members. Approval of a class action settlement involves, first, a preliminary hearing on fairness which can include information from expert witnesses designated by the parties or from court-appointed experts. If the settlement seems appropriate after the preliminary hearing, the court should order that notice of a formal fairness hearing be made to class members. *See* Fed. R. Civ. P. 23(e)(1)(C). The notice should invite class members who may have objections to the settlement to file written objections with the court. *See* Federal Judicial Center, Manual For Complex Litigation (Fourth) § 21.633 (2004). Rule 23(e)(3) now allows courts to offer class members in 23(b)(3) class actions a renewed opportunity to opt out of the action at the time of settlement. Barring that, objectors may not opt out of the class action at this stage, but they may notify the court of the reasons that they believe the settlement is unfair.

In the Agent Orange litigation, the court received numerous objections to the proposed settlement provisions. In the "Fairness Opinion" approving the settlement, the court explained that class consensus was virtually impossible to gauge and could not form the basis for a determination of the fairness of the proposed settlement. Thus, although the court received hundreds of responses to the proposed settlement, there was what the court called "an overwhelmingly large silent majority." Even though individual approval of the settlement provisions and individual execution of the settlement documents were not possible under the circumstances, the class members nevertheless were bound to its terms. *See* In re "Agent Orange" Prod. Liab. Litig., 597 F.Supp. 740 (E.D.N.Y.1984) (Fairness Opinion).

The court applied the following test in deciding whether the settlement was fair and reasonable:

"(1) The complexity, expense and likely duration of the litigation, ... (2) the reaction of the class [to] the settlement, ... (3) the stage of the proceedings and the amount of discovery completed, ... (4) the risks of establishing liability, ... (5) the risks of establishing damages, ... (6) the risks of maintaining the class action through the trial, ... (7) the ability of the defendants to withstand a higher judgment, ... (8) the range of reasonableness of the settlement fund in light of the best possible recovery, ... [and] (9) the range of reasonableness of the settlement fund to a possible recovery in light of all the attendant risks of litigation, ... "

Id. (quoting City of Detroit v. Grinnell Corp., 495 F.2d 448 (2d Cir.1974)). The court considered in detail the objections of the class members as well as the overall social effect of the Agent Orange litigation. The most important issue in determining the fairness of the proposed settlement was the plaintiffs' likelihood of success on the merits in light of the amount offered in settlement. The court considered the weaknesses of the plaintiffs' case, particularly causation ("[T]he evidence presented to the court to date suggests that the case is without merit."), the strength of the defendants' defenses, and other risks of establishing liability and damages and concluded that the settlement was fair.

5.   Class Counsel and Attorney Fee Awards

Rule 23 contains provision related to the appointment of class counsel and attorney fee awards. Rule 23(g)(1) provides that with class certification, the court must appoint class counsel that will "fairly and adequately represent the interests of the class." Factors in evaluating applicants for class counsel include: any work counsel has undertaken to investigate the claims and identifying potential class members; counsel's prior experience with complex litigation; and the resources available to counsel for use during the litigation. Fed. R. Civ. P. 23(g)(1)(C)(i). In selecting from multiple applicants, the court must choose "the applicant best able to represent the interests of the class."

Rule 23(h)(1) requires that a request for reasonable attorney fees and taxable costs be made by motion with notice to all parties and class members. If necessary, the court may hold a hearing to resolve fact questions related to fees. Fed. R. Civ. P. 23(h)(3).

C. CLASS ACTION FAIRNESS ACT OF 2005

After many years of heated debate, Congress passed the Class Action Fairness Act of 2005 (CAFA). The net effect of the law will be to move many, if not most, mass tort actions out of state courts and into federal court. CAFA achieves this by amending the federal diversity statute to add new subsection (d). *See* 28 U.S.C.A. § 1332(d) (West 2010). The new subsection expands federal diversity jurisdiction to include most class actions and mass actions by providing for minimal diversity and a $5 million aggregate amount in controversy requirement. In a coordinated provision, Congress loosened removal requirements to permit any defendant to remove a class or mass action to federal court without the usual limitations that apply to defendants who are citizens of the state in which the action was brought. *See* 28 U.S.C.A. § 1453 (West 2010).

CAFA applies to class and mass actions involving more than 100 persons whose aggregated claims exceed $5 million. A "mass action" refers to aggregate claims arising out of the same general circumstances, but which have not been brought as a class action. *See* Gilmore v. Bayer Corp., 2009 WL 4789406 (S.D. Ill. 2009) (slip op.) (holding that CAFA federal jurisdiction applied to a "mass action" consisting of approximately 100 cases for personal injuries based upon product liability claims relating to the prescription drug Trasylol). Two major exceptions are built into the Act that apply to controversies of a more local nature. The first, a mandatory exception, requires the federal court to decline to exercise jurisdiction where more than two-thirds of the plaintiffs are citizens of the state in which the action was originally filed, and the primary defendants are citizens of that state. 28 U.S.C.A. § 1332(d)(4) (West 2010). This is generally referred to as the "home-state controversy exception" to CAFA. A "primary defendant" is one whom the plaintiffs sue directly, as contrasted with contribution or indemnification claims. Kitson v. Bank of Edwardsville, 2006 WL 3392752 (S.D. Ill. 2006). The second exception grants the federal court the discretion to decline to exercise jurisdiction, "in the interests of justice and looking at the totality of the circumstances," where between one-third and two-thirds of the plaintiffs are citizens of the state in which the action was originally filed, and the primary defendants are also citizens of that state. *Id.* § 1332(d)(3).

In Anthony v. Small Tube Mftg. Corp., 535 F.Supp.2d 506 (E.D. Pa. 2007), a putative class action consisting of several thousand persons exposed to beryllium and seeking medical monitoring, the court declined to remand the case to state court under the home-state controversy exception. The court said that the plaintiff failed to provide evidence either that two-thirds or more of the members of the class were citizens of Pennsylvania or that the "primary defendants" were Pennsylvania citizens. The court emphasized that to rely on the exception, the plaintiff needed to address the citizenship of the entire membership of the class. It seems, therefore, that federal courts entertaining motions to remand will require more than mere conclusory statements about citizenship.

In addition, CAFA contains provisions for judicial scrutiny of so-called "coupon settlements." 28 U.S.C.A. § 1712 (West 2010). The provisions also require notification of certain public officials of the class action settlements and establish rules for attorney fees, contingent and otherwise, in coupon settlement cases.

The proponents of CAFA, which was heavily supported by business groups, viewed the state courts as friendly to plaintiff classes, and sought a means of moving these actions from state court to federal court at the discretion of defendants. This is exactly what CAFA allows. The strict application of Rule 23 in the federal courts, and the requirements of *Daubert* and the Federal Rules of Evidence for the admissibility of expert evidence, suggest that at least some class actions that might otherwise have succeeded in state court will not survive in federal court. For those class actions that survive, Rule 23 requires close monitoring by the court of both the management of the action and matters related to counsel. CAFA is filled with jargon—including such terms as "primary defendants," "significant relief," and "significant basis for the claims"—which assures that many judicial decisions will be required before patterns emerge to illuminate the meaning of the Act's language and the way that the Act applies in individual cases.

D. OTHER AGGREGATIVE PROCEDURES

1. Multidistrict Litigation Transfer

Congress has granted authority to the Judicial Panel on Multidistrict Litigation (MDL) to transfer actions "involving one or more common questions" pending in different federal districts to any single district for pretrial proceedings, provided that the transfer "will be for the convenience of parties and witnesses and will promote the just and efficient conduct of such actions." 28 U.S.C.A. § 1407(a) (West 2010). As the provision states, the panel is authorized to make such transfers for pretrial purposes only, including settlement. *See* Lexecon Inc. v. Milberg Weiss Bershad Hynes & Lerach, 523 U.S. 26 (1998).

The MDL transfer was used to aggregate more than 26,000 asbestos cases in the Eastern District of Pennsylvania before Judge Weiner. *See* In re Asbestos Prods. Liab. Litig., 771 F.Supp. 415 (Jud. Pan. Mult. Lit. 1991). Transfer was carried out even though a substantial group of plaintiffs objected. The rationales for the transfer to Judge Weiner's court were that the greatest number of the cases was already pending in that district and that Judge Weiner brought to the litigation a high level of experience in such matters. It is the responsibility of the transferee judge to establish procedures to expedite the litigation, and the judge may seek the assistance of other experienced judges in advancing the procedures.

Not every collection of similar toxic tort actions is appropriate for MDL transfer. In In re Ambulatory Pain Pump–Chondrolysis Prods. Liab. Litig., 2010 WL 1529487 (Jud. Pan. Mult. Lit. 2010), the panel declined MDL transfer for the second time, finding too many individual issues in the cases. One significant point was that the cases involved an "indeterminate number of different pain pumps made by different manufacturers." Some of the plaintiffs objected to transfer because their cases had progressed too far to benefit from the MDL procedures. Further, the plaintiffs disagreed on the appropriate transferee district. In In re Asbestos and Asbestos Insulation Material Prods. Liab. Litig., 431 F.Supp. 906 (Jud. Pan. Mult. Lit. 1977), the panel also denied MDL transfer on the basis of predominating individual questions. The panel noted that "the only questions of fact common to all actions relate to the state of scientific and medical knowledge at different points in time concerning the risks of exposure to asbestos." In contrast, numerous questions existed that were unique to each separate action. In addition, many of the actions were well advanced at the time of the proposed transfer, having been pending for several years. MDL transfer in this instance would hinder, rather than advance, the resolution of those actions. By 1991, however, the panel exhibited greater receptivity to MDL transfer in asbestos litigation, at least partly due to the apparent failure of individual adjudication to adequately compensate injured asbestos plaintiffs. *See* In re Asbestos Prods. Liab. Litig., 771 F.Supp. 415 (Jud. Pan. Mult. Lit. 1991).

2. Consolidation

In the federal courts, consolidation of actions is governed by Federal Rule of Civil Procedure 42(a), which provides that the court may order that actions with at least one common question of law or fact be consolidated. Consolidation may be for pretrial and trial purposes, or merely for discovery. Although use of this device has been attempted where many individual cases are involved, it appears that the device is most appropriate under relatively narrow circumstances.

In general, broad discretion is vested in the trial court to determine whether consolidation is appropriate in a given case. The need for judicial economy must be balanced against due process considerations. Consolidation must not be imposed at the substantial risk of prejudice or jury confusion. Attempts at the use of consolidation in asbestos litigation give some sense of the difficulties faced by courts. The asbestos litigation was particularly suited to innovative attempts at collective resolution. As one court observed: "Finding an appropriate forum to resolve all these [asbestos] claims with minimal delay is the goal.... Pre-trial consolidation for the purposes of discovery, the appointment of special masters to expedite settlement, and, especially, the liberal use of consolidated trials have ameliorated what might otherwise be a sclerotic backlog of cases." Malcolm v. National Gypsum Co., 995 F.2d 346 (2d Cir.1993). But the case law indicates that consolidation may not be appropriate in all circumstances in which multiple lawsuits threaten to seriously backlog the system.

In Johnson v. Celotex Corp., 899 F.2d 1281 (2d Cir.1990), the court upheld the district court's consolidation of two asbestos cases. The court applied a balancing test that weighed the risk of prejudice and confusion against the advantages of collective factfinding. These advantages included judicial economy, avoiding conflicting results on issues of fact and law, and reducing the hardship on the parties and witnesses. The court also stated that trial courts should explore the possibility of minimizing prejudice and confusion by providing specific instructions to jurors or employing other devices. The *Johnson* court followed other courts in employing the following criteria when deciding whether consolidation is appropriate in asbestos litigation: " '(1) common worksite [of plaintiffs]; (2) similar occupation; (3) similar time of exposure; (4) type of disease; (5) whether plaintiffs were living or deceased; (6) status of discovery in each case; (7) whether all plaintiffs were represented by the same counsel; and (8) type of cancer alleged....' " (quoting In re All Asbestos Cases Pending in the United States Dist. Court for the Dist. of Maryland, 1983 WL 808161 (D.Md.1983)). The court determined that these criteria were met.

A much larger number of asbestos cases was consolidated in In re Eastern & Southern Dists. Asbestos Litig. (Brooklyn Navy Yard), 1991 WL 270626 (E. & S.D.N.Y.1991). The court divided the consolidated action into three phases for trial, depending upon the percentage of each plaintiff's exposure to asbestos that occurred in the Navy Yard. The cases all arose out of exposure at that particular site, which during all relevant times was owned by the United States Government. Further, the sellers of the asbestos used at the Yard were somewhat consistent, as they were contractors hired by the Government and presumably required to comply with certain specifications. Also, due to the uniformity of the uses to which the asbestos products were put at the Yard, it was reasonable to assume that the circumstances under which the plaintiffs were exposed to asbestos were fairly consistent.

Not all consolidated asbestos cases exhibited the level of consistency that was present in the Brooklyn Navy Yard litigation. In Malcolm v. National Gypsum Co., 995 F.2d 346 (2d Cir.1993), the court reversed the consolidation of 600 asbestos cases in which each plaintiff had been exposed to asbestos through work in one or more of more than forty powerhouses. The court applied the criteria referenced in the *Johnson* case, but found that they were not met. The most significant problem for consolidation cited by the court was the lack of a "primary worksite" such as had existed in the Brooklyn Navy Yard case. The court determined that too many variables existed, which in turn would lead to an avalanche of evidence requiring a jury to make distinctions that were too difficult and confusing.

E. TRIAL MANAGEMENT

Regardless of the aggregative procedure employed to bring together numerous cases, issues remain as to management of the postaggregation course of the litigation. For a detailed exploration of postaggregative procedure in two case studies involving toxic torts, see Linda S. Mullenix, *Beyond Consolidation: Postaggregative Procedure in Asbestos Mass Tort Litigation*, 32 Wm. & Mary L. Rev. 475 (1991). One of the areas in which judges have been especially innovative is the management of trial.

Cimino v. Raymark Industries, Inc., 751 F.Supp. 649 (E.D.Tex.1990) provides an example of creative trial management, but also serves to highlight the pitfalls awaiting the judge who attempts to streamline mass tort litigation. In *Cimino*, Judge Robert

Parker of the Eastern District of Texas certified a
23(b)(3) class action involving the asbestos-exposure
claims of more than 3,000 persons. Judge Parker
established a procedure for trial in three phases.
Phase I addressed the fact questions in the issues of
product defect, appropriateness of warnings, state-
of-the-art, and punitive damages. Part of this process involved assigning a figure by which compensatory damages would be multiplied to obtain the
amount of punitive damages.

Phase II was to require the jury to make findings
regarding nineteen work sites; but instead, the parties entered into a stipulation on causation and
exposure. The issues in this phase involved determining the time frame when asbestos products were
used at each site, identifying the jobs in which the
products were used and whether the amount of
exposure in a job would be sufficient to produce
injury, and apportioning liability among the defendants. The stipulation regarding Phase II was based
upon a list compiled by the court of various work
sites and specific jobs. Judge Parker stated: "It was
contemplated that any plaintiff whose work history
did not include a threshold amount of time in any of
the worksites would have the exposure issue tried
in an individual mini-trial." Essentially, the parties
agreed to assess ten percent causation to each of the
nonsettling defendants and thirteen percent to the
settling defendant, Johns–Manville Corporation.

Finally, Phase III addressed damages by dividing
the class into five categories of disease. The court
randomly chose 160 sample plaintiffs, ranging from

fifteen to fifty persons for each category, to be tried to a jury. The amounts determined by the jury served as a basis for the awards to the remaining class members by extrapolation.

Judge Parker's efforts at economy of scale and efficiency of process ultimately failed, however. On appeal to the Fifth Circuit, and after judgment against it in a total of 157 of the cases, one of the defendants, Pittsburgh Corning, challenged the trial plan for failure to properly try the issue of individual causation in the sample cases and failure to individually determine damages in the extrapolation cases. *See* Cimino v. Raymark Industries, Inc., 151 F.3d 297 (5th Cir.1998). Pittsburgh Corning argued that these failures were fatal to the trial plan and were in violation of Texas substantive law, the Seventh Amendment right to a jury trial, and the due process clause. The court stated that neither the fact that this was a class action nor the massive scope of the asbestos litigation in this country alters the applicability of the Seventh Amendment to the case. Furthermore, the court determined that Texas law mandated individual determination of causation and damages with regard to Pittsburgh Corning's products. The court held that Phase III of the trial plan failed to individually litigate the issues of causation, exposure, and damages or to provide a jury trial on those issues. The flaws in the plan applied both to the sample cases and the extrapolation cases, the court ruled. Accordingly, the Fifth Circuit reversed the judgments.

Notwithstanding the result in *Cimino*, the use of various aggregative procedures will likely continue to be important in the future of toxic tort litigation. *See generally* Glen O. Robinson & Kenneth S. Abraham, *Collective Justice in Tort Law*, 78 Va. L. Rev. 1481 (1992) (proposing the use of statistical claim profiles derived from earlier cases and settlements, or models, to provide baseline values for individual claims). Legitimate concerns exist regarding matters of individualized justice, the right to a jury trial, and due process. Hopefully, future attempts by innovative judges to address the problems associated with collective resolution of mass toxic torts will result in a compilation of effective alternatives from which courts may draw when faced with similar challenges. For a discussion challenging the widely accepted notions of party control in traditional tort litigation and demonstrating that using such preconceptions as a standard against which aggregative procedures are measured may be faulty, see Deborah R. Hensler, *Resolving Mass Toxic Torts: Myths and Realities*, 1989 U. Ill. L. Rev. 89 (1989).

F. SETTLEMENT

Another area in which innovative approaches have been attempted is settlement. Toxic tort plaintiffs often seek remedies beyond traditional compensatory damages, or even punitive damages. Consequently, parties and courts have attempted to fashion creative settlements to accommodate these requests. The massive scope of much toxic tort litigation has inspired courts to use settlement and other options to resolve unprecedented numbers of claims efficiently and expeditiously.

1. Settlement Class Actions

For some time, plaintiffs in mass toxic tort litigation have been using the device of the "settlement class action." In these cases, the plaintiffs file the complaint and the proposed settlement agreement—previously negotiated between the parties—simultaneously. A request to certify a class action is accompanied by a request to approve the settlement. The settlement class action has the advantage of resolving large numbers of similar claims without the need for a protracted discovery and pretrial motion process or lengthy, perhaps multi-staged, trial. Critics of the device have argued that the classes of plaintiffs have become large and amorphous in recent years, and that parties have overreached in their zealous efforts to resolve thousands of claims.

In Amchem Products, Inc. v. Windsor, 521 U.S. 591 (1997), discussed in Section B, *supra*, the United States Supreme Court directly addressed the question whether settlement class actions are allowable under Rule 23 of the Federal Rules of Civil Procedure. The Court concluded that "settlement is relevant to a class certification" and that in settlement class actions, the district court should not analyze the case with trial in mind. Thus, "a district court need not inquire whether the case, if tried, would present intractable management prob-

lems ... for the proposal is that there be no trial."
The Court cautioned, however, that the portions of
Rule 23 designed to protect absent class members
may deserve "heightened attention" in a settlement
class action. This would include properly identifying
the class represented. Indeed, the Court was quick
to point out that in settlement class actions, class
certification will not necessarily be granted more
readily than in a case to be tried. Furthermore, the
Court stated that a determination that the proposed
settlement is fair does not lead to the conclusion
that class certification should automatically be
granted. Rather, the certification decision is
achieved through an independent analysis of the
23(a) and (b) criteria.

In *Amchem*, the Court held that the Third Circuit
had properly decertified the class action, consisting
of all unfiled asbestos personal-injury claims by
persons exposed to asbestos products, whether or
not those persons currently suffered asbestos-related injuries. Among other things, the Court determined that the predominance requirement of Rule
23(b)(3) was not met because the vast numbers of
claimants with potentially conflicting interests
raised a substantial number of factual and legal
questions that could only be resolved on an individual basis.

Notwithstanding the result in *Amchem*, settlement class actions are allowed in the federal courts
and offer an option for resolution of claims without
protracted litigation. Parties must use the device

with care, however, as it is not a means to circumvent the provisions of Rule 23.

2. Medical Monitoring

Plaintiffs concerned about future injuries associated with the defendants' conduct may seek to include some form of medical surveillance or ongoing medical care in the settlement agreement. Even in jurisdictions not recognizing medical monitoring claims without present injury, the parties may choose to include this kind of relief in their negotiated settlement.

In re Fernald Litig., 1989 WL 267038 (S.D.Ohio 1989) (approving settlement) involved claims by residents alleging exposure to hazardous substances, including uranium, as a result of the operation of the nearby Feed Material Production Center of the U.S. Department of Energy. The plaintiffs sought medical monitoring in the lawsuit. The settlement required the defendants to pay $73 million to the plaintiffs for future medical monitoring. The money was to be placed in a fund managed by trustees (special masters) who were also designated to establish the monitoring program. Appropriate uses of the funds included medical examinations, diagnostic tests, and epidemiological studies. Subsequently, in a separate class action brought by former employees of the Fernald plant against NLO Inc., which operated the plant for the Government, the parties reached a settlement during trial that included lifetime medical monitoring for the employees. As part of the settlement, an independent three-member panel would evaluate physical injuries or illnesses and determine whether they were sufficiently work-related to be compensable under workers' compensation. *See* Day v. NLO, 864 F.Supp. 40 (S.D.Ohio 1994) (transferring case for review of fairness of proposed settlement).

In the Three Mile Island litigation, which arose from a release of radiation at a nuclear facility in Harrisburg, Pennsylvania, a class of plaintiffs sought medical monitoring for all persons residing within a certain distance of the plant. Under the terms of the settlement, the defendants established and financed a Public Health Fund to conduct studies of the public health effects of the release at the facility and of the effects of low-level radiation generally, as well as public education programs. *See* In re Three Mile Island Litig., 557 F.Supp. 96 (M.D.Pa.1982).

In 2005, a West Virginia court approved a settlement in Leach v. E.I. du Pont de Nemours & Co., 2002 WL 1270121 (W.Va.Cir.Ct.2002) (certifying class action), which established a two-tier approach to medical monitoring. The first step was the establishment of a human health study, funded by the defendant, to evaluate the extent to which perfluorooctanoic acid from the defendant's plant harmed the class members or increased their risk of developing illness in the future. If harm or risk is found, the settlement authorizes a program for medical monitoring. *See* Bebe Raupe, *Court Approves Class Action Settlement with Possible $340 Million Du-*

Pont Payout, 20 Toxics L. Rptr. (BNA) 246 (March 10, 2005).

3. Bankruptcy Option

Many asbestos companies have filed for bankruptcy protection from toxic tort claims, with the number increasing yearly. The use of the bankruptcy laws to manage asbestos claims began in 1982, when the Johns–Manville Corporation, the major manufacturer of asbestos products, filed for protection under Chapter 11 of the federal bankruptcy laws on the basis of projected liabilities in then-current and future asbestos-related actions. The company estimated its liabilities at $2 billion dollars. The estimate was based upon both existing claims and future claims calculated on the basis of the number of persons who had been exposed to Johns–Manville asbestos-containing products, but who had not yet manifested disease symptoms. A reorganization plan was created in 1986 that involved establishing the Manville Personal Injury Settlement Trust to pay asbestos personal injury claims. All claims, present and future, were required to be presented to the Trust; no claimant could bring a tort action against Manville in court. No recovery for punitive damages was to be allowed by the Trust. *See* In re Johns–Manville Corp., 68 B.R. 618 (Bkrtcy. S.D.N.Y.1986). After the plan was approved by the Second Circuit in 1988, Kane v. Johns–Manville Corp., 843 F.2d 636 (2d Cir.1988), the Trust received an infusion of cash in the amount of $909 million, as well as stocks and bonds. The aggregate value of the Trust was in the vicinity of $2.5 billion.

The Trust began processing claims, but by 1990 the cash reserves were almost empty. Until that point, the Trust had provided compensation for more than 20,000 claims at an average value of $42,000. In 1990, the Plan came under the control of Judge Weinstein of the Eastern District of New York for restructuring so that the early claimants would not deplete the funds. A class was certified, and a settlement was proposed allocating the Trust payments with priority based upon seriousness of illness. The Second Circuit rejected the restructured plan in 1992, In re Joint E. & S. Dists. Asbestos Litig., 982 F.2d 721 (2d Cir.1992), in part because it identified certain subclasses—for example, those claimants who had held a higher priority under the original Plan—whose interests were not adequately represented by the class representatives. Later, however, the Second Circuit modified its ruling, holding that subclasses were not necessary and allowing further negotiations to go forward.

The result was a settlement plan approved by the court. In re Joint E. & S. Dists. Asbestos Litig., 878 F.Supp. 473 (E. & S.D.N.Y.1995). The settlement contained a scheduled value of claims based upon previous settlements under the Trust and recent settlements of tort actions. The settlement plan created a matrix of values for seven diseases on which the payments would be based. Nevertheless, claimants objecting to the scheduled amount could request individual claim review. The plan provided for initial payments to be made based upon ten percent of the scheduled value of claims, ranging from $1,200 to $20,000.

In addition to the scheduled values, another significant feature of the settlement was the inclusion of the claims of co-defendants who alleged that they were forced to pay to claimants the Trust's share of liability while the stay on Trust payments was in effect. The sum of $55.7 million was set aside to reimburse the co-defendants. The settlement also provided for the continued immunity of the new Manville Corp. and the Trust from asbestos-related lawsuits. Its scope was far-reaching, including claims by existing claimants, persons who may become ill in the future (represented by counsel), co-defendants, and Manville's distributors and judgment creditors. In a more recent development in the story of the Manville bankruptcy, the United States Supreme Court ruled, in Travelers Indemnity Co. v. Bailey, 129 S.Ct. 2195 (2009), that asbestos personal injury plaintiffs are barred from directly suing Manville's insurers on the basis of the insurers' alleged knowledge of the hazards of asbestos as early as the 1950s.

The settlement of the Manville Trust claims demonstrates the results that can be achieved through tenacious judicial management. The settlement's sweeping scope was intended to provide a mechanism to eventually put to rest the thousands of claims associated with the operation of Johns–Manville Corporation as an asbestos manufacturer and seller. It has also been a learning tool for subsequent bankruptcies of other asbestos product manufacturers.

4. Tobacco Solution

Perhaps the quintessential public law/private law toxic tort is tobacco. Private litigation and public regulation abound, and much of the discussion on the subject has centered on whether private litigation or regulatory action is the most effective means of addressing the public-health and legal issues that surround tobacco. Several state attorneys general commenced actions against the tobacco industry seeking reimbursement for public funds expended for medical care of persons with smoking-related diseases. In 1997, the states and the tobacco companies negotiated a global settlement with far-reaching implications. Not only would the deal have settled the existing lawsuits, but it contained numerous restrictions on future lawsuits, such as a ban on class actions and limits on damages. The proposal required Congressional approval to become effective. Despite months of debate and several proposed modifications of the settlement provisions, Congress could not reach a consensus on the tobacco settlement. In the wake of this failure, the states and the tobacco industry re-negotiated the settlement in 1998, this time with a narrower focus and without the requirement of Congressional approval. All states that had not yet independently settled their actions against the industry, including the states that had not yet filed actions, joined the settlement. Among the provisions in the settlement, known as the Master Settlement Agreement (MSA), were scheduled payments to the states, restrictions on cigarette advertising, and restrictions on tobacco company sponsorship of sports and entertainment events. Among the significant omissions from the settlement was any reference to limiting future actions by smokers.

The tobacco resolution used a private-law mechanism to solve a public health problem, and the settlement contained provisions that traditionally were the subject of public-law enactments. While the resolution does not end tobacco litigation, it does provide a model for resolving certain kinds of toxic torts that have a substantial regulatory component. For a discussion of the MSA in the context of mass tort litigation, see Jean Macchiaroli Eggen, *The Synergy of Toxic Tort Law and Public Health: Lessons From a Century of Cigarettes*, 41 Conn. L. Rev. 561, 600–607 (2008).

5. World Trade Center Solution

Immediately following the attacks of September 11, 2001, Congress enacted the Air Transportation Safety and System Stabilization Act (ATSSSA), Pub. L. No. 107–42, 115 Stat. 230 (2001) (signed Sept. 22, 2001). The purpose of ATSSSA was to protect the airlines from the financial burdens of lawsuits brought by the families of victims of the attacks. A major feature of ATSSSA was the creation of a no-fault Victim Compensation Fund "to provide compensation to any individual (or relative of a deceased individual) who was physically injured or killed as a result of the terrorist-related aircraft crashes of September 11, 2001." ATSSSA § 403. Application to the fund was voluntary, but if an eligible person used the fund for compensation, he or she waived the right to bring a tort action for damages. A subsequent amendment extended the tort liability limitation to other potential parties and limited the liability of New York City. In 2003, Congress appropriated $1 billion for a "captive insurance company or other appropriate mechanism for claims arising from debris removal" from the site. In effect, these public remedies were extended to first responders and other cleanup workers who have developed health problems as a result of exposures during their work during the protracted aftermath of the disaster.

ATSSSA also established a federal cause of action for damages and granted exclusive jurisdiction in the Southern District of New York for all disputes arising out of the 9/11 attacks. Judge Hellerstein of the Southern District was designated to handle the health claims of the first responders and other cleanup workers. *See* In re WTC Center Disaster Site, 414 F.3d 352 (2d Cir. 2005) (upholding the exclusive federal jurisdiction for 9/11 claims). The plaintiffs generally claimed injuries for respiratory illnesses during the rescue, recovery, and cleanup operations at the World Trade Center site and the Fresh Kills disposal site. Judge Hellerstein has made numerous rulings in the World Trade Center Disaster Site litigation, and in 2010 a proposed settlement was submitted to the court, to be administered by the captive insurance company, that would amount to payments from the fund of $575–657 million. The court rejected the proposal, in part out of concern that too much money was set aside for future claims. In June, 2010, however, the parties subnitted a renegotiated proposal, which appears to have the court's support, A.G. Sulzberger & Mireya Navarro, *Ground Zero Deal Gives Plaintiffs $712.5 Million*, N.Y.Times, June 10, 2010.

This approach to the exposure claims of World Trade Center cleanup workers is another example of a mixture of public and private legal remedies. Looking toward the future, it is likely that more resolutions of this nature will be fashioned for mass toxic torts.

6.   Contribution Claims

Successful settlement of a mass toxic tort action may be impeded by disagreement among defendants as to the contribution rights available to each. The situation becomes particularly complex when fewer than all of the defendants in a mass tort action reach a pretrial settlement with the plaintiff. The most hotly debated issue in this situation is the determination of the amount by which the subsequent judgment against the nonsettling defendants is to be reduced. This reduction, called a credit or set-off, is significant in that it defines the remaining liability that is the responsibility of the nonsettling tortfeasors. For a discussion of the many complex settlement and contribution issues that arise in mass tort litigation, see Jean Macchiaroli Eggen,

Understanding State Contribution Laws and Their Effect on the Settlement of Mass Tort Actions, 73 Texas L. Rev. 1701 (1995).

Many states provide a right of contribution among tortfeasors insofar as a tortfeasor has paid a judgment in an amount in excess of the tortfeasor's pro rata share. *See* Unif. Contribution Among Tortfeasors Act, 12 U.L.A. § 1(b) (2010). Many states interpret the term "pro rata" to mean the tortfeasor's equitable share of liability as determined according to the rules of comparative negligence in effect in the relevant jurisdiction. *See, e.g.*, Pesaplastic, C.A. v. Cincinnati Milacron Co., 750 F.2d 1516 (11th Cir.1985) (applying Florida law). But some states retain the original definition of pro rata as "per tortfeasor" equally.

The states are also split on the set-off effect to be given to the settling tortfeasor's payment. The majority employs the pro tanto rule, whereby the plaintiff's judgment is off-set by the dollar amount paid by the settling party, or any other amount so designated in the release. *See, e.g.*, Cal. Civ. Proc. Code § 877(a) (West 2010); Minn. Stat. Ann. § 604.01(5) (West 2010). Under this scheme, and assuming the applicability of joint and several liability, if the settling tortfeasor settles for less than its equitable share of the judgment, and the jurisdiction does not permit the nonsettling tortfeasors to seek contribution from the settling tortfeasor, the nonsettling tortfeasors could end up paying a share of the judgment in excess of their equitable shares without recourse. On the other hand, if a tortfeasor settles for an amount in excess of its equitable share, the nonsettling tortfeasors would enjoy a windfall by having less than the aggregate of their equitable shares left to pay. Thus, there may be little incentive for the remaining defendants to settle following a settlement by one defendant under the pro tanto rule.

A second, minority, approach is to reduce the plaintiff's judgment by the released tortfeasor's equitable share—percentage of fault—regardless of the amount that the tortfeasor paid in settlement of the claim. *See, e.g.*, Ky. Rev. Stat. Ann. § 411.182(4) (West 2009). This apportioned share rule protects the nonsettling defendants by assuring that the judgment is credited with the equitable share of the settling tortfeasor. If the settling tortfeasor settled the claim for an amount that turned out to be in excess of its equitable share, however, the plaintiff could realize a windfall by receiving the settlement plus the judgment (which judgment would be the equivalent of the aggregate equitable shares of the nonsettling tortfeasors). Nevertheless, some courts are undisturbed by this possibility. *See* Charles v. Giant Eagle Markets, 522 A.2d 1 (Pa.1987) (" 'Plaintiffs bear the risk of poor settlements; logic and equity dictate that the benefit of good settlements should also be theirs.' " (quoting Duncan v. Cessna Aircraft Co., 665 S.W.2d 414 (Tex.1984)). The United States Supreme Court has advocated the use of the equitable share rule in McDermott, Inc. v. AmClyde, 511 U.S. 202 (1994) (applying the equitable share rule in admiralty).

As a result of these and other problems in choosing between one of the above rules, some parties employ a release that allocates a specific set-off amount, sometimes designated as the settling tortfeasor's equitable share to be determined at trial. In addition, some states have developed a set-off rule that combines features of the pro tanto rule and the apportioned share rule. Thus, New York has enacted a rule that mandates that the plaintiff's judgment be reduced by the amount paid in settlement or by the settling tortfeasor's equitable share, whichever is larger. N.Y. Gen. Oblig. Law § 15–108(a) (McKinney 2009). This combined approach seeks to avoid windfalls to plaintiffs. *See* Williams v. Niske, 615 N.E.2d 1003 (N.Y.1993).

This array of contribution and set-off rules can create significant problems in mass toxic tort litigation. Some rules favor settling defendants, whereas others favor plaintiffs or nonsettling defendants. These problems may arise in relatively small litigation (one plaintiff, several defendants), but they are exacerbated in the situation in which numerous cases—perhaps hundreds—have been aggregated. Sometimes these cases arrive in the courts with some defendants having settled with the plaintiff, while others remain in the action. Defendants may resist settlement if they believe that the proposed rules do not benefit their cause. Because contribution and set-off rules vary from state to state, a defendant may feel that its own state's rules are more favorable than any rule chosen by the court to bind all defendants. This, in turn, raises choice-of-law questions in the mass tort litigation context. *See* Section G.2, *infra*.

7. Alternative Dispute Resolution

Some types of alternative dispute resolution (ADR) have appeared in mass toxic tort litigation to help move the parties toward settlement. Because the substantive and procedural issues in mass toxic tort litigation are typically quite complex, parties may not have a clear sense of their likelihood of success on the merits. Thus, they may resist reasonable settlement proposals for lack of their own ability to properly assess their litigation risks. ADR has been used to provide some of the information that they lack. The ADR methods used in this context are broadly defined, as the results would not necessarily displace the judicial process, but would supplement it and assist in the management of the litigation. In light of Amchem Products, Inc. v. Windsor, 521 U.S. 591 (1997), courts must be cautious in using ADR to resolve the rights of claimants in mass litigation, particularly as part of an administrative claims resolution scheme, and indeed some such uses of ADR may not be allowed. Arbitration may be less useful in mass toxic tort litigation because of the problems generated by the complex nature of the litigation. Nevertheless, it may serve an effective role post-settlement where the settlement agreement incorporates it. Other ADR methods may be useful in an interlocutory manner—to enhance communication, narrow the facts, and induce settlement.

a. Mediation

Mediation can facilitate negotiation, particularly when the parties are entrenched in their positions. Traditional mediation methods may not be appropriate for mass toxic tort cases, but the nature of ADR is that it may be customized for the particular case and the particular set of problems presented. For example, mini nonbinding discovery may advance the case at the pretrial stage in ways that could lead to settlement or clarification of the issues for trial, saving overall time and costs. If mediation is being incorporated into the case, it may be an opportunity to bring scientific expertise into the equation. A wisely chosen mediator knowledgeable in the science of the case could bring the parties together in a way that a judge in more formal proceedings could not. For a thoughtful argument on the uses of mediation in mass tort litigation, see D. Alan Rudlin, *Entropy or Opportunity? The Case for ADR in Mass Tort Cases*, 18 Toxics L. Rptr. (BNA) 550 (June 12, 2003).

b. Summary Jury Trials

The use of the summary jury trial (SJT) was initiated in 1981 by Judge Lambros of the Eastern District of Ohio, but has since been adopted by judges around the country. Its initial use to encourage settlement appeared to be quite effective. The summary jury trial is intended to result in an advisory verdict for use by the court and the parties in developing an approach to settlement. An actual jury is used, but both voir dire and "trial" are conducted by a truncated procedure that may relax the rules of evidence. Typically, each side has a set amount of time to present its case, with the overall time frame ranging from a day to a few weeks, depending upon the complexity of the litigation. Jurors may be asked to provide detailed information by means of interrogatories, with the possibility of the judge and parties being allowed to question the jurors after the verdict. During the SJT, the jurors may or may not know that the verdict will be non-binding. The participants then use this information for the purpose of fashioning a settlement.

By its nature, the summary jury trial requires that discovery and other pretrial procedures be completed by the commencement of the SJT. The procedure can be somewhat costly, but the cost may be warranted in cases, such as complex toxic tort actions, that are sure to be lengthy if they go to trial. In some instances, the SJT may just point out the arbitrariness of a jury's verdict, however. In Stites v. Sundstrand Heat Transfer, Inc., 660 F.Supp. 1516 (W.D.Mich.1987), a case arising out of the contamination of a drinking water supply with the chemical TCE, the court impaneled twelve jurors who deliberated in two separate groups of six. The SJT used one test plaintiff and consisted of closing arguments only, with use of discovery materials. The first jury found for the plaintiff in the amount of $2.8 million. The other jury found for the defendant; when asked, the second jury valued the case at $300,000. Despite such contradiction, this information in itself is valuable to the parties. When a case could easily go either way, settlement will surely be attractive. And, indeed, the *Stites* case settled after the SJT.

The SJT is a voluntary procedure. Courts may not require parties to submit to an SJT, at least in the absence of a court rule. *See* In re NLO, Inc., 5 F.3d 154 (6th Cir.1993); Strandell v. Jackson County, 838 F.2d 884 (7th Cir.1987). An SJT could require parties to divulge litigation strategy and privileged work product. But where used with the consent of the parties in cases that otherwise would be hard to settle, the SJT can be quite effective in its goal to achieve settlement.

c. *Mini–Trials*

A mini-trial is essentially the private sector equivalent of an SJT. Unlike the SJT, however, the parties in a mini-trial make their presentations of the evidence to the principals. Ideally, these individuals would have authority to enter into a binding settlement. A judge or a neutral mediator may preside over the mini-trial as a facilitator, but does not make legal rulings. *See generally* Green, *Growth of the Mini–Trial*, 9 Litig. 12 (Fall 1982). No advisory verdict results from the mini-trial. Rather, its chief advantages are in providing an early neutral evaluation of the case and in bringing the parties together to initiate settlement on equal ground.

G. OTHER PROCEDURAL ISSUES

1. Collateral Estoppel

a. Basic Concepts

The doctrine of collateral estoppel, or issue preclusion, operates to bar relitigation of certain issues
in subsequent litigation. The basic rules of collateral estoppel require that "once an issue is actually
and necessarily determined by a court of competent
jurisdiction, that determination is conclusive in subsequent suits based on a different cause of action
involving a party to the prior litigation." Montana
v. United States, 440 U.S. 147 (1979). Only parties
and their privies may be bound by a prior judgment.
See Restatement (Second) of Judgments § 29 (1980)
(does not use the term "privity," but adopts the
concept). Privies are entities whose relationship to a
party is so close that it does not violate due process
to bind the entity to the prior judgment. Typically,
privies fall into one of several categories. They may
be representatives of a party to the prior action,
such as the administrator of an estate. Privies could
also be successors in interest to property belonging
to a party, when the property was the subject of the
prior action. Or, privies could be entities that effectively controlled the prior litigation. Privity is not
established by a mere interest in the outcome of
litigation, but rather a true identity of interest is
required. Those entities that are not parties or
privies are considered "strangers" to the prior litigation; and strangers may not be bound to the
results in the prior litigation. Only a person who

was a party to the earlier litigation, or in privity with a party, may be bound by collateral estoppel, where it is allowed.

Traditionally, the doctrine of mutuality of estoppel limited the operation of collateral estoppel. Mutuality provided that because a stranger could not be bound to a prior judgment, the stranger would not be permitted to benefit from it. How might a stranger seek to benefit from the determination of a particular issue in the earlier litigation? If the issue had been decided in a manner favorable to the stranger's position in the subsequent litigation, the stranger may seek to prevent his or her opponent from relitigating the issue. The stranger may want to use the issue defensively—i.e., when the stranger is in the defensive posture defending against a claim brought by a party to the earlier litigation—or offensively—i.e., when the stranger affirmatively asserts a claim against the party to the earlier litigation. In any event, under mutuality, the stranger was not allowed to benefit from this situation, either defensively or offensively.

By now, mutuality has been largely abandoned in the states and the federal court system. *See, e.g.,* Blonder–Tongue Laboratories, Inc. v. University of Illinois Foundation, 402 U.S. 313 (1971); Bernhard v. Bank of America National Trust & Savings Assn., 122 P.2d 892 (Cal.1942). In general, jurisdictions have demonstrated more reluctance in abandoning mutuality when a stranger seeks to use collateral estoppel offensively, rather than defensively. Offensive, nonmutual collateral estoppel has been accepted when certain safeguards apply to prevent its abuse by parties or its inequitable application. In Parklane Hosiery Co. v. Shore, 439 U.S. 322 (1979), the Supreme Court set forth some significant limitations on the use of offensive, nonmutual collateral estoppel in the federal courts. In *Parklane*, the Court stated that the trial court has broad discretion in deciding whether collateral estoppel should be applied, but with some guidelines: "[T]he general rule should be that in cases where a plaintiff could easily have joined in the earlier action or where the application of offensive collateral estoppel would be unfair to a defendant, a trial judge ... should not allow the use of offensive collateral estoppel." *Accord* Restatement (Second) of Judgments § 29 (1982) (providing that offensive collateral estoppel should be allowed "unless the fact that he lacked full and fair opportunity to litigate the issue in the first action or other circumstances justify affording him an opportunity to relitigate the issue"). At least some states have incorporated the *Parklane* rule into their collateral estoppel doctrines. *See, e.g.*, Bichler v. Eli Lilly & Co., 436 N.E.2d 182 (N.Y.1982).

Courts have been especially concerned about the situation involving multiple plaintiffs with claims against the same defendant arising out of the same or related conduct. *See generally* Brainerd Currie, *Mutuality of Collateral Estoppel: Limits of the* Bernhard *Doctrine*, 9 Stan. L. Rev. 281 (1957). This is precisely the configuration of mass toxic tort litigation. A simple hypothetical will illustrate the problem. Assume a bus accident occurs and that all fifty passengers were injured. Passenger #1 brings an action against the bus company and driver, but cannot prove negligence. Passenger #2 (and any other passenger) has a right to bring an independent action against the same defendants, claiming negligence. This is because Passenger #2 is a stranger and cannot be bound to the result in Passenger #1's action. (Passenger #2 is not in privity with Passenger #1; their similar interests in holding the bus company negligent are not sufficient to constitute privity.) Suppose Passengers #2 through #15 all sue separately and all are unable to prove that the bus company was negligent. Then Passenger #16 sues and *wins*. Should Passengers #17 through #50 be allowed to use offensive collateral estoppel, based upon Passenger #16's favorable finding that the bus company was negligent, to prevent the bus company from relitigating the issue of negligence? Put otherwise, may Passengers #17 through #50 win on summary judgment on the issue of liability, on the basis of Passenger #16's favorable finding? The problems here are clear, not the least of which is the fact that a substantial number of cases had been tried earlier with a different result.

b. *Application to Toxic Torts*

Toxic torts compound the above problems. Because statutes of limitations have been relaxed to accommodate latent disease claims, actions accrue later and later. This does not create the "wait-and-see" scenario of the bus accident, in which all plaintiffs were injured at the same time and some chose to sit out and wait for a favorable verdict, then come in and attempt to use collateral estoppel. Rather, in latent disease cases, many plaintiffs have no choice but to wait, as their illnesses will be manifested at later dates. Further, in toxic torts, claims may arise from the same general conduct of the defendant, but the circumstances of the plaintiffs' exposures may vary considerably. In Hardy v. Johns–Manville Sales Corp., 681 F.2d 334 (5th Cir. 1982), the court applied the rule of *Parklane* and found enough problems with allowing the use of offensive collateral estoppel that its utility in toxic tort litigation is seriously in question.

Hardy involved consolidated actions brought by various asbestos workers against multiple manufacturers, distributors, and sellers of asbestos products. The plaintiffs alleged claims of strict liability, negligence, and breach of warranty. The trial court accepted a standard of industry-wide liability and issued an omnibus order approving the use of collateral estoppel on issues of marketing an unreasonably dangerous product, state of the art, and general causation. The plaintiffs sought to use issues determined in Borel v. Fibreboard Paper Products Corp., 493 F.2d 1076 (5th Cir.1973) that were favorable to asbestos workers seeking to recover damages from asbestos companies on product liability theories. On interlocutory appeal from the omnibus order, the Fifth Circuit in *Hardy* reversed the district court and held that the use of collateral estoppel was not appropriate.

The Fifth Circuit conducted separate discussions of those defendants in *Hardy* who had also been defendants in *Borel* (the "*Borel* defendants") and those defendants who had not been defendants in the *Borel* lawsuit ("non-*Borel* defendants"). The distinction was warranted because the *Borel* defendants, as parties to the earlier action, could be bound. The non-*Borel* defendants, on the other hand, appeared to be strangers, although the plaintiffs argued that they should be considered privies. The Fifth Circuit noted that the district court had not distinguished between these two classes of defendants.

The Fifth Circuit first addressed the collateral estoppel issues involving the non-*Borel* defendants. Initially, the court determined that no privity existed between the non-*Borel* defendants and the *Borel* defendants. A mere "identity of interests" between these two groups of defendants was insufficient to constitute privity. For privity to exist, the non-*Borel* defendants would have had to control the litigation in *Borel*. Quoting the Restatement (Second) of Judgments § 39, cmt. c (1982), the court stated: " 'To have control of litigation requires that a person have effective choice as to the legal theories and proofs to be advanced in behalf of the party to the action. He must also have control over the opportunity to obtain review.' " The mere fact that the non-*Borel* defendants, like the *Borel* defendants, were manufacturers of asbestos-containing products did not transform them into privies.

The court's analysis of the *Borel* defendants was different, as they clearly could be bound to the results in *Borel* under appropriate circumstances. Those circumstances were not present in this case, however. The court found that the basic requirements of collateral estoppel—that the issue be identical, that the issue was actually litigated in the prior action, and that the issue was necessary and essential to the judgment in the prior action—were not met because of the ambiguity of the findings on which the *Borel* judgment was based. *See also* Restatement (Second) of Judgments § 29, cmt. g (1982) (providing that collateral estoppel is not appropriate where the prior judgment is ambiguous). The Fifth Circuit closely examined the special interrogatories given to the jury in *Borel* and held that their lack of specificity made it impossible to determine the jury's precise findings on issues that were critical to the *Hardy* litigation (e.g., when the duty to warn attached, the exact composition of the various products). Because *Hardy* involved persons exposed to various products over differing periods of time, absolute clarity of the scope of the issues resolved in *Borel* was essential before collateral estoppel could be allowed. The Fifth Circuit stated that *Borel* did not decide that all manufacturers of asbestos-containing products knew or should have known their products were dangerous at all times relevant to the plaintiffs in *Hardy*.

Applying *Parklane*, the *Hardy* court held that application of collateral estoppel would be unfair to the defendants for two reasons. First, numerous other asbestos cases had been tried, at least half of which had resulted in verdicts inconsistent with *Borel*. As in the bus accident hypothetical above, the court was concerned that selecting *Borel* to provide the basis for offensive collateral estoppel was arbitrary and unfair. Second, the court concluded that the defendants could not have foreseen that their liability to the plaintiff Borel, amounting to $68,000 (even though Borel sought damages far in excess of that amount), would have grown to a multimillion dollar liability in *Hardy*. This lack of foreseeability may have meant that the defendants did not have sufficient incentive to vigorously litigate the issues in the earlier litigation.

Hardy reflects a circumspect judicial attitude toward use of offensive collateral estoppel in toxic tort litigation. The fact that some of the court's rationales for denying the use of collateral estoppel seem strained is an indication of just how strict courts are when faced with a stranger-plaintiff's proposal to prevent relitigation of key, disputed issues.

More recent cases have shown the same caution when it comes to applying offensive nonmutual collateral estoppel. For example, in Kessinger v. Grefco, Inc., 672 N.E.2d 1149 (Ill.1996), plaintiffs sought to preclude the defendant from arguing that diatomaceous earth could not cause pulmonary fibrosis. The issue had been determined against the defendant in an earlier lawsuit. In refusing to allow collateral estoppel, the Illinois Supreme Court emphasized that the current plaintiffs were not similarly situated to the plaintiff in the prior action. In Whalen v. Ansell Perry Inc., 2004 WL 840286 (S.D.N.Y.2004), the federal district court refused to apply collateral estoppel in a case in which a nurse claimed an allergic reaction to latex gloves. The court held that the gloves in the previous case on which the plaintiff relied were not identical to the gloves in the present case; thus, the requirement that the issue be identical was not met. In Smith v. Exxon Mobil Oil Corp., 64 Cal.Rptr.3d 69 (Cal. Ct. App. 2007), the plaintiff attempted to use collateral estoppel to prevent the defendant from relitigating the issue of exposure of the decedent to asbestos. The court refused to apply collateral estoppel because the defendant never had a full and fair opportunity to litigate that issue in the first action because its expert witness was unable to testify due to a personal emergency. In Mounce v. Sandoz Pharmaceuticals Corp., 2000 WL 33342378 (Ky.Cir.Ct. 2000), the court rejected the plaintiffs' request to apply offensive collateral estoppel on the issue of the health risk associated with the lactation-control drug Parlodel. The court said that numerous cases decided since the earlier case had either reached a contrary result or had held inadmissible the plaintiffs' causation evidence. Citing *Parklane*, the court ruled that collateral estoppel would not be allowed under those circumstances.

2. Choice of Law

The substantive law to be applied in mass toxic tort litigation is almost exclusively state tort doctrines. When brought in federal court, these actions are typically brought under the diversity jurisdiction of the federal courts. Pursuant to the *Erie* doctrine, state law, including state common law as well as statutory enactments, applies in diversity actions. *See* Erie Railroad Co v. Tompkins, 304 U.S. 64 (1938). The federal court sitting in diversity is under an obligation to apply the choice-of-law rules of the forum state. Klaxon Co. v. Stentor Elec. Mfg. Co., 313 U.S. 487 (1941). As a result, a different choice-of-law rule may apply in federal courts in different states. Moreover, when an action has been transferred to a federal district different from the one in which it was commenced, the transferee court is mandated to apply the law that the transferor court would have applied. *See* Ferens v. John Deere Co., 494 U.S. 516 (1990); Van Dusen v. Barrack, 376 U.S. 612 (1964). These basic rules make for some complicated choice-of-law questions in mass tort litigation.

Because tort law is a matter of high state interest, even generally recognized tort concepts have been subject to idiosyncratic interpretations and applications that vary from state to state. These state-to-state variations create an additional layer of complications when toxic tort actions have been aggregated. The claims of the individual plaintiffs may be subject to different state laws and, therefore, different tort rules. This may lead to conflicting results among similar claims that have been aggregated in one forum.

Further, practical problems arise from the stalemate that choice-of-law issues often create. When the choice of law is unclear, the litigation may be delayed while the parties and court attempt to sort through those issues. This is particularly true when there is an attempt to settle numerous actions. Judicial management issues become even more critical if the parties do not achieve settlement, for the court must determine an appropriate manner to handle the litigation when different state laws apply. Choice-of-law problems may prevent the court from certifying a class action because they render commonality and typicality problematic. *See* Ellington v. Philip Morris Inc., 2003 WL 22319075 (D.Nev.2003).

A few efforts have been made to supplant state tort doctrine with federal common law in mass tort litigation. In the Agent Orange litigation, Judge Pratt initially held that federal common law should apply to the product liability claims of the class members against the manufacturers of the defoliant. Applying the standard test, the court first identified substantial federal interests in the lawsuit in the relationship between the military service personnel and the Government and in the Government's interest in protecting its relations with suppliers of war materiel. Second, the court found that the federal interests would be adversely affected by the application of state law because state law would lead to inconsistent results and, ultimately, to uncertainty for all parties. Third, the court found no adverse effect on state interests if state law were to be supplanted by federal common law.

The Second Circuit reversed, finding that no substantial federal policy was at stake in the litigation. *See* In re "Agent Orange" Prod. Liab. Litig., 635 F.2d 987 (2d Cir.1980). The court examined the existing legal precedent and concluded that because the claims in the Agent Orange litigation were not brought by or against the Government, no rights or duties of the Government were directly raised by the litigation. The court stated that "there is no federal interest in uniformity for its own sake." Additionally, the court noted that the two federal interests cited by the court below competed with one another to some degree, thus fracturing the uniformity sought from a federal common law. *But see* Boyle v. United Technologies Corp., 487 U.S. 500 (1988) (developing federal common law in narrow area of Government contractor defense).

The Fifth Circuit reached a similar conclusion, but with respect to asbestos litigation. In Jackson v. Johns–Manville Sales Corp., 750 F.2d 1314 (5th Cir.1985), the Fifth Circuit reaffirmed the state interest in tort litigation, even when the litigation occurs on a massive scale. Further, the court expressed concern for the unfettered spread of federal common law. Accordingly, the court concluded that in the absence of legislative action, use of federal common law was inappropriate. Of some significance, however, was the existence of a substantial dissent in *Jackson*, thus demonstrating judicial interest in a federal law alternative for asbestos.

In the Manville Trust litigation, Judge Weinstein ultimately reached the same conclusion. *See* In re Joint E. & S. Dists. Asbestos Litig., 129 B.R. 710 (E. & S.D.N.Y.1991). Judge Weinstein identified substantial federal interests—upholding the reorganization plan under the Bankruptcy Code and effecting a settlement of a tort action of massive scope, encompassing more than 150,000 claimants. Nevertheless, he rejected the application of federal common law mostly for reasons of federalism. Even though the states had individual tort laws that could cause choice-of-law problems, a legislative enactment by Congress, not a rule imposed by judicial edict, was the appropriate solution.

Earlier, however, in the Agent Orange litigation, Judge Weinstein did take steps to create and apply what he referred to as a "national consensus" law. Similarly, commentators have offered strong arguments in favor of considering federal common law as a solution to the choice-of-law problem in mass torts. *See, e.g.*, Georgene M. Vairo, *Multi–Tort Cases: Cause For More Darkness on the Subject, or a New Role For Federal Common Law?*, 54 Fordham L. Rev. 167 (1985). *See also* Linda S. Mullenix, *Federalizing Choice of Law for Mass–Tort Litigation*, 70 Tex. L. Rev. 1623 (1992) (stating that "the legal profession has a longstanding, collective psychological block with regard to even the mention of federal common law"). While all are in agreement that something must be done to remedy the problems associated with choice of law, it appears for the moment that no clear solution has emerged.

INDEX

References are to Pages

----

†